From Web to Workplace

From Web to Workplace

Designing Open Hypermedia Systems

Kaj Grønbæk and Randall H. Trigg

The MIT Press
Cambridge, Massachusetts
London, England

© 1999 Massachusetts Institute of Technology

This book was set in Sabon by Wellington Graphics.

Printed and bound in the United States of America.

Library of Congress Cataloging-in-Publication Data

Grønbæk, Kaj.
   From Web to workplace: designing open hypermedia systems / Kaj Grønbæk and Randall H. Trigg.
      p.   cm.—(Digital communication)
   Includes bibliographical references and index.
   ISBN 0-262-07191-6 (hardcover: alk. paper)
   1. Interactive multimedia. 2. World Wide Web (Information retrieval system). I. Trigg, Randall H. II. Title. III. Series.
QA76.76.I59G76   1999
006.7—dc21   98-34700
                                                                            CIP

Contents

Series Foreword

Digital Communication is one of the most exciting, rapidly expanding fields of study and practice throughout the world, as witnessed by the increasing number of Web sites and users of the Internet, as well as publication and use of multimedia CD-ROM titles in schools, homes, and corporate environments. In addition, Web and multimedia publications have created a vast secondary literature of scholarly analysis in a range of subject areas. Professional societies and degree-granting programs devoted to digital communication have steadily increased. And the language and concepts of digital life have become central in popular culture. In cyberspace the roles of writer and audience are no longer static but dynamic; the concept of text is no longer fixed but fluid. Computational technology has delivered us a powerful tool for the creation, presentation, exchange, and annotation of a text (in words, images, video, and audio)—so powerful that we speak in terms of transparent and seamless information environments that integrate all media.

We are witnessing a profound revolution in communication and learning in a post-Gutenberg world. The MIT Press series on Digital Communication will present advanced research into all aspects of this revolutionary change in our forms of expression, thought, and being. This research will be published in traditional book format or as Web sites or multimedia CD-ROM titles as demanded by content. As this series finds its expression in hardcopy or in digital format, it will seek to explore and define new genres of thought and expression offered by digital media.

Edward Barrett

Preface

Our goal is to make the legacy of 50 years of hypermedia research available to today's system designers. Drawing on the groundbreaking Dexter Hypertext Reference Model of the late 1980s and current research related to the World Wide Web (WWW), this book offers design principles and candidate object-oriented frameworks that address problems ranging from the locating and placing operations at the heart of hypermedia to problems of distribution and multiuser support. The principles and frameworks reflect our belief in the power of an open systems approach, one that can integrate applications and software across networks, platforms, and environments. Moreover, our design practice encourages active user involvement throughout the design and development process.

In the late 1980s, the most significant contributions in the hypermedia field were captured in the Dexter Hypertext Reference Model, based on a series of meetings among the foremost hypermedia designers of the time. Though the Dexter model was not intended as a specification for system developers, it has nonetheless served as a starting point for the design of many hypermedia features and a few systems. We have ourselves experienced both the power and the weaknesses of the Dexter model in the design and implementation of a hypermedia design framework and several applications. In the years since its publication, we and others have extended the Dexter model to support cooperative and distributed work practices, multimedia, and, most important, open systems and integration.

In this book, we offer design principles and object-oriented frameworks based on both the Dexter model and developments in the field since the publication of that model in 1990, including, of course, the WWW. In addition to supporting our proposals with accumulated wisdom from the field, we show how they can be used to tackle critical problems for today's system designers.

Though we do not advocate particular systems, we do take a strong stand in favor of an open systems approach. It is our belief that hypermedia can be the key ingredient in development projects whose goals include the integration of applications and software across networks, platforms, and environments.

We are also firm believers in the value of involving future users of technology in its design. This participatory approach is just as important for the design of infrastructure technologies like hypermedia as for domain-specific applications. Therefore, we offer proposals, grounded in concrete work settings, for ways to involve users in the development of hypermedia systems.

Our intended audience includes researchers, professional system developers, teachers, and students who are interested in hypermedia design and the application of object-oriented design principles and frameworks. Our book also briefly recounts the history of hypermedia and shows how the WWW, today's foremost hypermedia system, is one point in a large space of design options. With regard to current practice, the book should be valuable for graduate students or advanced undergraduates as they gain experience using and programming on the web.

For a course on the World Wide Web, the book could contextualize and motivate student projects that build multipage structures, links for collaborative authoring and annotation, graphical browsers, and synchronized multimedia materials. For a course on integrating workstation-based applications, relevant projects could integrate independent third-party software through linking and other forms of cross-application structuring. Finally, students could bridge the worlds of the workstation and the WWW, say, by modifying an off-the-shelf spreadsheet program so that its cells continuously monitor quantities retrieved from the Internet.

The body of the book is composed of four parts and an epilogue. Part I introduces, in separate chapters, the sources of our proposals: the goals and principles of the open hypermedia approach, a particular set of engineering users and their needs for support for linking and application integration, and finally the accomplishments and outstanding problems of the Dexter model.

Part II begins by describing the building blocks of open hypermedia, the various means of locating in and pointing across third-party material. Subsequent chapters cover the fundamental concepts of hypermedia: anchors, components, links, composites, and hyperspaces. Part II contains chapters on the runtime behavior of hypermedia, both link traversal and other forms of navigation, and issues related to multimedia. The second part closes with a chapter summarizing and exemplifying our design principles with candidate object-oriented frameworks.

Part III uses the extended Dexter framework to model modern-day hypermedia concepts, many of which have been introduced since the publication of the original Dexter model in 1990. The chapters in part III address issues concerning the design of "industrial-strength" hypermedia, including among others, distributed hypermedia databases, collaborative use of hypermedia, and open architectures.

The chapters of parts II and III include concise design patterns, each meant to capture an essential concept or design choice likely to be faced by the developers of open hypermedia systems. The patterns range from the means to connect program data structures with online text and multimedia materials, to principles for providing hypermedia functionality to collaborating users who are geographically separated.

Part IV draws on our experiences designing applications for real users based on our principles and frameworks. It starts from an assumption that the work of system development should be organized so as to bring the realities of technical and organizational contexts to bear on concrete design choices. The first chapter describes our cooperative design and prototyping activities with a set of engineering users, while the second outlines how those activities informed our open hypermedia frameworks and design principles.

Finally, the book's epilogue presents our view of the current trends in hypermedia and system design, and identifies new areas in which to apply our design principles. Two appendices offer capsule summaries of selected hypermedia systems and our open hypermedia protocol.

Those readers familiar with the Dexter model and the goals of open systems may want to skim chapter 1 and browse the chapters in part II. All readers, however, should take a look at chapter 11, whose object-oriented frameworks are an important resource for understanding the subsequent applications of the concepts and principles in part III. Readers with particular interests may choose to skip around in part III rather than read each chapter in order.

We hope the concrete experiences and proposals this book offers will make knowledge about hypermedia design more widely available, encourage developers of future systems to use these concepts in their own designs, and spark further research on open systems.

Acknowledgments

At Aarhus University in 1989 we began the collaborative research, prototyping, and conceptual system design that culminated in this book nine years later. We shared interests in prototyping and computer-supported cooperative work from the start; and over the years, we taught each other and learned together about hypermedia, participatory design, and system development methods. Our collaboration has stood the test of time (9 time zones, to be exact) and we hope it will continue for years to come.

This book would not have happened without the help of many colleagues and friends on both sides of the Atlantic. A number of people have been directly involved in our work on designing open hypermedia systems; we have had valuable discussions, arguments, and hacking sessions with Heine Alsaker, Peter Andersen, Jakob Bardram, Niels Olaf Bouvin, Søren Brandt, Jens Arnold Hem, Lars Jakobsen, Niels Jakobsen, Nikolaj Kolte, Morten Kyng, Ole Lehrman Madsen, Jawahar Malhotra, Cathy Marshall, Jakob Mathiesen, Preben Mogensen, Kim Jensen Møller, John V. Nielsen, Rasmus Pagh, and Lennart Sloth.

We are grateful to Frank Halasz and the members of the Dexter group for fun and inspiring discussions. This book depends on the theoretical groundwork they laid in the late 1980s.

The Open Hypermedia Systems Working Group (OHSWG) provided a forum for intense discussions of open hypermedia system issues during several workshops over the past four years. In particular, we thank OHSWG members Ken Anderson, Hugh Davis, Wendy Hall, Pete Nürnberg, and Uffe Kock Wiil.

The Devise team at Aarhus University and the Work, Practice and Technology area at Xerox Palo Alto Research Center provided supportive and stimulating environments that helped us ground our research and development in the work of real people as well as cutting-edge technologies. In particular we would like to thank our colleagues Jeanette Blomberg, Susanne Bødker, David Levy, Kim Halskov Madsen, Cathy Marshall, Susan Newman, and Lucy Suchman.

The software engineers at Mjølner Informatics in Denmark provided ready support when our Devise Hypermedia framework overstepped the boundaries of Mjølner's software development environment.

The engineers at Great Belt Ltd. who participated in the EuroCODE project provided us with valuable challenges and feedback on each of our prototypes. In particular, Quality manager Kurt Lauvring played a central role in our collaboration.

Our thanks to Bob Prior and Deborah Cantor-Adams, our editors at MIT Press, for their understanding and support in producing this book.

Lauren Rusk, our copy editor, took on a variety of tasks not the least of which were harmonizing our writing styles and reducing our use of the passive voice. Whatever coherance and readability the book has is due in large part to her patient diligence. Thanks also to Marianne Dammand Iversen, Lene Holst Mogensen, and Jane DeLong for the crucial roles they played in the cross-oceanic pipelined editing and proof-reading process.

Our dearest thanks to Iben and Jane for their love and support throughout the multiyear writing and publishing process.

The book is dedicated to Bill and Louisa for their years of support and encouragement, and to Jens-Emil and Asbjørn for their lively disinterest in all things hyper.

The work behind this book has been supported by various grants: The Danish Research Programme for Informatics, grant number 5.26.18.19; EU Esprit II— the EuroCoOp project; EU Esprit III—the EuroCODE project; the Danish National Science Research Foundation, grant number 9502631; and the Danish National Centre for IT Research, CIT project number 123—COCONUT.

I

Hypermedia in Support of Integration

The fundamental technique of hypermedia–creating associative links between online materials–shows great potential for knowledge work. Nevertheless, few users enjoy hypermedia support that is seamlessly integrated into their work environment, that is, into their favorite editors and tools. Working with hypermedia still requires a separate set of computer tools. In our view, the need for integration constitutes the biggest single challenge hypermedia designers face.

Since the late 1960s many variants of the fundamental hypermedia concepts have been proposed and implemented. To varying degrees, the resulting systems all support authoring and navigation in networks of interlinked textual and multimedia information.

Today, two examples of hypermedia and multimedia dominate. The first is the World Wide Web (WWW), the major system for organizing and navigating information on the Internet. The second popular form of hypermedia is "canned" multimedia–educational packages, novels, encyclopedias, and the like–distributed on CD-ROMs.

Some might conclude that hypermedia systems have reached their peak, and thus question the need for a book on their design. We believe, however, that the basic concept of hypermedia has much more to offer. Hypermedia should provide powerful support for sharable materials organized in complex structures beyond the simple jump link. Moreover, this support should be seamlessly integrated into the users' working environments.

The WWW and CD-ROMs, as well as most of the classical hypermedia systems such as NLS/Augment, KMS, NoteCards, Intermedia, HyperCard, and Guide, are what we call *monolithic systems;* that is, they require almost full control over the data format, rendering algorithms, and user interface. These systems all have limitations and anomalies in the way they support knowledge work. To offer better support in multiple domains, researchers need to develop hypermedia systems as efficient *integrators* of heterogenous material, applications, and platforms rather than attempt to force an entire domain into a predefined box. Among other things, this book offers a framework for developing hypermedia systems that support a rich variety of integration tasks.

Part I first illustrates the need for an integrationist approach, with examples of various hypermedia challenges in complex industrial work settings. We then introduce the main ingredients of our approach: open systems technology, object orientation, and the famed Dexter Hypertext Reference Model.

1
Open Hypermedia in a Historical Context

Everything is Deeply Intertwingled. . . . In an important sense there are no "subjects" at all: there is only all knowledge, since the cross-connections among the myriad topics of this world simply cannot be divided up neatly. . . . Hypertext at last offers the possibility of representing and exploring it all without carving it up destructively. (Nelson 1974, p. DM45)

Carefully examining the systems created to date, uncovers a single common thread that explains why hypertext/hypermedia systems have not caught on: virtually all systems have been *insular, monolithic packages* that demand the user disown his or her present computing environment. (Meyrowitz 1989, p. 107)

Today, the terms *hypertext* and *hypermedia* often bring to mind the Internet and the World Wide Web (WWW) and their ability to interconnect far-flung sites of online material at the click of a mouse. Indeed, link following across the Internet is one of the breakthroughs of the WWW. But hypermedia includes much more than Internet pointers embedded in HTML-tagged text. This book builds on the past forty years of research in the field and introduces approaches to the design of *open hypermedia*, that is, advanced hypermedia structuring models and architectures that make hypermedia support available from the users' favorite computer applications. Along the way, we propose patterns for hypermedia system design, specifically oriented to the design of open systems that support application integration.

This chapter introduces the notion of open hypermedia and related hypermedia topics as well as relevant design methods that we take up later in the book. First we give a brief overview of the evolution of hypermedia from an open systems perspective. We limit our examples to a few of the best known hypermedia systems, Augment, ZOG/KMS, NoteCards, Intermedia, and Microcosm. Appendix A contains capsule summaries of these and other systems. Interested readers should also refer to Conklin (1987) and Nielsen (1990). We then introduce three themes that have occupied researchers and designers in the field of open hypermedia: tailorability, cooperation, and distribution. Finally, we discuss the design and implementation methods of greatest relevance to open hypermedia.

1.1 Hypertext and hypermedia

The field of hypermedia concerns the design and use of systems that support authoring, managing, and navigating networks of interlinked textual and multimedia information (Conklin 1987; Nielsen 1990). The word *interlinked* is essential; hypermedia's advance beyond multimedia authoring and document management systems is its explicit support for representing interconnections among online materials. At their simplest, these interconnections take the form of traversible links connecting a source with a destination. As we'll see, today's hypermedia systems have evolved to support a variety of structures, both link- and nonlink-based, both explicit and computed.

Research in the field of hypermedia over the past forty years has ranged from creative writing to software versioning, from help systems to remote collaboration, and from Petri Nets to spatial information structures. Ted Nelson (1965a), who coined the terms *hypertext* and *hypermedia* in the 1960s, envisioned a world-wide "docuverse" whose users would reuse material, adding their own links and annotations to what they read. Hypermedia also spans the linked "trails" of Vannevar Bush's memex and the human-readable "viewspecs" of Doug Engelbart's Augment, the separable link "webs" of Brown University's Intermedia and the graphical network browsers of Xerox's NoteCards.

These landmark systems and others were captured, in the late 1980s, with the Dexter Hypertext Reference Model (Halasz and Schwartz 1990). The Dexter model combines the best ideas of these systems with a few conceptual breakthroughs of its own.

In the late 1980s and early 1990s, a number of so-called link services and hyperbase systems emerged. These systems applied variants of a basic principle of the Dexter model: the link and other hypermedia structures should be separated from the data. A link service is an independent server that provides hypermedia links for second- and third-party editors and viewers through a communication channel. Examples include Sun Link Service (Pearl 1989), Microcosm (Hall et al. 1996), Multicard (Rizk and Sauter 1992), Devise Hypermedia (Grønbæk et al. 1997a), and Chimera (Anderson et al. 1994).

A hyperbase is a special purpose database that manages the storage of hypermedia objects and, in some cases, data contents. A hyperbase can support long- and short-term transactions, versioning, collaboration, and distribution of hypermedia objects. Examples of hyperbase systems are HAM (Campbell and Goodman 1988), HB1–4 (Wiil 1993), Hyperform (Wiil and Leggett 1992), and HyperDisco (Wiil and Leggett 1997).

The World Wide Web, which appeared on the scene in the early 1990s, represents a different line of development, in which the hypermedia structures are embedded in the data. Almost overnight, the simplicity of the WWW brought hypermedia to end users all over the world.

Recently, the field has seen several attempts to merge the ideas of link services and hyperbases with the WWW. This merging is a key component of what is called *open hypermedia*. This book takes up design issues raised by the tension between sophisticated Dexter-based notions of hypermedia and the simpler but highly scalable WWW approach.

1.2   The evolution of open hypermedia

Reviewing the history of hypermedia systems development, we can identify a shift from the design of integrated environments–monolithic systems that include all the editors and databases a user may need–to open systems that provide hypermedia structures for standard editors and applications.

1.2.1   Integrated environments

The first working hypertext system was NLS/Augment (Engelbart and English 1968), a monolithic system that attempted to support all the user's application needs, including email, programming, and text editing. At that time, assembling already existing applications was not a viable option. For one thing, few applications could surpass those provided by Augment. Moreover, no infrastructure for application integration was available; Augment had no choice but to provide its own. Nonetheless, Augment did at one point live on the Internet, presaging the World Wide Web by some 25 years (Engelbart 1984b).

Several later systems shared Augment's monolithic approach to integration (Meyrowitz 1989). For example, KMS provided its own email and text/graphic editor (Akscyn et al. 1988), in addition to import and export support for a few data formats. NoteCards, another monolith, was profoundly tailorable, but to give it credit for true application integration would be misleading. NoteCards ran in a sophisticated Lisp environment (Masinter 1981), which meant that it could be integrated with practically any application written in that environment (Trigg et al. 1987). In a sense, it was the Lisp workstation rather than the hypermedia system that supported application integration. The same basic argument holds for Intermedia (Haan et al. 1992), which was built in the MacApp Application Framework (Wilson et al. 1990) and thus could only integrate applications based on that framework.

1.2.2 Separating structure from content

A crucial step in the evolution of open hypermedia was the recognition of the importance of separating structure from content.

The Intermedia system (Garrett et al. 1986) achieved this separation with its "web" databases, which allow links to live separately from the text and the graphical material being linked. Intermedia was built from a common object-oriented framework that supported construction of different editors for specific document types. The framework ensured that the editors supported the maintenance of identifiable "blocks" of data in the different document types. Blocks were the predecessors of what are called *anchors* in this book; both are objects with an identifier and some specification of a location in a given document. Links in Intermedia were symmetric relationships between block objects; both blocks and links were stored in the web database. In this way, Intermedia supported a user's private link structures overlaid on an existing public information structure without disturbing it. For instance, Intermedia enabled library users to maintain a personal web with notes and references on top of a public read-only library with references, reviews, and so on. Intermedia also supported partial multiuser access to webs by allowing the user to enter nodes and links in the database in either read, annotate, or write mode.

Intermedia represented a first step toward openness, but, as with NoteCards, both web and material had to live within the overall Intermedia environment. This weakness was pointed out by one of the developers, Meyrowitz, in his famous "missing link" article (1989). Nonetheless, the block idea has had a lasting influence on both the Dexter model and later open systems.

1.2.3   Open hypermedia services

The first efforts to move beyond the monolithic nature of NoteCards and Intermedia took the form of *link services*. For example, the Sun Link Service (Pearl 1989) and LinkWorks from DEC (Clark 1992) support links using a separate server. In these systems, APIs for link creation and traversal support communication between the link service and third-party applications.

Open hypermedia services take the further step of integrating standard applications not written specifically for use with hypermedia systems. This deep application integration was perhaps first attained by Microcosm in the late 1980s (Hall et al. 1996). In that system, the ability to locate links within a document depended on the degree of "Microcosm-awareness" of the controlling application. As we'll see in chapter 6, Microcosm's "generic links" and "link filters" provided a significant degree of hypermedia functionality for any application on the workstation platform. This was a step beyond the Sun Link Service's requirement that "compliant" applications abide by certain protocols.

The Devise Hypermedia (DHM) system first described by Grønbæk and Trigg (1992) is another example of an open hypermedia service that provides support for a rich set of hypermedia structures for third-party applications. We use the DHM system as a reference example throughout this book, especially in chapters 13–20.

1.3   Open hypermedia research issues

The ability to provide hypermedia structures for arbitrary data types, though an important advance, is not sufficient for real life work practices, as we will see in chapter 2. Tailorability, collaboration, and distribution support are not new issues for hypermedia researchers but they are becoming ever more pressing. The next three sections review historical research on these issues, which part III discusses in depth.

1.3.1   Tailorability

Tailorable systems support modifications and improvements to an installed system by users or software developers not involved in the original system development. Tailorability has been considered a crucial feature of many of the best known hypermedia systems. For example, NoteCards provided a range of tailoring options, from preference sheets to the ability to create new "card types" specialized for particular applications (Trigg et al. 1987). Intermedia also offered support for the integration of new applications, though it required compilation and relinking of the core system (Haan et al. 1992). HyperCard employs the programming language HyperTalk, which supports a wide variety of tailoring (Goodman 1987). KMS includes a scripting language (Akscyn and McCracken 1993), as does MultiCard (Rizk and Sauter 1992) and, most recently, WWW browsers and servers.

Tailorable systems are able to augment or integrate new applications or editors with an installed open hypermedia service. Such integration usually involves tailoring both the new application and the open hypermedia service. The application is augmented with new user interface elements and procedures to communicate with the hypermedia service, and the hypermedia service is augmented with objects that model the new application. Many applications provide application programming interfaces (APIs) or scripting languages, and some hypermedia services are open for configuration by users. As we discuss in part III, we are nearing the point where new applications registered with an open hypermedia service can be made to support hypermedia seamlessly.

1.3.2   Cooperation

Augment was the first system to offer hypermedia support for cooperative work. An often cited film made in 1968 shows Doug Engelbart, the creator of Augment, performing real-time collaborative writing on a shared hypermedia substrate with a colleague 30 miles away (Engelbart and English 1968). The KMS system also enables collaboration by operating in a kind of client-server mode that allows users to share parts of a hypermedia structure (Akscyn et al. 1988). Intermedia and NoteCards made advances in asynchronous collaboration, including hypermedia annotation of coauthored papers (Catlin et al. 1989), and cooperative reorganization of shared project materials (Irish and Trigg 1989; Trigg et al. 1986). The ABC system provided similar support for collaboration through a common server (Smith and Smith 1991). Later work included support for synchronous collaboration, as in Sepia (Streitz et al. 1992), and for awareness notification (Wiil 1991). Recently, there have been attempts to add CSCW support to the WWW (Bentley et al. 1997b).

However, cooperation support has mainly been investigated in integrated environments, and open hypermedia systems of today are still mainly single-user systems with little or no support for collaborative manipulation of hypermedia structures and contents. Part III presents our proposals for cooperation support in an open hypermedia context, particularly in the areas of concurrency control and event notification.

1.3.3 Distribution

Distributed hypermedia was almost unheard of before the arrival of the World Wide Web. Aside from a short period in the 1970s when Augment was available to collaborating authors over what was then the ARPANET, hypermedia systems have predominantly used centralized storage. This is just as true for today's link services like Microcosm as it was for the monolithic systems of the preceding era. Xanadu has envisioned world-wide distributed hypermedia since the 1960s (Nelson 1965b), but to our knowledge, no working systems beyond prototypes have been made available.

With the emergence of the WWW, we are seeing a renewed focus on distributed hypermedia. This is an exciting time for the hypermedia field, in which open systems at the workstation are meeting global hypermedia in the form of the World Wide Web. Early experiments on distributing hypermedia structures by means of the WWW infrastructure appear in systems such as Hyperwave (Maurer 1996), Microcosm (Hall et al. 1996), Devise Hypermedia (Grønbæk et al. 1997a) and others. The hope is that such distributed hypermedia services will change the WWW from a browsing system into a full-blown hypermedia environment with support for collaboration and the design of hypermedia structures. Part III addresses the issue of distributing and replicating anchor-based hypermedia services across local area networks and the WWW.

1.4 Methods of open hypermedia design

Open hypermedia systems impose significant requirements on the infrastructure of applications and platforms. At the same time, these systems are highly dependent on the flexible modeling and implementation techniques needed to meet the requirements of dynamically changing software and hardware platforms as well as a rich variety of use contexts.

1.4.1 Open systems approaches

In hypermedia as well as much of computer science, the last ten years have seen a marked increase in the perceived value of an open systems approach to software development. A major benefit of this approach is the increased adaptability of the resulting software to the needs of its users (Trigg et al. 1987). Adapting can range from an end-user's selection from menu-driven property sheets to a value-added reseller's (VAR's) integration with a new application by means of APIs.

To support adaptability, systems can be open along three dimensions. They can have *horizontal* integratability with other applications, *vertical* integratability with networks, databases, middleware, and the like, and *tailorability*, to support changes to the system by users after installation. To illustrate the three forms of openness, we'll use examples from the WWW and from the Emacs text editor, which first appeared on UNIX platforms in the early 1980s (Stallman 1984).

Application integratability   An open system serves as a means of integrating applications and data formats. At the same time, it should have the ability to be integrated into other applications itself. Both forms of integratability are partially supported by Emacs. First, Emacs is often used as an overarching framework within which text-based applications run. For example, the "rmail" electronic mail program is an integration of UNIX "mail" into an Emacs-based email browsing and management environment. Emacs can also be incorporated into other systems. For example, the Allegro Lisp programming environment incorporates a specialized version of Emacs as its underlying program text editor, both for user composition of new functions and for display of code fragments in the debugger. The designers of that environment not only incorporated Emacs at several points in the environment; they also extended Emacs functionality in significant ways, for instance, by adding simple font faces like bold and italics.

Both forms of application integratability are important for hypermedia systems. Consider, for example, a World Wide Web browser like Netscape Navigator. On the one hand, the plug-in architecture of Navigator supports the ability to integrate new applications (such as 3D animation and sound), as does the extensibility of the WWW addressing protocols. On the other hand, up to this point, Netscape has not supported integration of its browser into other applications and environments, in part because it offers only limited support for inter-application communication protocols such as AppleScript, DDE, OLE, and the like.

System integratability Integratability at the system level involves a variety of capabilities, some of which are invisible to users. For example, an open system should be able to store its data in a variety of different "back ends," say, databases from different vendors. System integration can also be supported by a client-server architecture, as well as distribution of storage over a network of platforms. Allowing intercommunicating clients on the network offers further support for multiuser cooperation.

The World Wide Web provides a striking example of system integratability. With the help of CGI scripts, data from a wide variety of back ends (such as file systems, databases, and other servers) can be retrieved and displayed in HTML on a page. The web uses a client-server architecture to support distribution across the Internet. As of this writing, multiuser cooperation over the WWW is still rare. Although WWW clients are currently not interconnectable, a few experiments are taking place in cooperative asynchronous web authoring. See, for example, Röscheisen, Mogensen and Winograd (1994).

Tailorability As we mentioned in the discussion of history in section 1.3.1, a tailorable system is one that supports limited changes after installation, usually by users or others not involved in the original system implementation. One can think of a tailorable system as a "gray box," in contrast to a "black box" or "glass box." That is, a tailorable open system does not expose all its inner workings all the time for all users. Rather, it is partially open for certain users as needed. Beyond inspection of the system's structure and processes, the system's behavior can also be changed in carefully bounded ways (Kiczales et al. 1991; Nardi 1993). In Emacs, for instance, users can inspect and modify various options related to line wrapping, indentation, and buffer saving. Values for such options are also aggregated into modes among which users can select. Emacs also supports more advanced tailoring. For example, users willing to learn Emacs Lisp, a dialect of the Lisp programming language, can create their own modes either from scratch or by modifying existing modes. Emacs Lisp was perhaps the world's first scripting language.

WWW browsers also serve as an instructive case in point. The earliest browsers lacked support for tailoring, in part because HTML strictly constrains the appearance of a page. JavaScript, an advanced scripting language built into HTML tags, and Java, a full-fledged programming language, are changing that situation dramatically. JavaScript enables users with HTML experience to embed advanced client-side behavior in their Web pages (Goodman 1996). Java supports even more sophisticated tailoring for users who program (Gosling and McGilton 1995).

1.4.2   Object-orientated application frameworks

In this book, we advocate the use of hypermedia frameworks to support the design of open hypermedia systems. But what exactly is a framework? How does it relate to other approaches, in particular, reference models such as Dexter's, and standards such as HyTime?

A framework is an object-oriented conceptual design that explicates the fundamental concepts of hypermedia and their interrelationships (Meyrowitz 1986). Usually, the framework includes representations of policies for the runtime behavior of hypermedia entities at some level. Unlike reference models and standards, however, a framework is oriented toward the work of design (Johnson 1997). Frameworks thus rarely use the mathematical formalisms common in reference models like Dexter, nor do they attempt the conceptual coverage of a comprehensive standard like HyTime (DeRose and Durand 1994). Of greatest concern is that the structural representations be readily amenable to the work of design. Toward that end, this book employs object-oriented design diagrams combined with historical and design-oriented justifications.

With a framework, it ought to be possible for a designer to choose the concepts and behaviors she wants to support and then ascertain the basic requirements of an object-oriented implementation.[1] At the same time, a framework is not a prescription. Rather, it offers a design-oriented means of making available the lessons learned in building earlier hypermedia systems. In short, a framework is a resource for design that offers the best experience of past systems in the service of future designs. Though we are not engaged in a standardization process based on our framework, we do believe in the importance of standards like HyTime (DeRose and Durand 1994) and build on them whenever possible.

The best-known example of a hypermedia design framework to date is that presented by Norm Meyrowitz (1986) and his codesigners of the Intermedia system. For hypermedia designers interested in using object-oriented techniques, this framework offered concrete representations of the design decisions underly-

---

1. Compare for example, HyTime's description of multimedia synchronization in (DeRose and Durand 1994) with ours in Chapter 10.

ing Intermedia. The frameworks we present in this book are also object-oriented and directed toward the work of design. However, they differ from Intermedia's in two ways. First, like the Dexter reference model, they are general enough to model many of the features of today's hypermedia systems. Second, each concept we present is accompanied by a design rationale based on the history of work on the issue that concept addresses.

1.4.3   Design patterns

In recent years, the object-oriented programming language community has taken up the notion of *design patterns* (Coplien and Schmidt 1995; Vlissides et al. 1996). First introduced by Christopher Alexander (1964; Alexander et al. 1977) in the realm of architecture, patterns act as nuggets of distilled experience, applicable to the practical work of design. Each pattern is based on corroborating experiences gained by designers working independently in a variety of settings. At the same time, a pattern explicitly identifies a context in which its application makes sense. A collection of patterns can interrelate, building on one another to form what Alexander called a *pattern language*.

Researchers and practitioners in the object-oriented community have used design patterns in a variety of projects, from a catalog of tips for good object-oriented design (Gamma et al. 1994) to a collection of recommendations for organizing software development projects (Cockburn 1996). The patterns we propose in this book summarize and structure the hypermedia design principles we have gathered. These principles are based on the Dexter model and on the research and development that have taken place in the hypermedia community since 1990. Our patterns range from the low-level design for specifying locations that must underlie any linking infrastructure, to strategies for applying hypermedia concepts to particular work situations.

1.5   An open hypermedia design pattern

We use design patterns throughout the book to summarize the main points of each chapter in a concise format and to encapsulate one or more related design recommendations and strategies. This chapter's pattern presents hypermedia as a tool for integration.

In the next chapter we focus on the use context for open hypermedia and identify challenges from a real workplace.

Title: Hypermedia as Integration

Context: Heterogeneous data, applications, and platforms applied to a single application domain. The third-party applications are tailorable with APIs, communication interfaces, and built-in macro languages.

Problem: To establish organizing conceptual structures such as links, collections and paths for such heterogeneous data, and to support structuring of data that you do not own.

Solution(s): Use object-based hypermedia in which conceptual structures are supported as entities separate from the data. The structures are anchored in the data through a unified mechanism for specifying locations in data. The structures are maintained persistently in dedicated databases.

Examples: Intermedia, Sun Link Service, Microcosm, Devise Hypermedia, Chimera, and HyperWave.

Related patterns: N/A

2

Hypermedia at Work

It is tempting to describe the essence of hypertext as its ability to perform high-speed, branching transactions on textual chunks. But this is a little like describing the essence of a great meal by listing its ingredients. Perhaps a better description would focus on hypertext as a computer-based medium for thinking and communication. (Conklin 1987, p. 32)

[U]sers do not see hypermedia as an alternative to their desktop environment; rather, they see it as an integral technique tying together documents in that environment. (Yankelovich, Haan, Meyrowitz and Drucker 1988, p. 90)

Hypermedia technology has the potential to contribute to most areas of human work with computer-based materials and information, from project management to online education, from creative writing to industrial engineering. Each area poses challenges to hypermedia technology and how it should be designed. Among the examples of domain-specific requirements for hypermedia in the wider hypertext literature, Malcolm et al. (1991) and Grønbæk et al. (1993) discuss engineering domains while De Young (1989) investigates the auditing domain. This chapter builds on these efforts with scenarios drawn from engineering work at a bridge construction site in Denmark. Though the names of the engineers have been changed, the work practices we describe are taken from a specific engineering group within the project. Each of the scenarios poses specific challenges for our open hypermedia design.

Between the islands of Zealand and Funen in Denmark, what will be the world's largest suspension bridge was under construction. Great Belt Link, Ltd. manages the work on this bridge as well as the accompanying railway tunnel. The characters Susanne and Søren in the scenarios that follow are supervising engineers (hereafter called *supervisors*) at the Great Belt office in Knudshoved at the west end of the bridge. Søren and Susanne's typical tasks include on-site

Figure 1
Building a fixed link between two islands in Denmark.

inspection at the construction site, as well as handling two main types of cases, nonconformance reports and change requests, which they receive from the Contractor, a consortium responsible for performing the construction. Nonconformance reports describe unexpected situations that occur during the construction process. Change requests are sent when the Contractor wants to carry out a construction process different from that described in the design specification. Processing these two kinds of reports plays a significant role in the supervisors' daily work, as the scenarios that follow illustrate.

2.1   Heterogeneous materials, applications, and platforms

Supporting heterogeneity has long been a major goal for open hypermedia system developers. The problem is how to support the integration of existing materials across existing platforms, without requiring wholesale conversion of users' practices, materials, and tools.

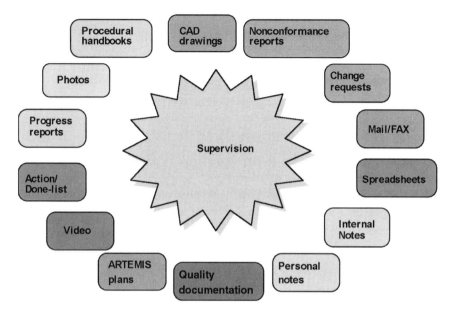

Figure 2
The work materials of an engineer at Great Belt, Ltd.

In particular, a supervisors' case handling and documentation of onsite inspections involves dealing with a rich variety of materials, as depicted in figure 2. The materials used for daily work represent gigabytes of text, scanned letters, Computer-Aided Design (CAD) drawings, spreadsheets, planning diagrams, videos, and photos. Supporting efficient online access to all shared materials could reduce the need for multiple archiving, decrease the workload of the secretaries responsible for archiving, and support the engineers in sharing materials needed for their work.

At Great Belt, these heterogeneous materials are managed by an almost equally diverse set of office and technical applications. Many of the applications are quite advanced, and require a high degree of skill to use. The first scenario illustrates the cross-referencing that is sometimes needed between two documents viewed simultaneously in separate applications.

Providing hypermedia support that can become an integrated part of a work practice like Susanne's is a challenge. Great Belt engineers, like other sophisticated computer users, are reluctant to throw out their favorite tools just to get hypermedia linking, even though it may improve their work practice. Whereas

---

Scenario 1: A diversity of applications
Susanne composes a report in Microsoft Word while inspecting engineering drawings in the Microstation CAD system. In the Word document, she refers to the
positions of damaged bridge elements using locations in the CAD drawing.

---

most monolithic hypermedia systems developed in the past included a set of
proprietary editors, our approach is to provide an open hypermedia service that
augments the engineers' current applications with hypermedia support.

The success of such an open hypermedia service approach depends on the
openness of the applications it integrates. Thus the general requirement for open
hypermedia includes specific requirements for open systems that can be integrated both with each other and with value-adding open hypermedia services.
Fortunately, many recent off-the-shelf applications take significant steps in this
direction.

While cross-application linking is practically synonymous with open hypermedia, the notion of cross-*platform* links is less often discussed.[1] Our next scenario
offers a graphic example of the problem of cross-platform linking. Interestingly,
rather than a collaborative task, the second scene is a single user attempting to
link his own materials across platforms.

Let's suppose Søren wanted to create a link between his Windows text document and the OS/2 database. Suppose further that the online architecture consists of networked clients and servers. (For more on hypermedia system
architectures, see chapter 13.) Søren's link would have to be started from one
client and completed from another, which requires the link to be incrementally
constructed at the server (or at a middleware system between client and server).
This requirement, in turn, seems to necessitate that active links be maintained on
the server, on a per user or possibly per workgroup basis. A benefit of such
incremental link creation is that it enables users on separate platforms to cocreate
links and perform other fine-grained collaborative tasks.

It is unlikely that any single computer system vendor or consortium will ever
be able to provide unified system packages that support arbitrary work environ-

---

1. A notable exception is Kacmar and Leggett's PROXHY system (1991). Based on a
process model of links and anchors, PROXHY was able to link across platforms and
applications.

Scenario 2: Multiple platforms
Søren has been assigned the task of handling a particular nonconformance report. Søren is also responsible for managing the quality documentation, a large Oracle database on UNIX servers with OS/2 PCs running the client interface. Since the office software packages used at Great Belt run on the Windows platform, Søren has to deal with two different machines on a daily basis. A special purpose box built by the systems staff allows Søren to have a single screen and keyboard on his desk and switch the connection between a Windows and an OS/2 PC, both located under his desk. Søren moves back and forth between his two machines while writing his recommendations in a word processor on the Windows machine.

---

ments. Thus, we must cope with heterogeneity when designing hypermedia systems. Fortunately, the web offers presentation modules for an increasing number of data formats. However, most of these modules behave like black boxes for users who might prefer to manipulate them to modify relationships among parts of the data, for instance, between a video segment and an object in a CAD drawing.

In short, a hypermedia system for an engineering environment needs to support links between different types of material, maintained by multiple special-purpose applications, possibly running on different types of machines.

2.2   Linking and grouping materials

During workshops with a research team from a Danish university, the supervisors handling complex technical cases at Great Belt expressed the need to maintain relationships among the documents in a case, some of which appear in figure 2. The designers proposed the use of links and other hypermedia structuring mechanisms as a means of representing and reifying these relationships. Subsequent experiments with hypermedia prototypes led the supervisors to conclude that they would benefit from a hypermedia system in which they could dynamically create links between their heterogeneous working materials (Grønbæk et al. 1993).

At present, the only online means of finding documents is keyword search in the Journalization system. This method is insufficient even if the assignment of keywords is highly standardized. In contrast, marked links in the material would support immediate access without the supervisors having to guess, say, which date or keywords were assigned to the desired document. Currently, some of the existing materials are manually interlinked with cross-references. For example, half of the letters refer to sections or paragraphs in the Work Procedure Handbook, called SAB in Danish, which supervisors often consult for standard wording. Links could increase the efficiency of handbook access from other documents. Moreover, when a supervisor accepts a change request, she is required to add appropriate modification notes to the handbook. These notes could be linked to relevant sections of the handbook and to the instigating change request.

The supervisors feel a need to be able to distinguish among different types of relationships between working materials. Two desired link types are "In-reply-to" and "Refers-to," to connect incoming mail and existing materials such as previous letters, drawings, and the Work Procedure Handbook. Two others are "Reject" and "Accept" links for connecting a change request sent by a contractor to a note explaining the decision on the request. The engineers also want to see who established a given link, since knowing who made an annotation helps them assess the status of an active document or case.

Another important link-related issue for Great Belt engineers concerns the need to annotate documents that legally should not be altered. Such documents include scanned letters or pictures, and certain CAD drawings and procedure descriptions. The engineers need to annotate the images of these protected documents online as they might on the hardcopies. The challenge for hypermedia systems is to support links and other annotations in overlays on top of such scanned images and pictures. This issue also arose in DeYoung's studies of the auditing domain (DeYoung 1989).

In addition, the engineers' needs go beyond simple linking to include groupings or collections of documents, some of which overlap as in scenario 3.

This scenario illustrates the need for engineers and secretaries to maintain different groupings or views of the material, making the same letter, for example, accessible from multiple contexts. Currently, they meet this need by filing multiple copies of the letter. A grouping or collection facility would avoid redundant copying and archiving of materials by allowing the same document to be a member of several collections. For instance, the Master File is a collection determined by the physical decomposition of the bridge into bridge elements. It includes each piece of material relevant to a certain bridge element. Many of

Scenario 3: Overlapping groupings

During an inspection visit, Susanne observes damage to a bridge element caused by a temperature differential where two castings meet. She makes notes on the damage and photos of the area. Upon returning to her office, Susanne must record her observations and apprise her colleagues of the situation in order to make them aware of the initiated repair activity. She registers the pictures in a spreadsheet database, types her notes in a word processor, locates the damage on the CAD construction drawings, and looks for any relevant incoming nonconformance report from the contractor. Susanne creates a list of all the material she might need when following up on the case. Finally, she looks at the plan in the Artemis system to see whether the damage and the repair procedure will affect the overall construction schedule.

When Susanne finally completes the case, she inserts a copy of the relevant material into the Master File folder for the bridge element in question.

these documents also belong to other collections, such as that of materials identified with a particular activity described in the construction plan.

Because of the need for such cross-application collections, the hypermedia server in a client-server architecture must serve structure as well as links. As we'll see in the next chapter, the Dexter notion of composites and its extensions (Grønbæk 1994; Hardman et al. 1994) is a good candidate for the conceptual entity underlying such a structure service. In particular, composites can represent overlapping structures in ways that complement links.

2.3   The need for cooperation support

Hypermedia system developers have long linked their work with that of the Computer-Supported Cooperative Work (CSCW) community, arguing that hypertext is particularly well-suited to the requirements of cooperating users. The document-related work at Great Belt is rich with examples of cooperation, coordination, and distribution, to which hypermedia support might fruitfully be applied.

One of the recurring tasks that requires coordination is the handling of incoming mail. Many of the incoming letters need to be assigned to particular supervisors, who then take appropriate actions. As scenario 4 illustrates, they register the actions they take in a small database maintained by the area manager.

Scenario 4: Tracking distributed work
Helle, the area manager, analyzes incoming letters, assigns them priority, and decides who should have copies and who should be responsible for taking action. The letters are registered in an "action list" together with a deadline and the initials of the person responsible. The deadline is either two days, a week, or two weeks. The weekly reminders the responsible engineers receive consist of copies of the most recent action list. When they complete an item on the action list, they move the item to a "done-list."

Scenario 5: Coordinating work on complex documents
Søren has just received a draft of the contractor's progress report. He is responsible for assessing whether the draft reflects reality at the construction site. This task requires copying and distributing parts of the contractor's reports to the appropriate supervisors in order to get their responses within a few days. Søren is responsible for making the final version of the progress report, based on contributions he receives from the supervisors by email and floppy disk. Performing the assessment thus involves assembling the original report, revisions, and the supervisors' comments.

Sometimes, several engineers collaborating on a task need to share materials. In scenario 5, an incoming document is processed and annotated by people distributed throughout the organization. Søren then gathers their input and uses it to produce new documents.

As this scenario shows, even if one person has overall responsibility for a document's production, the work can involve coordinating contributions from several people. In this case, Søren needs to access the information supplied by others and monitor when their contributions arrive. In terms of hypermedia, it would be helpful if the supervisor managing a progress report could create links between the original document and the background documents supplied by other supervisors. Private sets of documents and links for both shared and individual materials—like Intermedia's separate webs (Garrett 1986)—should also be supported.

It is often the case that particular individuals need to be notified when a document changes or when new links are established. Awareness notifications

> **Scenario 6: Serendipitous cooperation**
> Susanne has just accepted a Change Request from the contractor. She must now add an addendum to the Work Procedure Handbook, hard copies of which have been distributed to all the supervisors. At the same time, Jens is working with another Change Request on a different type of bridge element with a duct at the connection points. He consults several sections of the Work Procedure Handbook and is about to write his conclusion. One day he talks with Susanne in the canteen, and she tells him that she thinks he has a copy of her addendum to the section on ducts sitting in an internal mail envelope somewhere on his desk, since she asked a secretary to distribute the addendum last week.

(Grønbæk et al. 1994; Halasz 1988; Wiil 1991) alerting users to changes in documents and hypermedia structures could help Søren keep track of contributions linked to critical parts of the contractor's progress report. The sixth scenario describes another situation involving the creation of links that the use of awareness notifications could improve.

In this situation, Jens could benefit from an awareness notification. Ensuring that addenda to the Work Procedure Handbook are linked into the relevant sections and that the supervisors are notified upon the creation of such links, would reduce the risk of missing a recent update.

Together, these scenarios and work descriptions suggest that hypermedia systems ought to allow cooperative authoring of contents as well as structures like links and collections. Moreover, the hypermedia database should support monitoring changes and distributing notifications to users who indicate particular interests or whose jobs require staying informed.

2.4   Envisioning an open hypermedia service architecture

The scenarios in the previous sections draw on current practice at Great Belt to pose problems and requirements for hypermedia support. In this section, we turn to the future, envisioning an architecture in which open hypermedia services are plugged into a network to support interlinking of materials maintained by the different applications, as illustrated in figure 3. The hypermedia service supplements existing database structures rather than replacing them. For instance, the overall system continues to support the sorting and indexing of various types of material in the service of conventional query facilities.

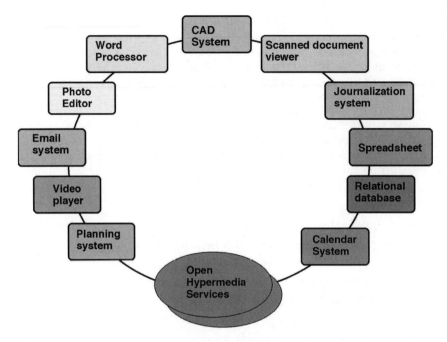

Figure 3
An approach to integrating materials at GBL. Rounded rectangles represent archives of specific types of materials; ovals represent link databases.

As we'll see in the next chapter, a crucial consideration for any hypermedia system is the means by which links are *anchored* in the material at each endpoint. The kinds of anchors depend on the particular application. At Great Belt, for example, the existing CAD systems and word processors present very different sorts of anchoring options. Once anchors in the material are defined, links connecting them can be created through a user interface, and stored by hypermedia database servers managed through an open hypermedia service. Such servers allow the whole organization, a particular department, or the members of a work group to share materials and hypermedia structures, including links and collections.

The hypermedia services are made available to all workers connected by the company network, subject to appropriate access restrictions. For performance reasons, separate hypermedia database servers may be required for each site, in which case it must be possible to establish links between documents at different sites.

In accord with Engelbart's (1984a) original notion of hypermedia, a journalization system should be integrated with the hypermedia system. This allows the secretaries currently responsible for registering correspondence to create hypermedia links as well. These links between new and existing materials supplement and, in part, substitute for keyword registration. When, for example, an incoming letter is a response to a letter already stored in the network, the secretary might establish a "Refer-to" link between them.

Instead of having to photocopy incoming materials for manual distribution and filing in multiple local archives, the entry of material into the hypermedia triggers automatic notification to employees who subscribe to that type of material. Thus, there is less photocopying, but more printing, to enable people to generate hardcopy just when they need it. In addition to the links created during journalization, workers who receive the material can add links and annotations of their own, thereby offering their reactions to other subscribers.

For instance, a supervisor assigned to carry out an action might want to find all relevant correspondence and notes. If the existing materials were entered and interlinked during earlier work on the case, then the relevant materials can be accessed directly by following links. Specialized structure browsers could support semi-automatic gathering of materials from the hypermedia (chapter 7). Finally, users might specify a linearization of subsets of the material for making printouts.

To conclude, let's briefly consider the degree to which such a vision of hypermedia support at Great Belt is realizable.

2.5   Impending challenges for hypermedia design

No existing hypermedia system or open hypermedia service can meet the challenges posed by the foregoing scenarios. These scenarios call for cross-linking of heterogeneous materials managed by existing applications on diverse platforms, support for nonlinked overlapping structures, annotation of nonwritable material, sharing of materials and hypermedia structures in collaborative settings, and support for monitoring ongoing changes to both content and structure.

A WWW-based intranet would help overcome some of the problems of publishing and regularly updating material meant to be accessible to all the employees in an organization. But the WWW fails to support users in creating links into and from materials that they do not own. Moreover, creation of links in nontext-based data is hard. The available open hypermedia services can support the dynamic link creation provided by some of the best-known applications, but these applications are generally still oriented to single users. As yet, no open hypermedia service supports the integration of cooperative link creation with these applications. In short, current systems cannot integrate dynamic and cooperative creation of hypermedia structures with the applications that users want to apply in a work context.

Even when such support becomes available, a huge effort will be needed to integrate old materials into the new hypermedia structures. Automatic generation of link structures (Bernstein 1993) can only partly solve this problem. Some of the most valuable relationships among documents are particular rather than generically specifiable and thus require manual identification. In many organizations, it will not be realistic to convert the entire information corpus into hypermedia. In all likelihood, only new incoming materials would be organized in hypermedia structures; links to old materials would be added as needed. At the end of the book, we return to the topic of links from online to offline worlds, which remains an open research question.

3

The Dexter Model and Beyond

The [Dexter hypertext reference model] provides a standard hypertext terminology coupled with a formal model of the important abstractions commonly found in a wide range of hypertext systems. Thus, the Dexter model serves as a standard against which to compare and contrast the characteristics and functionality of various hypertext (and nonhypertext) systems. The Dexter model also serves as a principled basis on which to develop standards for interoperability and interchange among hypertext systems. (Halasz and Schwartz 1994, p. 30)

At the heart of this book lies a set of proposed principles and frameworks for the design of open hypermedia systems and functionality. Rather than starting from scratch, we have formulated these principles and frameworks on the basis of the hypermedia design research that precedes us. Fortunately, a large part of that design history is captured in the Dexter hypertext reference model. This ground-breaking conceptual model includes a formal specification of hypertext entities and their relationships, as well as informal descriptions and motivations. This chapter gives a brief overview of the goals of the Dexter group, who participated, what they accomplished, and why we find it so appropriate as a foundation for the open hypermedia design we want to support. At the same time, we have found the Dexter model to be insufficient as it stands. Hence, the chapter concludes with a discussion of some of the problems we and others have identified and why we believe solving them is critical for our open systems goals.

3.1 The goals of the Dexter group

The Dexter group was a collection of hypermedia researchers and developers who met several times during the late 1980s and are now best known as the creators of the Dexter hypertext reference model. At the start, however, the goal of the Dexter group was not to design such a reference model. Rather it was to compare experiences and arrive at a shared terminology that could encompass the variety of conceptual apparati in the field. In the process, the group discussed the history and ongoing concerns of the various hypermedia projects they had developed.

It was only later that the group took up the task of jointly designing a hypertext reference model. Eventually, their intents moved beyond creating an agreed-upon terminology and conceptual framework, to

· unifying the notions of node and link
· augmenting link-based networks with other structures
· integrating hypermedia with existing environments and content editors
· representing and enforcing different data models and runtime behavior
· storing properties of node presentations
· interchanging hypertexts across systems
· and even defining what *counts* as hypertext/hypermedia

Before taking a closer look at these goals and the degree to which the Dexter reference model met them, let's review the participants and their collaborative efforts.

3.2   The participants and their systems

The Dexter meetings started in the fall of 1988, when John Leggett and Jan Walker invited a carefully selected group of hypermedia designers to a meeting at the Dexter Inn in Sunapee, New Hampshire. Jan and John chose members of the community who had played a key role in the development of a well-known and/or ground-breaking hypermedia system, people who understood first-hand the rationale as well as the technical details of their system's design.

Perhaps most crucial to the success of the group was its coverage of existing systems, at which the organizers succeeded astonishingly well. The attendees represented 17 systems encompassing a wide variety of hypermedia design philosophies and strategies. [The best known systems that were not represented were Guide (Brown 1987) and Xanadu (Nelson 1974; Nelson 1981).] After the first meeting, three others took place over the next two years, as well as a few *ad hoc* meetings of subgroups. Aside from two replacements and one addition, the

Participants	Hypermedia systems
Organizers: John Leggett, Jan Walker	
Rob Akscyn, Don McCracken	ZOG, KMS
Doug Engelbart	NLS, Augment
Steve Feiner	IGD
Mark Frisse	Dynamic Medical Handbook
Frank Halasz, Randy Trigg	NoteCards, TextNet
Norm Meyrowitz, Karen Smith	FRESS, Intermedia
Tim Oren	HyperCard
Amy Pearl	Sun Link Service
Catherine Plaisant, Bill Weiland	HyperTies
Mayer Schwartz	Neptune, HAM
Jan Walker	Concordia, Document Examiner

Figure 4
Participants at the Dexter meetings and the systems they represented.

group of thirteen people present at the first meeting also attended the three subsequent meetings, an organizational feat in itself.[1] Figure 4 lists the attendees and their systems.

The striking diversity of approach and design across these systems was apparent to the participants. In light of their differences, was it at all reasonable to try to define hypermedia? What, if anything, did Doug Engelbart's groundbreaking Augment system and Apple's brand-new HyperCard program have in common? At the first meeting, the participants compared their work and found some surprising connections and shared roots. During the second meeting, they created a graphical representation of the history of their field. As the photograph in figure 5 indicates, this graphic is itself a hypermedia structure. Each system is depicted as a line whose length corresponds to duration in time. Two kinds of arrows connect the lines. One represents direct ancestry (as when the FRESS group at Brown became the Intermedia development team); the other, less direct influence (as when Doug Engelbart first talked to the Brown University researchers).

The participants then proceeded to the business of design. After several more meetings, Frank Halasz and Mayer Schwartz crafted the group's conclusions into

1. Sources of funding for the Dexter meetings included Digital Equipment Corporation, Texas A&M University, and Apple Corporation.

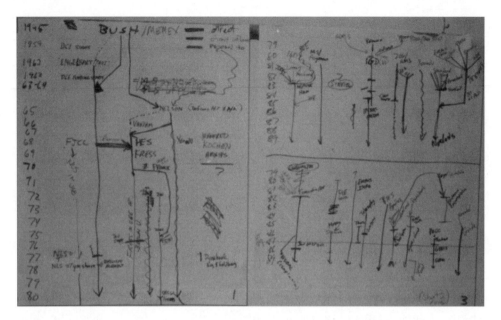

Figure 5
The Dexter group's representation of the early history of hypermedia research.

a formal reference model, which they subsequently presented at the 1990 National Institute of Standards and Technology workshop (Halasz and Schwartz 1990).

3.3   Dexter's recommendations

In the end, the reference model that resulted from the Dexter group's deliberations accomplished both less and more than the group had hoped. This section lists the main conclusions of the reference model, which the group articulated as requirements, and explains the premises that underlie them. Some of the conclusions were controversial, a few were new, and most were inherited from one or more existing systems and then generalized to apply across the board. The next section adopts a critical perspective on the Dexter model, identifying issues and problems that the rest of this book explores. Interested readers can also check the original sources (Halasz and Schwartz 1990; Halasz and Schwartz 1994).

We cannot expect hypermedia systems to manage the "content" of the material whose interconnections they support. In most cases, this is the province of applications outside the control of the hypermedia system.

It was clear to the Dexter group that while most systems used the term *link,* the naming of the entities connected by the links of a hypermedia system varied from system to system. These entities were variously called *nodes, cards, documents, frames, files,* and so on. In chapter 5, we'll return to these terms and the different behaviors and world views they represent. Considering hypermedia's fundamental goal—integration—it was hardly surprising that much of the material to be integrated would already exist and have its own rich terminology. The Dexter group's awareness of the variety of preexisting material to be interconnected led to the realization that the management of such materials was essentially "out of the hands" of the hypermedia system. These observations arose, in particular, from Amy Pearl's (1989) experience with the Sun Link Service, perhaps the first open integrative hypermedia system.

The Dexter model's high-level architecture reflected the group's recognition of the limited scope of a hypermedia system. Borrowing loosely from operating system terminology, the Dexter group defined the *within-component layer* to be that part of a user's online environment that is under the control of application programs. This architectural design decision marked the first time that theorists of hypermedia took an anti-monolithic stance.

A conceptual framework for hypermedia must distinguish between aspects of the storage of electronic material and its runtime behavior.

Also clear to the Dexter group and computer science researchers generally was the need to distinguish between information storage and runtime interfaces to that information, in other words, between the persistence of electronic materials and their behavior. Such distinctions are analogous to that between client and server in distributed systems. Again, the Dexter group conceived of the distinction in terms of layers. In the Dexter model, layers are architectural divisions between parts of the system as well as areas of concern. In particular, the model distinguished between a storage and a runtime layer. In the next section, we'll discuss how the concept of layers led to problematic associations for some readers of the Dexter model.

Link anchoring, connecting link endpoints to content, constitutes much of the action in a hypermedia system. Therefore, anchoring must be explicitly represented in the model.

One of the most important problems taken up by the Dexter group involved link *anchoring.* That is, given the premise that we cannot control the content of material in the system, how can we create and manage links that connect points within that content? The Dexter group generalized Intermedia's notion of the block (Meyrowitz 1986), a data structure representing points or spans in the material of online documents. The result was the *anchor,* an abstract object that straddles the boundary between the storage and within-component layers.

Certain aspects of the runtime behavior of particular links and nodes must persist across uses of the system, and thus must be stored with the hypermedia content and structure.

The Dexter group defined *presentation specifications* (pSpecs) to be an entity associated with every component that retains information related to the runtime behavior of the component and its linked neighbors. Like the anchor, pSpecs straddle a layer boundary, here between the runtime and storage layers. The example most often used to justify pSpecs involved varying the interface to material depending on the link the user traverses to access the material. Figure 6 depicts a computer-assisted tutoring scenario. It illustrates two means of arriving at the animation: one used by students who by default should run the animation, and one by teachers who by default should edit it.

In the Dexter model, pSpecs stored with each link capture the distinction by representing the two choices. In this way, pSpecs provide a means of recording and saving choices made about runtime behavior.

Nonlink structures should be represented as full-fledged parts of the model.

Frank Halasz asserted in his landmark "Seven Issues" paper (1988) that most applications of hypermedia require structures beyond purely link-based networks. These structures include hierarchies, outlines, tables, objects with attributes, database relations, and the like. Moreover, he argued against building these representations out of links. Instead, he proposed a new hypermedia entity called the *composite* to represent non link-based structures. The notion of the composite was taken up by Dexter and became one of its best-known features. In the Dexter view of the world, composites and links are equivalent in status.

The various objects involved in representing hypermedia structures should be specializations of a single generic entity, which models the wrappers around material, the links used to interconnect it, and the composites used to structure it.

Rather than adopt one of the many terms in use at the time for the "nodes" of a hypermedia system, the Dexter group chose a new one, the *component,* to

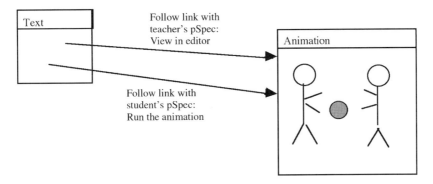

Figure 6
Two links with different instructions (pSpecs) for the destination interface.

express a concept that unified the ideas of the link and the node. This consolidation in the model made it easy to capture the commonalities of links and nonlinks, providing a single entity with which to model the structural and behavioral aspects common to all objects modeled by the framework. Searching and the assignment of unique identifiers could thus be defined once for the Component object, ensuring coverage for all objects in the hypermedia. Furthermore, links could connect other links as well as nonlink components. This idea was attractive to many hypermedia researchers, though practical applications were hard to imagine. Finally, the component was also used to model composites, material organized with nonlink structures.

The Dexter model distinguished three fundamental kinds of components: atomic components, link components and composite components. Atomic components were meant to wrap content that would typically be managed by a third-party application. They were called *atomic* to underscore the fact that the structure of this content was not visible to, that is, represented in, the hypermedia system.

Computed link endpoints are best modeled by separating the work of specifying a location from that of accessing material at that location.

Over the years, many researchers in the hypermedia community have argued for the notion of a link whose destination is computed. Rather than depending on hard-wired endpoints, computed links execute a small program in order to determine the result of a traversal. Though few systems at the time of the Dexter meetings had found extensive use for the concept (that would come later with the

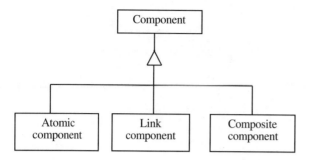

Figure 7
An object-oriented depiction of the original Dexter concepts.

World Wide Web), the group agreed that any comprehensive model should be able to represent both computed and noncomputed links.

The Dexter group eventually arrived at a powerful generalization that could have wider application. First, they stipulated that computation be associated with endpoints of links rather than with the link as a whole. This means that a link's source can be computed or that multiple endpoints can be simultaneously computed.

Second, the Dexter model distinguishes between specifying locations and accessing them. In fact, these activities are embodied in the model by two functions, called the *resolver* and the *accessor*. The resolver models the processing of executable scripts as well as hard-wired endpoint identification. The result of the computation is a unique identifier (UID) of a component, which optionally includes an anchor identifier to locate a position within the component's contents. The UID is then handed to the accessor function, which returns the actual component/anchor. This model of hypermedia computation was particularly well suited to supporting links whose endpoint computations involve searching the hypermedia for components with certain attributes.

Directionality should be associated with link endpoints, rather than with links. Links should also have an unlimited number of endpoints.

In attempting to encompass the systems represented by the Dexter participants, the group ran into a knotty problem involving the semantics and traversal behavior of links. Some systems like HyperCard implement links as "embedded go-tos." With HyperCard, every link is computed, in the sense that its destination is found by running the accompanying HyperTalk script. HyperCard's links are thus one-way in that traversal backward from a link's destination is almost impossible. This is also largely the case with HTML links on the web, which has prompted some to refer to the web as a distributed version of HyperCard. Intermedia represents the other extreme. In that system, links are separate, two-way objects for which neither traversal direction is privileged. The behaviors of the other systems the Dexter participants worked on lie somewhere in between.

As with computed links, the Dexter group decided to associate directionality with a link's endpoint rather than with the link as a whole. They adopted four directionality constants: TO, FROM, NONE, and BOTH. Though the model didn't offer a semantics for all (or even most) of the possible assignments of directionalities to endpoints, the group was able to model the semantics of HyperCard, Intermedia, and the other systems represented at the meetings. We'll return to the topic of link directionality in chapter 6.

In addition, the group decided after some debate to include in the model links with more than two endpoints. Though hypermedia researchers at the time had even less experience with multiheaded links than with computed links, the Dexter group felt the generalization to be important for future sytems. Figure 8 depicts a link component with three endpoints interconnecting three other components. The atomic component at the upper left acts as a source for the link (the endpoint has FROM direction) while the other two components act as destinations (TO direction).

Any hypermedia system should be able to export a representation of the structure and content of its hypermedia in a standard way that allows other hypermedia systems to import that representation.

Supporting interchange between hypermedia systems was a key goal of the Dexter model at the start of its design. However, no one in the Dexter group had experience translating hypermedia representations between systems. It was only after the last Dexter meeting that co-organizer John Leggett and others conducted the first concrete experiments (Leggett and Schnase 1994).

All these premises should be represented formally in a reference model that allows hypermedia systems to be compared, in terms of their capabilities, both to each other and to a defined standard.

The Dexter group intended their model to provide a "Good Housekeeping seal of approval," as they put it, so that designs of future or existing hypermedia

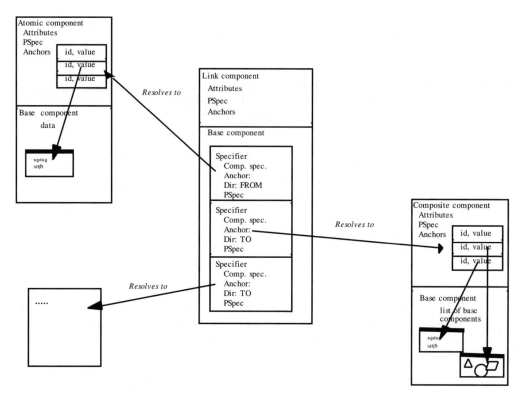

Figure 8
A Dexter link and its relationship to other components.

systems could be compared with the Dexter model as a kind of compliance check. To enable such comparison, the group formally represented the Dexter model using Z, a formal syntax for reference models (Spivey 1989). In addition to representing the conceptual framework, this formalism also expressed certain rules of good hypermedia behavior, the best known being the rule outlawing "dangling links," shown in figure 9.

DeleteComponent is a function that, given a hypertext H and a component UID, returns a new hypertext H' from which the component has been removed. The components of H' are those of H, minus the given component and all link components pointing at it. The accessor and resolver functions of H' are suitably restricted to the reduced set of components. We'll have more to say about the Dexter rules in chapter 6.

Despite the limitations of Dexter's choice of formalism and its goal of strict rule enforcement, many readers welcomed the formal representations of the concepts. Those unfamiliar with Z found that they could puzzle out most of the syntax in the context of the issues they cared about. In addition, the formal descriptions enabled readers to take up and criticize the Dexter group's work as well as to understand the proposed conceptual framework.

3.4   Dexter and open systems: Problems and issues

Let us now turn to the question of the relevance of the Dexter model for the design of open hypermedia systems. The recommendations of the Dexter group arguably represented the state of the art in hypertext research and development in the late 1980s. However, the Dexter group never intended their model to be used as a design specification, nor were they particularly concerned with open systems issues. Yet, somewhat to our surprise, we have found the Dexter model to be a valuable starting point on both accounts. On the one hand, its clear articulation of architectural and process recommendations serves well as input to design. On the other hand, several of its conclusions and premises align with our open systems agenda.

Nonetheless, Dexter was inadequate for our project as it stood. Indeed, this book emerges from our efforts to reconstruct, revise, and extend Dexter to better

---

2.4   Deleting A Component

In deleting a component we must ensure that we remove any links whose specifiers resolves to that component.

$$DeleteComponent : HYPERTEXT \times UID \rightarrow HYPERTEXT$$

$$DeleteComponent = (\lambda\, H : HYPERTEXT;\ uid : UID \bullet$$
$$(\mu\, H' : HYPERTEXT \mid \exists\, uids : \mathbf{F}\ UID \mid$$
$$uids = \{uid\}\ \cup\ linksTo(H, uid) \bullet$$
$$H'.components = H.components \setminus H.accessor(\!|uids|\!)\ \wedge$$
$$H'.accessor = uids \unlhd H.accessor\ \wedge$$
$$H'.resolver = H.resolver \unrhd uids))$$

Figure 9
Dexter's rule outlawing "dangling links."

support open systems, cooperative use, and global distribution. The rest of the chapter lists some of the outstanding questions that confronted us as we tried to use Dexter as a basis for design. Parts II and III revisit each of these questions in greater detail.

What is the role of Dexter's reference model in design?

The fact that the Dexter reference model was formalized using the Z syntax (Spivey 1989) enables readers to compare system capabilities and behavior. But use of Z syntax alone cannot serve as a specification for system design. As we will see in part II, the challenge that remains is to map these concepts into object-oriented patterns and frameworks that are more amenable to the practical work of design.

What's in a layer?

Modeling a hypermedia system with the three layers shown in figure 10 was an important step toward supporting integration with existing applications. But the Dexter three-layer architecture is awkward and inadequate as the basis for a real open systems architecture. The first problem involves the term *layer,* which many readers associated with operating systems, though this was not the Dexter group's intention. The storage, within-component and runtime layers name the three high-level concerns of the Dexter model. Though they overlap in interesting and important ways, they are not ordered by degree of abstraction as are, for example, the ISO operating system layers. In presenting the architectural concepts of Dexter, we have often found it useful to turn the diagram on its side, so that the three divisions are depicted horizontally explained in chapter 13.

Moreover, aside from the orientation adopted, there are problems with the juxtapositions of layers in the Dexter model. Though the placement of storage between the runtime and within-component layers helps to underscore the borders between them and the interactions and objects used to manage those borders, it imposes two important limitations. First, the runtime and within-component layers wind up far apart in conceptual space, which implies that the applications "wrapped" by Dexter components are responsible for content definition and storage, but not runtime behavior. In fact, the integrative open systems approach we advocate requires runtime interfaces as well.

A second limitation is the Dexter model's locating of the anchor concept on the border between storage and within-component layers, which suggests that an-

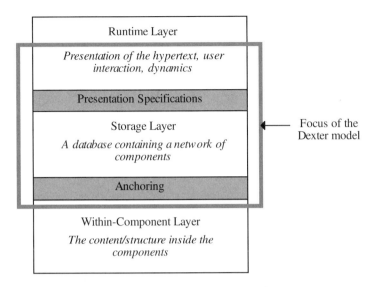

Figure 10
Dexter's three-layer architecture.

chors are not involved in runtime behavior. In fact, an important issue in open hypermedia research involves the proper management of runtime updates to anchors when users modify the components' contents (Davis 1995). As described in part III, in our architecture, the within-component notion as well as concepts like the anchor are incorporated throughout both storage and runtime layers.

Should hybrid components be allowed?

Dexter's elegant unification of links with nodes opened up intriguing possibilities for hypermedia designers, such as the ability to link to a link. Ironically, however, the notion of the component included the restriction that hypermedia objects must be either composite, link, or atomic. In fact, there had been experience within the Dexter group with hybrid components. For example, in NoteCards, the FileBox is a composite component in the sense that it represents hierarchical structure, but it is atomic in that it can be used as a text component. A current example is HTML, where the page is the only kind of component. Though in HTML there is technically no support for composite structuring, web pages often serve that function even as they also include contents. Such hybrid components are difficult to represent in the Dexter model.

Who stores a component's contents?

One of the Dexter group's breakthroughs was the modeling of components as wrappers, which help distinguish the hypermedia system's responsibilities from those of applications. However, the model overlooks the fact that some applications may need to manage the storage of their contents. An excellent source of examples are today's multimedia applications. They often manage large data files whose optimized storage requires complex compression algorithms. It would clearly be inappropriate to require that the hypermedia system take over the management of such forms of data. As we argue in chapter 12, the ideal approach for open hypermedia is to *offer* storage support for those applications that need it, and otherwise manage only the storage of component wrappers as well as links and composites.

Exactly what does a composite "compose"?

One of the Dexter group's best-known contributions was the elevation of the composite, used to model nonlink-based structures, to full-fledged status alongside links. Unfortunately, the definition of a composite reflects only one kind of composition, overlooking certain important common cases. The Dexter composite was meant to model components that have internal structure into which one might want to link. The Dexter group's favorite example was a graphics component whose editor managed the layout and construction of groups of graphical objects. The intention was to allow the anchoring of links in particular graphical objects, as illustrated in figure 11.

However, this limited sense of composition does not, for example, support the modeling of collections of other components. Such collection composites include overlapping structures of other components, in the style of NoteCards "guided tours" and "tabletops" (Trigg 1988). Collection composites even appeared in Frank Halasz's "Seven Issues" paper (1988), though not by that name. A more versatile definition of the composite would model the Dexter group's notion of intra-component structure as well as the inter-component structures represented by collection composites. And the discussion doesn't end there, as chapter 7 reveals. Interpreting composites as a kind of *encapsulation* of structure opens up other useful possibilities.

What's in an anchor?

Both fans and critics of the Dexter model now widely recognize the importance of anchoring. The Dexter group called attention to the fact that the concept of

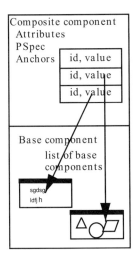

Figure 11
The Dexter composite component.

anchoring lies at the heart of hypermedia's fundamental goal of integrating online materials. However, the definition and use of anchors in the model left something to be desired. For example, although the Dexter group supported the use of computation to find the components identified by a link endpoint, the location of anchors within those components was assumed to involve no computation; a link endpoint always named a particular anchor ID. This means that the Dexter model overlooks a particularly useful (and in some systems, prevalent) form of anchor that specifies searches within its component's contents in order to identify the linked material.

The Dexter group's definition is deficient even for anchors that specify their locations directly. The case of a composite with several layers of nested structure illustrates the problem. The Dexter definition says nothing about how to identify an anchored object deep within that structure. For example, let's suppose we're implementing the collection composite described in the preceding section. One option is to store local anchors in each component of the collection, which then are identified by anchors in the collection composite. This approach has the advantage of keeping anchors local to the components to which they refer. Such indirect referencing from a composite's anchors through the anchors of subcomponents is not supported in the Dexter model.

Which way does a link go?

As we've seen, the Dexter group's notion of directionality properly associates a direction attribute with endpoints instead of links. In addition, it provides a way to represent radically different approaches to link implementation. Unfortunately, this is one of the areas in which the Dexter model may have confused more than it helped. The four constants, TO, FROM, BOTH, and NONE are used to distinguish separately stored link objects from "go-to" style embedded links. But this mistakenly conflates the notions of link directionality and link embeddedness. In chapters 4 and 6, we unhitch directionality from embeddedness and in the process expand the design possibilities inherent in both.

Is your hypermedia system Dexter-compliant?

As we've seen, the Dexter model can be read as a kind of standard. Unfortunately, no existing system, including those developed by members of the group, was Dexter-compliant! The group did, however, consider the possibility of Dexter subsets and partial compliance. For example, they recognized that the requirement that links never be dangling, even temporarily, was too strict, as we discuss in chapter 6. But the group never specified a semantics of partial compliance.

Our approach in this book is to give up the goal of a standard that supports compliance checking for current and future open hypermedia systems. Rather, we argue in favor of a set of design principles that can guide the development of a variety of tunable object-oriented frameworks. We believe that the wisdom of earlier hypermedia systems captured in the Dexter model is most useful as design input, as a resource rather than a prescription.

In parts II and III, we explore the questions raised by the Dexter model more deeply and in relation to today's best known hypermedia system, the World Wide Web, with the goal of formulating principles and frameworks for open systems design.

II

Hypermedia Fundamentals

Hypermedia is often thought of as contributing one significant new entity to information structuring, the link, and one new activity to the work of document management, navigating through and among links. But closer inspection reveals the link as a richer, more subtly faceted entity than first meets the eye. Likewise, the field of hypermedia, especially open hypermedia, includes work on structuring and navigation possibilities that go well beyond simple link creation and traversal.

The situation is similar in the case of the World Wide Web. Its design includes not only links added to Internet ftp, but careful attention to issues of addressing, anchoring, browsing interfaces, and distribution. As we'll see, however, web design still has a ways to go in areas like document structuring and support for collaboration.

In this part of the book, we explore some of the richness that underlies the simple characterization of hypermedia as "linked information space." We start in chapter 4 at the foundation of open hypermedia, its infrastructure of addressing, pointing and "locating" in diverse online materials. Chapter 5 looks at components, hypermedia's primary means of packaging or "wrapping" these materials. Chapters 6 and 7 take up the two primary means of structuring, links and composites. And in chapter 8, we discuss the superordinate entities that correspond to information networks, which we call hyperspaces.

Following these chapters on basic hypermedia entities, chapter 9 considers issues involving the behavior of a hypermedia system, what Dexter called the *runtime layer*. In this context, we explore variants of the most basic form of hypermedia navigation, link traversal. Chapter 10 continues the discussion of navigation with more advanced navigational aids like guided tours. This chapter also raises issues related to the organization and synchronization of dynamic

multimedia materials like animations and audio/video streams. Finally, chapter 11 sums up part II by proposing an object-oriented design framework with variants and extensions, based on the principles presented in the preceding chapters.

Each of these eight chapters includes a historical perspective that evaluates the contributions of the Dexter model as well as of other relevant foundational research. Our approach to addressing outstanding issues, including Dexter's shortcomings, is summarized at the end of each chapter with one or more design patterns. These patterns encapsulate the principles we believe should inform the design and development of any open hypermedia system. Each pattern identifies the context in which it applies and the problem it addresses. The solutions we recommend are drawn from the experience of multiple independently developed systems. Like the Dexter group, our goal is to take fullest advantage of the wisdom and experience in our field. The patterns build on one another to form the dependency graph shown in figure 12.

The examples that appear in our patterns are drawn primarily from a small set of past and present hypermedia systems that includes DHM, HyperCard, Hyper-G, Intermedia, KMS, Microcosm, NoteCards, TextNet, and, of course, the World Wide Web. For short descriptions of each system and selected references, see appendix A.

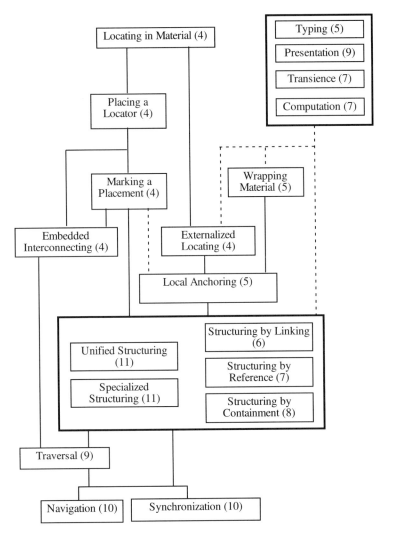

Figure 12
Design patterns for part II. Chapter numbers appear in parentheses.

4

Locations, Placements, and Interconnections

There is a consistent set of addressing features that a worker may use in any command to designate a particular structural node or some element of text or graphics attached to that node. It adds appreciably to the power and flexibility of the system commands to have a rich, universally applicable vocabulary for directly addressing particular entities within the working files. (Engelbart 1984a, p. 467)

For most people, the term hypermedia is associated with webs and links, and the activities of building and traversing connections across diverse material. What can go unnoticed is the less visible infrastructure that supports the work of anchoring and pointing. Though important for any hypermedia system, such infrastructure is especially critical in an open systems context. As we've seen, a major goal of open hypermedia is the interconnecting of third-party applications that make up a user's environment and the wide-area network that comprises its larger context. In open hypermedia, the action is in the details of how links and other structures refer to and are accessible from the material managed by applications and services.

In this chapter, we introduce three concepts—locators, placements and interconnections—that are fundamental to the work of integrating hypermedia with applications and material. A locator is an address or pointer that identifies, more or less precisely, points or regions of material. It is through such locators that hypermedia structures are able to refer to the material. But pointers *into* the material are not enough. It must also be possible to gain access and traverse the hypermedia structures from *within* the material. Placements are the data structures or user interface mechanisms that associate access to hypermedia structures with a position or span of material. Finally, interconnecting is the means of bringing instances of these fundamental concepts together to create traversable structures.

In the sections that follow, we'll discuss how these concepts interact to provide a foundation for open hypermedia. We start with a brief look at early hypermedia systems that supported embedded locators, that is, pointers embedded in the online material. Next, we review the Dexter group's proposal to separate the notions of linking and placement and the impact this separation had on the field. Then we present our approach to supporting locations, placements, and interconnections, which is summarized at the end of this chapter with five design patterns. These patterns provide the basis for the discussions of hypermedia structuring and traversal that comprise the rest of part II.

4.1 Links as embedded locators

Early hypermedia systems focused on the work of locating, that is, addressing arbitrary portions of online material. Less attention was paid to the problem of placement, how to provide access to the locator from inside the material. By choosing the simplest form of placement, links became synonymous with embedded locators. This does not mean, however, that these systems weren't sophisticated at many levels. For example, the Augment system (Engelbart 1984a) included advanced notions of reference that could pick out remote spans of hierarchically structured text, direct the presentations of that material during traversal, and specify multihop traversal through intermediate links. Many of Augment's capabilities would be valuable today if supported on the WWW.

Since Augment embedded its locators directly in the textual material, readers of the text saw the links in all their syntactic complexity. Systems like ZOG/KMS (Akscyn et al. 1988) and HyperCard (Goodman 1987) employ a similar notion of links as embedded locators. Unlike Augment, however, these systems shield readers from the details of the locator syntax. HyperCard, for instance, uses buttons and other user interface widgets behind which the locator information is stored in HyperTalk scripts. Likewise, KMS links are implemented by means of the scripts lying behind each frame. (For brief introductions to all three of these systems, see appendix A.)

Augment, KMS, and HyperCard are all monolithic systems. In other words, the material being interlinked is for the most part created and managed within the hypermedia system. There is no expectation that users will integrate material managed by third-party applications without first translating it into the formats supported by the system. In such situations, embedding locators directly in the

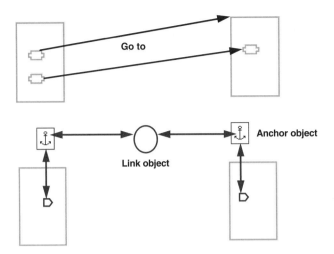

Figure 13
Two kinds of interconnecting: embedded locators and external link objects.

material can enable linking with less overhead than, say, maintaining a separate link database.

In an open hypermedia context, however, the embedded locator approach is less obviously applicable. For example, it may not always be possible to gain write permission for the material one wants to link *from*. As described in the next section, there is an alternative to links as embedded locators, though it incurs the cost of a bit more infrastructure.

4.2   Separating links from placements

One of the Dexter group's major contributions was the realization that the use of links to model different sorts of connections ought to be separated from the question of the link's placement, that is, how the link is accessed from a component's content. Figure 13 illustrates the difference between two forms of interconnecting that the Dexter model distinguishes. The top diagram depicts embedded locators, such as those in Augment, HyperCard, KMS, and the WWW. All information about the link is stored in the placement at its source end. The bottom diagram illustrates the second form, familiar to Dexter participants primarily through the Intermedia system. In Intermedia, links interconnect block objects that manage the link's endpoint connections. In such a system,

	Embedded locator approach	**External link approach**
Storage of links	Jump addresses inside content.	Link objects in separate database.
Openness with respect to linking	Closed, requiring special content formats like HTML or VRML.	Open, requiring no special content formats; material in the applications' formats can be linked.
Media support	Links are mostly supported from text-based data.	Links may interconnect segments in any data-type, e.g., video.
Maps of link structures	It's difficult (often impossible) to see the links to a specific document (search engines give only partial answers).	Link relations can be inspected and maps generated.
Distribution	Simple—only content has to be distributed.	More complicated—links have to be stored and accessed separately.
Collaboration	Collaborative manipulation of the link network is difficult.	Collaborative manipulation of links is easier, because it requires no write permission for the content.

Figure 14
Comparison of the embedded locator and external link approaches.

the links are stored and accessed separately from the content of the linked components.

Let's take a closer look at the advantages and disadvantages of these two approaches in the context of the WWW, as summarized in figure 14. Indeed, the best known examples of embedded locators today are the jump addresses on the WWW. An example of such an HTML tag is:

```
<a href="http://www.host.org/file1.html#loc1">click here</a>
```

where `www.host.org` names the server where the file `file1.html` containing the label `loc1` appears. The biggest advantage of embedded links on the WWW is their simplicity; a specialized link server is not needed, thus the WWW only has to manipulate tagged ASCII files. This simplicity comes at a cost, however, since only the owner of a document can create links from the document. At the same time, links to specific parts of a document can only be created if target tags already exist at the desired point in the document. It is impossible to see which documents point to another document. Finally, there can only be one set of links from a given document. If two users wish to have different links from the same document, they must maintain two copies of the document, identical apart from the different links. Doing so requires extra maintenance if the original document is likely to change.

The situation is further complicated if the original document is not a simple ASCII file. To use a document in a WWW context, it must first be converted into HTML. The problem of document format has been addressed by a variety of conversion programs, from simple RTF to HTML converters to large-scale WWW publishing systems such as Interleaf's Cyberleaf (Baldazo and Vaughan-Nichols 1995). Powerful as some of these systems are, their existence indicates the restrictive nature of HTML. In addition, links as defined in HTML are unidirectional, which makes them difficult to traverse backward. Finally, semantic link types as recommended by Nelson (1974), Trigg (1983), and DeRose (1989) among others, though supported in HTML, are largely ignored by web browsers and are thus unavailable to most users.

Although external links are more complicated, they offer advantages over embedded locators. Because the original document is unaffected by link creation, users can create, maintain, and share their own links, regardless of who owns the document. In hypermedia systems where links are first-class objects stored in a database (Halasz and Schwartz 1994), links to and from a document can be traced from it by querying the link database. Links can be named and assigned types, which the user can inspect and manipulate from the user interface. Unlike the WWW's embedded locators, external links can have more than one target. Finally, since linking is handled outside the documents, the documents can be represented in any format.

Fortunately, the WWW is likely to move beyond these constraints. The proposed protocol, WebDAV,[1] if adopted, will allow properties of a "resource" (e.g., a web page) to be stored and accessed separately from its content. In principle, WebDAV properties could be used to construct a link resource, or even a link server devoted to managing such resources.

4.3   Anchoring

The entities called *anchors,* as defined in the Dexter model, act as reference objects for links and are responsible for encapsulating location information for

1. See www.ics.uci.edu/~ejw/authoring.

Microcosm: "In Microcosm, link source and destination anchors are recorded in terms of absolute position within a document" (Davis, et al., 1992).

Multicard: "An anchor *represents* a sensitive portion of the content of a node. The associated anchor is the hypermedia object that carries the links, scripts, and other hypermedia properties. The sensitive portion is editor dependent" (Rizk & Sauter, 1992).

PROXHY: "[A]nchors connect *application objects* to *links*. *Links* are connectors among anchors. Together links and anchors are used to represent associations among the application objects in a hypertext" (Kacmar & Leggett, 1991). Though anchors in PROXHY are processes rather than objects, they share with Dexter anchors the quality of being represented externally from the nodes.

MacWeb: "[A]n *Anchor* is a reference to a small part of a text that denotes a valid concept" (Nanard & Nanard, 1993).

ABC: "An anchor identifies part of a node's content, such as a function declaration in a program module, a definition in a glossary, or an element of a line drawing. An anchor can be used to focus an HS-link onto a specific place within the content of a node" (Shackelford, et al., 1993).

WEBS: As in early Intermedia publications, the term *block* is used: "A block represents any selection made inside a document (e.g. a string of characters in a textual document). The connection between two blocks is created by a link, which the user may follow" (Monnard & Pasquier-Boltuck, 1992).

Chimera: "An anchor tags some portion of a view as an item of interest. Anchors are tailored by a viewer to the particular view of the object being displayed" (Anderson, et al., 1994).

HyTime: "Hyperlinks connect data items known as anchors. . . . an anchor can literally be anything that can be unambiguously located by a human or computer using a formal or informal notation" (DeRose & Durand, 1994, p. 110).

Figure 15
Anchor references in current and recent hypermedia systems.

material inside a document. Locating via anchors is limited only by the methods applications provide for accessing parts of their data. Anchors can refer to segments of sound and video, areas of pictures, or rows in a relational database.

Today there is widespread acceptance of the importance of anchoring for hypermedia. Figure 15 lists instances of anchor-like entities in a variety of recent systems.

In the Dexter model, the identification of an anchor is always relative to a particular component. An anchor consists of an identifier, unique within the associated component, and an anchor value that specifies a place or region, sometimes called a *span*, in the component's material. The Dexter group assumed that the means of locating varies from application to application, and thus did not further specify types of anchor values.

4.4   Problems with the Dexter approach

Though the notion of separating links from placements was a breakthrough for hypermedia design, the Dexter group's concrete recommendations were insufficient and at times confusing, especially from a design perspective. We'll discuss a variety of problems in subsequent chapters, but it is worth briefly mentioning two that are particularly related to the issues of location and placement under consideration in this chapter. The first issue concerns the use of directionality to model embeddedness. Rather than seeing embedded locating as an essential concept in its own right, the Dexter group attempted to incorporate it into the concept of directionality. As we'll argue in chapter 6, this confusion led to problematic models of both directionality and linking.

A second problem is the inconsistent treatment of entities that refer or point in the Dexter model. For example, the Dexter group recognized the importance of computability in hypermedia, but associated support for computation only with link endpoints, not with anchors or composites.

4.5   New forms of specification: refSpecs and locSpecs

One of the Dexter group's primary contributions was the distinction between the operations of identifying a component and accessing it. They defined an abstract operation, called a *resolver,* that takes a specification and returns a unique identifier for a component. The specification can be the title of a component, or a script that performs a search on the basis of a user-provided query. The Dexter group left open the precise format of the specifications. The *accessor* operation then retrieves, say, from a hypermedia database, the component with the given identifier. Separate resolver and accessor operations let the Dexter group intermix computation with direct addressing, and locate computation at the endpoints of links rather than with links as a whole.

In thinking about extending the Dexter model to support computability for anchors and composites as well as links, our first idea was simply to reproduce its specification formalism within these other entities. On the other hand, the success of the WWW has demonstrated the power of a portable specification like the URL that can exist independently of the web, in email messages or on highway billboards. As a result, we decided to rebuild the internals of the Dexter model's fundamental entities to use a uniform means of specification, but also support the portability of that specification. In addition, we wanted to disentangle embedded linking from link directionality.

Our deliberations resulted in two new entities, which we call *location specifications (locSpecs)* and *reference specifications (refSpecs)*. A locSpec is a description of a location that can live independently of the hypermedia system and thus resembles a URL. Like a URL it can specify absolute locations in material as well as computations like searches. In principle, a locSpec can also include arbitrary attributes, though for the moment, we leave unspecified the explicit form of a human-readable locSpec syntax.

A refSpec is a uniform means of packaging a locSpec for use within the hypermedia system. For example, it might be an object defined according to the hypermedia system's class hierarchy. RefSpecs provide the foundation for hypermedia structuring. For example, a link endpoint is comprised of a refSpec, a direction, and a pSpec. A composite "endpoint," is comprised of just a refSpec and a pSpec, since composites traditionally have no notion of directionality.[2]

At the same time, anchors can also be built from the basic refSpec. Because anchors "belong to" components, a fuller discussion must wait until the next chapter. Suffice it to say here that the crucial difference between endpoint refSpecs and anchor refSpecs is that the locSpec underlying an anchor's refSpec is restricted to identifying a location within the parent component's content.

Figure 16 shows several examples of refSpecs. The overarching composite C1 has three refSpecs that point to each of the other three components. There are two text components, T1 and T2. T1 includes one anchor refSpec (T1.A1), which points to the material making up the content of T1. Finally, the link L1 has two endpoints, one refering to the anchor in the T1 component and the other refering directly to the content of T2 (for instance, via a computed locSpec).

2. In chapter 11, we present the idea of a hybrid link/composite that we call a *structure component*. For such a component, the quality of link-ness or composite-ness is a property of an endpoint rather than of the component as a whole.

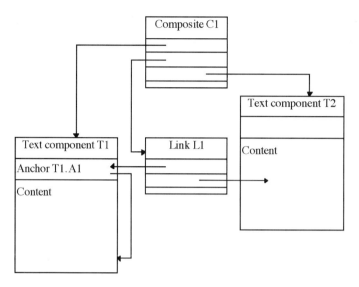

Figure 16
Uses of refSpecs as link endpoints, composite endpoints, and anchors.

4.6   RefSpecs and the HyTime standard

At a conceptual level, our approach can be compared to that of the HyTime standard (DeRose and Durand 1994). We are concerned with data models for hypermedia systems, while HyTime is best thought of as a representation and interchange language for hypermedia documents. Nonetheless, parts of the HyTime standard cover similar conceptual ground.

For example, the HyTime hypermedia standard makes a conceptual distinction between what they call i-links and c-links that is related to our distinction between locSpecs and refSpecs. The i-links are so-called independent links, or in our terms, links based on refSpecs placed outside the document content, whereas c-links are contextual links, or locSpecs placed inside the data in the style of HTML links.

4.7   RefSpecs and the World Wide Web

The WWW employs an advanced form of the locSpec (the URL), one that is portable and human-readable, yet powerful enough to represent certain kinds of computation as well as absolute addressing across the Internet. Without the notion of a refSpec, however, it is almost impossible to package these embedded locSpecs into objects that can be refered to programmatically. We believe that the refSpec provides a powerful conceptual means of bringing new functionality to the web. We also hope that the refSpec/locSpec distinction will help those who are trying to design hypermedia support that connects the web with applications supported on individual workstations. Chapter 14 discusses application integration in more depth.

4.8   Patterns for locators, placements, and interconnections

This chapter has introduced several concepts that form the underpinnings of hypermedia design. We close with patterns that summarize each of them. First, any open hypermedia system must have the means to identify or locate points in online material. In addition, such locators must be somehow placed in the material. The resulting placements generally need to be marked so as to be accessible to the user. Finally, interconnections between points in the material can either be embedded directly in the material or captured in structures stored separately from the material.

Title: Locating in Material

Context: A system meant to work in the presence of and in conjunction with a body of online material in a variety of media, possibly managed by third party applications, with varying degrees of access rights.

Problem: To specify locations, places in the material, in terms that make sense for the given material. Sometimes the names are absolute and static; at other times they need to be dynamic, able to reflect changes in the material, perhaps by being recomputed at each access.

Solution(s):   Use the location specifier, locSpec, to package several kinds of naming conventions in one entity, including fixed identifiers known to the application managing the material, calculations in terms known to the application (e.g., location offset in a text stream), and arbitrary invokable scripts. These conventions can serve either as alternative naming options, or as redundant specifications that improve robustness in the face of changes to the material (see the Anchor Maintenance pattern in chapter 14).

A locSpec can be represented in a portable, readable format, that lets it float freely both outside the material and outside the hypermedia system (e.g., a URL). As we'll see in the Externalized Locating pattern (this section), the locSpec can be the core of a reference specification, or refSpec, which is embedded in the data structures of a running hypermedia system.

Examples: In the hypermedia community, HyTime manifests the most sophisticated conception of a locSpec. HyTime's location description formalism includes a syntax for units of measurement, dimensions, and even a search language. Other versions of the locSpec can be found in the emerging Open Hypermedia Protocol (www.csdl.tamu.edu/ohs), as well as hypermedia systems like Microcosm, DHM, Augment, and, of course, the WWW.

Related patterns: Placing a Locator and Externalized Locating in this section.

Title: Placing a Locator

Context: A system, together with heterogeneous online material, meant to support the creation and management of new entities that structure and interconnect the material.

Problem: To gain access to the hypermedia entities that structure and interconnect material from within that material. The Locating in Material pattern (this section) identifies the problem of naming locations in material. Here we take up the second major problem for any hypermedia infrastructure: how access entities are placed in the material.

Solution(s): Use a placement such as the link tag of HTML, the means of placing URLs in textual web pages. There are four common types of placements, which depend on the degree to which modifications to the material are permitted and desirable:

1. Direct embedding (Augment, WWW). This is the approach taken for standard links (embedded URLs) on the web. The structural entity is directly embedded in the material, and thus the relevant material must be writable by the user. It should also be reasonable on aesthetic and practical grounds to modify the material and its appearance.

2. Embedded marker (Intermedia). The entity is not itself embedded; rather, a marker or proxy is. This approach entails less radical changes to the material, but still requires write permission. Embedded markers also require a means of mapping from the marker to the object, and vice versa.

3. Nonembedded reference (Microcosm, DHM). The location is maintained using a resolvable specification, rather than by embedding a marker. Hence, no change to the material is required. As with embedded markers, the approach requires a means of mapping back from the material to the objects placed there.

4. Display-time markup (HyperWave). This approach is a combination of the other three approaches. Systems that support display-time markup maintain a nonembedded reference to allow storage of the material without modification, but insert a marker of some kind in the material at the time of its display.

Note that with 1, 2, and to some degree 4, either the application or the material itself keeps the entity properly placed. In contrast, hypermedia systems using nonembedded references must maintain the integrity of location specifications across changes to the material.

A useful means of comparing the practical implications of the approaches is the deletion test: if material that includes the placement is deleted, what happens to the anchored entity? With direct embedding, it's gone for good. For a direct embedding, say, a URL deleted from a web page, we might have wanted the chance to reposition the object elsewhere, depending on how bound the semantics of the object is to that particular placement. The dangling placements that result from deletions with embedded markers and nonembedded references can allow the author of the structural entity to reposition it elsewhere in the material or delete it, as appropriate. The deletion test is less relevant for the web, where most readers can't delete material from the HTML pages they visit.

Examples: Augment, WWW, Intermedia, Microcosm, DHM.

Related patterns: Depends on Locating in Material in this section. See also Marking a Placement in this section.

Title: Marking a Placement

Context: A system for structuring and interconnecting heterogeneous online material, along with locators to be placed in the material.

Problem: To mark placements so that they appear (and behave) in a user interface. Of the four design options presented in the Placing a Locator pattern (this section), only the third, nonembedded reference, is not relevant to marking a placement.

Solution(s): Use one of four means of marking a placement depending on the applications that manage the viewing of the material and the access permissions available to the hypermedia author.

1. Embedded icon (NoteCards, Intermedia, HyperCard, HTML, Microcosm) or text (Augment). Embedding a clickable icon or text in an editor or viewer is a common technique in hypermedia systems for indicating the presence of a link endpoint. One issue raised by embedding icons in text involves how to indicate the span of text, if any, with which the icon is associated. In NoteCards, and for Microcosm and HTML buttons, there is no relevant span of text associated with the placement, although in NoteCards the embedded icon can display a short string of text that might form a readable part of the surrounding text.

In Intermedia, the endpoint does have an associated span, but the small arrow icon that is generally placed to the left of the span gives no indication of the length of the linked text string.

In Augment, text representing the placement is inserted directly into the material. That approach exposes the details of the placement to the user at the risk of hindering readability. (In HTML, placement is in the form of a text string, or link tag, embedded directly in the source of the document. In that sense HTML placements are reminiscent of Augment, although the tags are not visible to users of web browsers.)

2. Highlighting (HyperTies, HTML). Highlighting is a form of placement marking, familiar to us from the text of HTML pages. The various means of highlighting text include underlining, bold, italics, and color. Color and shading are also used to highlight placements in graphics.

3. Active regions (HTML). Sometimes the placement is invisible, but nonetheless active. For example, the placements in an HTML image map are often invisible. Moving the mouse over the image can, for example, display link information in the preview area of the web browser. Or a Java applet can dynamically highlight active regions of the image in response to mouse movements. HyperCafe supports such active regions in running video (Sawhney et al. 1996).

4. Separate but juxtaposed marks (placements in video and audio streams). It is sometimes the case that marking the material is inconvenient, or even impossible if write access isn't available. In such cases, some systems place markers nearby and closely aligned with the relevant material. For example, a running video stream might have clickable markers appearing in an aligned scroll bar (Roschelle et al. 1990).

Examples: Augment, WWW, Intermedia, Microcosm, DHM, HyperCafe.

Related patterns: Depends on Placing a Locator in this section. See also Embedded Interconnecting in this section, Local Anchoring in section 5.5, and the structuring patterns in chapters 6, 7, 8, and 11.

Title: Embedded Interconnecting
Context: A system for structuring and interconnecting heterogeneous online material. Access permissions are such that we can modify the material at the source of the interconnection to be created.
Problem: To gain access from a given source point in the material to one or more destinations elsewhere in the material. The goal is to do so with low-overhead linking; we don't want to have to create extra structure outside the material in order to insert a link.
Solution(s): Use the first of the options in the Placing a Locator pattern. That is, directly embed an entity containing one or more locSpecs that pick out the destination(s) of the interconnection in the material at the source.
Examples: The simplest and most familiar example comes from the web—an embedded URL, which is a locSpec wrapped in an HTML link tag. Normally, a URL picks out only one destination. Other examples include Augment, Hyper-Card, and KMS.
Related patterns: Depends on Placing a Locator and Marking a Placement in this section. See also Externalized Locating in this section and Traversal in section 9.5.

Title: Externalized Locating
Context: A system for structuring and interconnecting heterogeneous online material. Access permissions may restrict modifications to the material itself.
Problem: To build structures that live apart from the material and yet interconnect one or more source points in the material with one or more destinations elsewhere in the material. In contrast to the problem addressed by the Embedded Interconnecting pattern, we require separate, even centralized, access to the structures in order to build link browsers, follow links backward, and the like. In return for such facilities, we're willing to pay the costs of higher overhead linking.
Solution(s): Implement the *refSpec,* a locSpec that is packaged to exist as an object in the system outside the material. A refSpec belongs to the hypermedia system, not to the material. When the system isn't running, the refSpec doesn't exist, though it can be saved, say, in an object-oriented database.

In general, structural entities in a hypermedia include locSpecs for each endpoint, packaged as refSpecs. As shown in the Local Anchoring pattern in section 5.5, these refSpecs can also serve as anchors in a component, offering potential connections for structuring entities.
Examples: Intermedia, HyperWave, Microcosm.
Related patterns: Depends on Locating in material, and Placing a Locator in this section. See also Embedded Interconnecting in this section, Local Anchoring in section 5.5, and the structuring patterns in chapters 6, 7, 8, and 11.

5

Components: Structuring Primitives

Our experience . . . has encouraged us to practice a design philosophy of *voluntary simplicity,* striving to make do with fewer concepts and mechanisms. (Akscyn et al. 1988, p. 834)

Not surprisingly, hypermedia systems tend to take a link-centric view of the world. This view is reflected in the terminology—the underlying body of online material is sometimes called *data,* as though it exists solely to serve the linking operation at the heart of hypermedia, or *content,* as though hypermedia consists of linked containers that need to be filled. This gloss of the variety inherent in the online material also reflects one of the field's earliest goals, that of supporting all of the user's work under the umbrella of a single monolithic hypermedia system.

The emergence of open systems has replaced this goal with one of integration, leaving us with the significant problem of how differently to conceptualize the variety of online materials hypermedia systems hope to interlink. Designers need to consider how and to what extent our hypermedia systems can communicate with applications that manage the storage and behavior of the material. Where should the lines of responsibility be drawn to support a reasonable division of labor? For example, should hypermedia or applications handle the management of link markers to appear in the material?

In the first section of this chapter, we briefly review the metaphors hypermedia systems have used to conceptualize the material to be interlinked. We next consider the Dexter group's notion of the component, the advantages that concept offered, and the new problems it raised. We conclude with design patterns that make explicit how online material can be wrapped to support structuring. Our patterns address some of the problems with Dexter components.

5.1   Nodes, cards, and documents: Unpacking the metaphors

There are almost as many terms used to designate material to be interlinked as there are hypermedia systems. In the link-centric world of hypermedia, these terms reflect designers' views of how that material can or should be organized, and more broadly, their perspectives on the work of authoring.

Jeff Raskin (1987) captured the prevalent points of view in the late 1980s with his twin notions of "card sharks" and "holy scrollers." Systems based on the card shark metaphor assume that the material to be organized is divided or divisable into relatively small chunks. Links often interconnect cards as a whole without requiring internal anchoring. HyperCard is the premier example; because of the generally small sizes of cards, the destinations of HyperCard links are almost always entire cards. The runtime behavior of these systems is characterized either by the shuffling of many windows, as in NoteCards, or by the rapid replacement of the content of a single window, as in HyperCard.

The holy scroller systems assume that material is organized into one or more documents of arbitrary length. Linking involves interconnecting points in the documents or possibly spans of sequential text or graphics. The preeminent example is Owl's Guide system (Brown 1987), HyperCard's primary competitor in the commercial PC market in the late 1980s. Guide's runtime behavior is typified by rapid scrolling induced by link following in a single large document.

Though valuable for their evocativeness and the fruitful discussions they engendered, Raskin's characterizations masked the complexity of these systems. The size of a card in NoteCards is in fact unlimited; at times multipage documents are written in single cards. Guide includes small pop-up cardlike notes in addition to both intra- and inter-document links. Though the metaphors and accompanying terminology reveal important design assumptions, the actual systems have tended in practice to support more complex possibilities.

Let's consider the World Wide Web, a current hypermedia system that is at least as hard to classify. There are various styles of web use. Some web page designers try to keep the contents of their pages entirely visible without scrolling. For such card-like networks, links tend to point at entire pages. Other designers, who prefer entire documents to appear in single pages, include links within the document, for example, from an opening table of contents. In such cases, a single page resembles an article or even an entire magazine.

The task of web page printing reveals some of the advantages and disadvantages of Raskin's card shark and holy scroller approaches. Material organized in single large documents is easy to print using the default ordering of the text provided by the document, but problematic when alternative orderings are desired. On the other hand, organizing material in small chunks raises issues of selection as well as sequencing. Often, a web user needs access to just those pages that comprise a subnetwork, corresponding, for example, to the document's table of contents. In particular, she would not necessarily want to follow arbitrary links to other sites in gathering material for the print. NoteCards addressed this problem 10 years ago with its DocumentCard, which supports user-defined aggregation on the basis of link types and depth-first traversal of parts of the network (Trigg and Irish 1987). To our knowledge, no such support is yet available for page aggregation on the web.[1]

5.2   The Dexter approach: Atomic components as wrappers

Instead of specifying a metaphor or style of interaction, the Dexter group's notion of the atomic component left responsibility for the material in the hands of application designers. An atomic component was meant to wrap a body of material of arbitrary size. In this way, the Dexter model proposed a concrete division of labor that separated the responsibilities of application developers from those of hypermedia system developers. The atomic component provided an entity that could be linked to (and anchored in, as we'll see) and could communicate with the programs responsible for opening, browsing, and editing its content.

In some cases, the Dexter group intentionally blurred the line between hypermedia and application. For example, they recognized the need for the hypermedia system to influence the behavior of the applications managing component content. An example from the web is HTML's support for specifying the "target" window or frame within a window in which to display a link's destination. We'll consider the design of presentation support further in chapters 9 and 10.

---

1. The recent support for style sheets on the web has taken the important step of adding structure to web pages, and thus may well ease the printing problem for documents with predefined structure. It leaves open, however, the question of how to support reader-defined aggregations according to aspects of links or pages.

5.3   Problems with the Dexter component

In spite of its power, the Dexter group's concept of the atomic component as wrapper has several significant limitations. First, it presumes that the hypermedia system will take over storage of the content, or data, of the component. This assumption has turned out to be impractical in cases where the application uses special storage algorithms, say, for large objects like compressed audio and video. Similarly, the Dexter model assumes that the hypermedia system will oversee the runtime behavior of the components, using display editors called *instantiations*. In fact, most third-party applications provide their own environments, including editors and browsers. To successfully integrate with such environments, a hypermedia system must somehow enable linking and structuring within existing interfaces. Examples of such systems are LinkWorks (Clark 1992), Microcosm (Hall et al. 1996), and DHM (Grønbæk and Trigg 1994).

The Dexter group's conceptual framework comes dangerously close to requiring material to be atomized into types of entities with mutually exclusive capabilities. It is especially hard to imagine implementing an entity, like the NoteCards filebox, that can contain both hierarchical structure and text or graphics, which, in other words, is both a composite and atomic component.

Just as controversial is Dexter's lack of support for explicit typing of components. Systems like HyperCard and KMS have a single component type; components differ only in their contents and attribute-governed behavior. In fact, the designers of KMS have argued eloquently against component typing (Akscyn et al. 1988; McCracken and Akscyn 1984). They start by pointing out that their single component type, the frame, supports a wide variety of materials—text, graphics and images. They go on to argue for unifying what are normally separate levels in user interfaces; directories, files, menubars, and pull-down menus are all provided by frames. Furthermore, KMS provides a single interface for both frame editing and navigation, which reduces the need for multiple command contexts.

At the other extreme are systems like NoteCards and MacWeb (Nanard and Nanard 1991), which support component types that users can extend. Types have been used to distinguish components on the basis of the semantics of their contents as well as its form, for example, video and text components.[2] The

2. The World Wide Web's component types correspond to MIME types: text/html, image/gif, image/jpeg, and so on.

Dexter group expected component attributes to represent such distinctions. However, without an object-oriented framework, type encapsulation and inheritance is difficult.

Other problems involve the anchors associated with components. Anchors, according to the Dexter group, lack support for computability and transience. The anchor value, unlike link endpoints, was to be an absolute address into the component's material. The group assumed that it was sufficient to support computability using specifications in link endpoints. However, restricting computability in this way precludes certain valuable kinds of sharing and reuse of computational specifications across links and composites.

Consider, for example, a text document that is expected to change outside the control of the hypermedia system. In this dynamic context, one might decide that searching within the document for a particular keyword or phrase is more appropriate than maintaining an absolute location in the document. A computable keyword anchor could be configured to include a search specification, in this case, the text of the search phrase. After the user follows a link to the anchor, a search is carried out within the component to resolve the location. Because this computation is associated with the anchor, any links or composites refering to that anchor share the single copy of the search specification.

Also missing from the Dexter model is the notion of transient anchors. Such anchors usually persist for the duration of a navigation operation. A typical example is a computed source endpoint of a link, arising when the user makes a selection in an editor that does not correspond to an existing anchor. The system creates a transient anchor on the fly and matches it with links that have computed source endpoints. The anchor can then be deleted once the matching links have been traversed.

5.4 Designing flexible components

In this book, we consider the component the basic hypermedia entity through which online material is grouped, interlinked, and structured. As the first design pattern in the next section shows, *atomic* components reflect the existing organization of the material. A component might, for example, wrap a paragraph in a structured document. We sometimes refer to the paragraph as the *content* of the component. As discussed in the next two chapters, other sorts of components are used to capture hypermedia structures that are not reflected in the online material.

Whether they correspond to structure inherent in the material or not, all components can have types and attributes as described in our second pattern. Depending on the nature of the implementation, these properties might appear as classes and slots in an object-oriented framework, or relational tables in a database. The second pattern in the next section outlines some of the possible typing mechanisms.

In addition, components include a set of anchors, refSpecs that point internally, within the content of the component. These anchors act as entry points, that is, potential destinations for the endpoints of structuring components (such as links) in the hyperspace. Typically, anchors are found in atomic components, but they can also provide entry points for complex structuring components as explained in section 11.8. Like link endpoints, anchors package a pSpec together with the refSpec. When a user follows a link to an anchor, the system combines the pSpecs from the anchor and the link endpoint to direct the presentation of the linked material. Chapters 9 and 10 discuss presentations in more detail.

The issue of how to keep location specifiers up to date with changing material is one of the hardest to deal with in an open hypermedia environment. Users of the web confront the problem every time they encounter a URL whose location is no longer valid. As chapter 6 explains, our prefered approach to such dangling links is not to view them so much as a problem to be solved once and for all, but as a fact of life, a defining characteristic of hypermedia environments that are open and diverse.

An important advantage of the notion of components is that decisions concerning division of labor and the management of runtime behavior can be made on a per application basis. For example, link components might be stored by the hypermedia system while most text editors wrapped by components could remain responsible for their own storage (as is the case in DHM).

5.5 Patterns for components and anchors

Three design patterns serve to sum up the important ideas of this chapter. The Wrapping Material pattern embodies the basic idea of an atomic component. The Typing pattern embodies the design choices involved in distinguishing among components. Finally, the Local Anchoring pattern proposes the use of refSpecs as component entry points for the endpoints of links and composites.

Title: Wrapping Material

Context: Material that varies with respect to form, medium, size and degree of structure. The hypermedia system needs to reveal this inherent structure, as well as any additional structure.

Problem: To refer to bodies of material as single entities. The entities may be (or correspond to) preexisting divisions in the material, or they may subdivide the material in new ways.

Solution(s): Use the atomic component, a hypermedia entity that refers to, or wraps, a body of online material. Generally, online material comes with its own structure; atomic components pick out and wrap elements of this structure, for example, documents or entities in structured documents.

In monolithic systems, where online material generally has no independent existence outside of, or prior to, the hypermedia system, atomic components are the primary means of defining structure.

In open hypermedia systems, on the other hand, most atomic components identify existing bodies of material using the structures already present, although extra material may be created in the course of building new hypermedia structures, e.g., (Marshall and Irish 1989; Trigg 1988).

Examples: Examples of open hypermedia systems where the material comes with its own structure are DHM, Microcosm, Intermedia, and WWW browser plugins. Examples of monolithic systems where the material is primarily structured through the hypermedia mechanisms are Augment, NoteCards, HyperCard, and HTML pages on the WWW.

Related patterns: See also Typing and Local Anchoring in this section, Transience and Computation in chapter 7, and Presentation in chapter 9.

Title: Typing
Context: Hypermedia structures that interconnect and organize a body of heterogeneous material.
Problem: To distinguish the semantics and behavior of different structural entities.
Solution(s): Assign types and attributes to components according to one of these approaches.

1. Types as labels. This is the simplest approach, often used for link components (e.g., NoteCards link types). More generally, the structural entities can include arbitrary attribute-value pairs.
2. Types as object classes, with attributes as slots. This object-oriented approach offers the benefits of inheritance, especially important when there is code of some kind to reuse. Structural entities may be stored in an object-oriented database.
3. Combined labels, attributes, and classes. Labels and attributes are used when storing the hypermedia structures, but object-oriented class instances are created at runtime.

Examples: Intermedia document types, NoteCards card types, and DHM component types.
Related patterns: See also Wrapping Material in this section.

Title: Local Anchoring
Context: Heterogeneous material which changes as the hypermedia system is used. Hypermedia structures exist outside the material and point into it.
Problem: To design an entity that is responsible for keeping the placement's locSpec up to date with the changing material.
Solution(s): Use the atomic component, the hypermedia entity that refers to or wraps online material, as a home for maintainable placements. We call such a placement an *anchor*, a refSpec belonging to a particular component and refering into the online material wrapped by that component. Hypermedia structures like links and composites that refer to this component can use its anchors as endpoints, rather than point directly into the material. Anchors can be thought of as entry points into the component, in other words, as advertised locations of candidate structural endpoints.

Anchors can also be used in nonatomic components, where they refer to points in the structural component. For example, an anchor in a link component might refer to one of its endpoints. In this way, a hypermedia system can support not just links to other links, but links to the endpoints of other links.
Examples: DHM.
Related patterns: Depends on Placing a Locator and Marking a Placement in section 4.8, and Wrapping Material in this section. See also the structuring patterns in chapters 6, 7, 8, and 11.

6

Links: Traversable Components

We believe that fast system response to selecting a link is the most important parameter of a hypermedia system. (Akscyn et al. 1988, p. 829)

We resolved to build a hypertext system which imposed no mark-up on the data to which the links are applied. We defined a spectrum of dynamic link types, in particular the generic link, which enable the destination of a link to be resolved at runtime calculated on the basis of the content of a source anchor rather than simply its location in a document. . . . All aspects of the model were to be totally extensible. (Hall et al. 1996, p. 7)

Over the last 30 years, hypermedia system designers have taken a variety of stands on the functions of linking, considering it as *pointing* from one document to another, *associating* points in related documents, *representing* relations between things, or *structuring* information. Often the same system supports more than one of these perspectives. For example, the WWW uses links both as pointers and as a means of structuring documents, usually hierarchically.

Regardless of the function originally assigned to a link, it is almost always also traversable. That is, the joined points can be brought into active juxtaposition for a reader or the author herself at a later time. It is for this reason that support for link traversal is such an important part of any successful hypermedia system.

Almost as important is support for link creation. Sometimes links are added to preexisting material, but often, their creation is an integral part of the work of authoring new material. On occasion, the new links can serve as placeholders that mark work yet to be done. Sometimes pejoratively labeled "dangling," these links serve as reminders of the need to write a new section, or create another piece of a multimedia presentation.

In this chapter, we review some of the ways links have been used in past and current hypermedia systems, and consider issues of link directionality and the

Dexter group's rules of "good behavior." Along the way, we revisit an ever popular topic in the field, the concept of links as locations of computation rather than as static connections or associations. We close with a design pattern that integrates links into our component-oriented conceptual apparatus for hypermedia.

6.1 Link metaphors

Links have been interpreted in a variety of ways over the years and across very different systems. The following list is not meant to be comprehensive, nor are we suggesting that a hypermedia system adopt only one of these perspectives. Rather, this section aims to give a sense of the rich variety of possibilities. As designers, we may want to support several perspectives.

6.1.1 Links as addresses

In the style of linking made popular by NLS/Augment and later HyperCard and the WWW, a link is simply an address of a destination, embedded directly in the material—in our terminology, an *embedded interconnection.* In Augment, the address is human-readable and visible in the text, like a reference in a research paper (Engelbart 1984a). Augment's addressing scheme depends on an "outline" view of all the text ever stored in the system. It is even possible to link into archived material. Following such a link triggers a request that the file be retrieved. Augment notifies the user by email when the link becomes traversable.

The link format of Augment additionally enables the specification of a wealth of display directives. Indeed, these directives inspired the Dexter group's notion of the pSpec. Over time, some of these options are making their way into the HTML definition. For example, specifying the subwindow target of a link was supported in the earliest NLS/Augment systems.

In HyperCard, links can appear as buttons in a card's layout, but the destination of the link is hidden in the HyperTalk script behind the button. Likewise, in the WWW, links can be associated with graphical objects or with text, which then appears highlighted. To see the link's definition, its locSpec, requires viewing the source HTML, as shown in figure 17.

6.1.2 Links as associations

In the style of linking perhaps best typified by Intermedia, links represent associations between two points or regions of text or graphics (Haan et al.

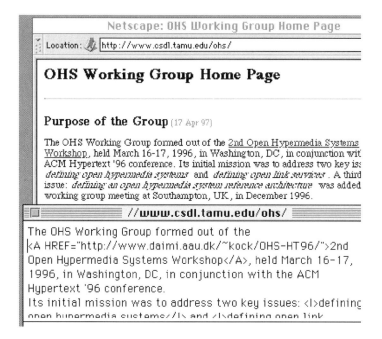

Figure 17
Two ways of viewing an HTML link: its locSpec definition shown in the foreground text editor, and its rendered component in the background web browser.

1992). Traversal in Intermedia is two-way, with no privileged direction. In Intermedia, links are stored apart from the material in relational database tables. Links are represented visually in a graphical browser that captures the local neighborhood of the currently active document; the current document is shown along with documents one link away.

Intermedia also broke new ground in enabling such links to be active. Using a metaphor of temperature, Intermedia distinguishes three degrees of activity: *cold, hot,* and *warm.* A cold link is a traditional traversable association. A hot link maintains a constant relationship between the material at both ends of the link. For example, a link between a text document and a spreadsheet's bottom-line cell might keep the current value of the cell visible in the text. As the numbers change, so does the bottom-line figure in the text. Today, Microsoft supports hot links among its office products using OLE and publish/subscribe. Xanadu's transclusion is a hot link used to keep separated copies of material up to date across changes (Nelson 1995).

Finally, Intermedia introduced the idea of warm links. Though again serving as traversable associations, material at one end can, under user control, be "pushed" or "pulled" across the link. For example, in a case of two authors collaborating on a shared hypermedia network, one of the authors can make annotations to the other's text and link them using a warm link (Catlin et al. 1989). The second author can later pull the annotations through the link to replace the affected text. Alternatively, the second author can start from a browser showing all the annotations and push multiple changes back into the documents.

Although certain kinds of active links can be supported with an embedded address style, the implementation is easier when links are represented and stored separately from the contents, as they are in Intermedia. Though this approach sacrifices the simplicity and human-readability of embedded addresses, the advantages of links as active objects may be important for applications like collaborative writing.

6.1.3   Links as structuring elements

Links have often been used in hypermedia systems to capture various kinds of structure. A typical example involves hierarchical organizations of material orthogonal to nonhierarchical link-based network structures. TextNet (Trigg and Weiser 1986) and NoteCards both use link types to distinguish hierarchical from nonhierarchical links. Although any two points can be linked hierarchically, in practice these systems enforce structural rules at link-time. Thus, a filebox link in NoteCards is disallowed if it results in a cycle of filebox links. Moreover, NoteCards alerts the user when cards become disconnected from any hierarchy, and automatically adds a filing link from a special "orphans" filebox. This enforced filing has been the subject of debate among both designers and users (Monty and Moran 1986).

In the end, Frank Halasz, the original designer of NoteCards, argued against the overloading of links with structural semantics. In his landmark "Seven Issues" paper, he proposed separate structuring support in the form of composites. Chapter 7 explores how this call was taken up by the Dexter group, as well as other designers.

6.1.4   Links for rhetorical representation

Rhetorical links have been common in systems like Intermedia, NoteCards, TextNet, and, on occasion, HyperCard. The idea is to use links as representations of argument structure, that is, as rhetorical devices. Cathy Marshall made extensive use of rhetorical links to represent Toulmin argument structures in NoteCards (Marshall 1987). Links tied together the five part of a Toulmin argument: datum, warrant, backing, claim, and entailment. Similarly in the GIBIS system, Jeff Conklin used links to tie together the positions and pro and con arguments comprising multiperson design debates (Conklin and Begeman 1988). When hypermedia is used to represent rhetorical structures, the links are often given types (DeRose 1989; Trigg 1983).

Like Frank Halasz, however, Cathy Marshall came to doubt the efficacy of representing complex relations with binary-valued links. In Marshall and Halasz's subsequent work on the AquaNet system, argument structures were represented by structured tailorable relational objects, rather than by links (Marshall et al. 1991). We'll look more closely at such composite structures built without links in chapter 7.

6.2 Link directionality

The issue of directionality arises for each linking style. The first case is the simplest; an embedded address link is traversible from its source in the embedding material to its destination in the addressed location. Associational links can indicate a traversal semantics by labeling endpoints as either source or destination. In systems like Intermedia the link can also be traversed backward, from destination to source. But links can have direction that is not traversal-based. For example, a support link in TextNet captures a rhetorical semantics—say, that the claim in the starting, or left, component (reading from left to right) is supported by the arguments in the ending, or right component. Reading the link in the other direction requires shifting the semantics from *is supported by* to *supports*.

The Dexter group's approach to supporting directionality constituted an architectural advance, though its proposed collection of directionality types was confusing. The architectural breakthrough was to assign directionality to the endpoints of links rather than to the link as a whole. This turned out to be especially valuable when generalizing the notion of directionality to multiheaded links. Unfortunately, however, the taxonomy of kinds of directionality provided by the Dexter group proved inadequate for most purposes. The Dexter model provides only four directionality constants: TO, FROM, BOTH, and NONE. They can represent constructs like embedded address links, and links with one source and multiple destinations, as well as behaviors like bidirectional traversal.

However, the model of directionality raises several questions. What is the meaning of a link with only two FROM endpoints? Two BOTH endpoints can be used to model Intermedia links, but how should one interpret a link with two NONE endpoints? Although we agree that links ought to have directionality associated with endpoints, we seek a more precise way of distinguishing traversal and representational semantics.

6.3 Computed links

By the time the Dexter group convened it had become clear to many that static hypertext was not sufficient for all applications (Halasz 1988). Several systems supported links that could take various runtime conditions into account and calculate a destination on the fly. A radical example is the StrathTutor (Kibby and Mayes 1989), a hypermedia-based tutoring system. Each card is assigned a binary vector that characterizes its content along various dimensions. Students follow special nearest-neighbor links from any card. The system calculates dynamically the closest card according to a distance metric based on the vectors, and opens that card as the link's destination. (StrathTutor calculated efficient paths through the entire hyperspace using similar strategies.)

One of the most important contributions of the Dexter group was to associate computation with link endpoints. This meant that computation could be triggered on any (or all!) endpoints of a link, something that no system at that time supported. In fact, the group used the term *specification* rather than *endpoint* to underscore the potentially computed quality of the link's location. A specification could be either an absolute identifier or a description of a computation to be run at traversal time.

Recently, computed links have been popularized through the use of CGI scripts and other executable programs on the WWW. For example, these programs often invoke web searches. On the basis of a query string embedded in the link's URL, the program typically looks up the elements of the query in indices of word occurences. It then builds a page containing links to the pages found by the search. Thus, the computed link not only searches for a destination, but also constructs a new transient page that presents the results.

A variant of this kind of search link is supported in the HyperTies system (Shneiderman 1987), in the hypertext version of the Oxford English Dictionary (Tompa et al. 1993), and in Microcosm where it is known as a *generic* link (Hall et al. 1996). The idea is that any word found in any document can serve as a link source. Following the link causes the source word to be treated as though it were a query into a database of linked material, say, a dictionary of word definitions. HyperTies uses a similar form of generic linking in an online museum application. In each case, the computed link searches among and brings up existing destinations, possibly by way of an intermediate component that acts as a results browser. Alternatively, a computed link can construct one or more new components as destinations. This can happen on the WWW where the new pages are usually assembled at least in part out of material found elsewhere on the web.[1]

Computed links also provide a means of automatically constructing new material. For example, the IDE project (Jordan et al. 1989) added computed links based on customizable templates to the NoteCards system. By choosing which computed links to follow, the user incrementally builds up new structures of arbitrary size. She then manually fills in these template structures with text and graphics. In chapter 7, we'll encounter an analogue to computed links: composite structures that recompute themselves as needed.

6.4 The Dexter group's "no dangling links" rule

Using a formal specification language, the Dexter group presented several rules to be enforced by "Dexter-compliant" systems. The most well-known and controversial of these was the "no dangling links" rule. It specifies that whenever a component is deleted, all links with endpoints in that component must be found and also deleted. Similarly, new links cannot be created unless they have at least two endpoints, each of whose specifications are resolvable.

Though the conclusion of the original Dexter paper mentions the possibility of Dexter "subsets" in recognition of the fact that no existing hypermedia systems met the Dexter specification, the Dexter model came to be associated with a strict adherence to such rules. Elsewhere we have argued that the "no dangling links" rule was one of the Dexter group's gravest errors (Grønbæk and Trigg 1994). Dangling links are not only unavoidable in various open and distributed system situations, but are also valuable as placeholders during the work of authoring. Indeed, the need for a link may well arise before the linked material is constructed.

1. For example, the Dynaweb system can dynamically build HTML out of SGML structures (www.inso.com/products/publishing/dynatext/dtweb.htm).

6.5   Issues in link traversal

Regardless of whether links are interpreted as addresses, associations, or argument representations, they invariably support some form of traversal. One of the earliest design questions concerned whether a traversal should cause a link's destination to replace the currently displayed material at the link's source. In Augment this choice can be specified in the link itself. In ZOG/KMS, HyperCard, and the WWW, the default action is replacement, while NoteCards and Intermedia typically display the destination in a new window. Xanadu's notion of transclusion captured, among other things, the more complex idea of keeping two linked displays synchronized during processes like scrolling (Nelson 1995). The designers of hypermedia support for interlinked media streams adopted similar schemes (Hardman et al. 1994; Roschelle et al. 1990). We'll have more to say about synchronization of time-based media in chapter 10.

Another important issue for designers of link traversal support is what George Landow (1987), in a landmark paper calls the *departure* and *arrival rhetoric* of a link. An example of departure rhetoric is HyperTies' link preview mode, a summary of a link's destination that can be displayed quickly to help the user decide whether the link is worth following. A simpler variant of HyperTies previewing is a web browser's display of the URL of the link indicated by the cursor.

Arrival rhetoric concerns how best to provide context for a user who has just followed a link, and thus just arrived at a new place in the interlinked material. The WWW exemplifies the situation as it exists in most hypermedia systems. Although web pages can include extensive and informative departure rhetorics, representations of context upon arrival are rarely supported. One approach is to provide a "you are here" graphical browser depicting the structure of the network surrounding the current web page, similar to Intermedia's local map (Utting and Yankelovich 1989). Such browsers are sometimes manually constructed and maintained by webmasters for particular sites, but are usually accessible only from the top nodes of the site. The WWW could benefit from site-specific graphical overviews, maintained by a combination of manual and automatic means, which are accessible (that is, a mouse-click away) anywhere within the site.

The generality of Dexter's architecture raises several other issues related to traversal. For example, what exactly should be the semantics of following a multiheaded link? Can one be followed backward? Dexter's architecture allows linking to arbitrary components, including other links. What might traversal mean in such cases? We take up some of these questions in chapter 9 when we discuss our proposed model of link traversal, and in chapter 10 when we discuss advanced forms of navigation including browsers, paths, and guided tours.

The design pattern for links includes a policy for interpreting directionality values during traversal. In contrast to the Dexter group, we use directionality constants exclusively to model traversal behaviors, rather than confounding directionality with embeddedness. For example, we diverge from the Dexter group in our interpretation of the NONE constant. We use NONE as a means of temporarily hiding certain endpoints during traversal, rather than as a means of modeling embedded endpoints. Nevertheless we recognize the value of other forms of semantic direction unrelated to traversal and propose using attributes at the link component or endpoint to model them.

6.6   A pattern for link structuring

Title: Structuring by Linking

Context: Hypermedia structures over diverse online material, in particular, links that connect multiple locations using external interconnections.

Problem: To interconnect multiple locations using structures that live outside the data and support computability.

Solution(s):   Implement the link as a structuring component that includes zero or more endpoint refSpecs, each labelled with a traversal directionality value. The set of possible values should be extensible, but must at least include Source, Destination, Both, and Neither. Traversal forward opens all endpoints labeled Destination or Both; traversal backward opens those labeled Source or Both. The Neither endpoints are hidden from these two traversal operations.

A link endpoint editor might invoke a separate operation to open all endpoints regardless of their directionality. Hypermedia system designers can assign other semantically meaningful labels and directions as attributes to the link component as a whole, or to individual endpoints.

Because refSpecs are used as endpoints, each endpoint can be independently computable. For example, Microcosm's "generic links" consist of a computed source and a fixed destination (e.g., in a dictionary).

Examples: DHM, Intermedia, and Microcosm.

Related patterns: Depends on Local Anchoring in section 5.5 and Externalized Locating in section 4.8. See also Navigation and Synchronization in chapter 10.

7

Composites: Structured Components

[T]he basic hypermedia model lacks a composition mechanism, i.e. a way of representing and dealing with groups of nodes and links as unique entities separate from their components. (Halasz 1988, p. 843)

Virtual structures are a particularly powerful mechanism when combined with the notion of composites. A virtual composite allows the user to create nodes that are dynamically constructed at access time from other nodes, links, and composites that are stored in the network. Such virtual composites are true hypermedia entities and not simply a display of results from a query. (Halasz 1988, p. 846)

Structuring has long been a part of hypermedia systems, from the hierarchies of Augment statements and KMS frames, to the relations of Aquanet. These hierarchical and relational structures were meant to supplement and complement the network structures provided by links.

In a recurring criticism directed at the design of HTML, members of the hypertext community decry the lack of support for just such structures (Bieber et al. 1997; Instone 1996). As a concrete example, consider hierarchical structures that could serve to aggregate web pages into larger documents. Though users could still follow links into individual pages of the document, hierarchical structures would enable other activities such as printing, which are appropriate to the document as a whole. At the moment, web page designers are forced to choose between creating long pages that are easy to print and short interlinked pages that are easier to browse but harder to print as an aggregation.

Another structure missing from the web, but well-known to hypermedia researchers, is the graphical link browser. Though insufficient by themselves to solve Conklin's "lost in hyperspace" problem (Conklin 1987), link browsers are a significant help in many cases. Graphical link diagrams can, of course, be created and maintained manually, and some web sites do just that. As we discuss in this chapter, link browsers require sophisticated structuring support and the ability to compute these structures on demand.

Within the field of hypermedia, however, the debate has not so much concerned the value of such structures, but whether to implement them using links. In systems like KMS, Intermedia, and NoteCards, the basic link facility supports structures that go beyond the references or associations that links are meant to support. KMS's frame hierarchies, for example, are built using tree items, a form of link conceptually and syntactically distinct from the annotation items used to construct nonhierarchical cross-references. Similarly, FileBox cards in NoteCards support hierarchical structures using a *FiledCard* link type to identify the cards contained in a FileBox. Links are also commonly used to implement structures comprising the "hits" returned by a query-based search. In KMS, Intermedia, NoteCards, and the WWW, atomic result components are created with links to all the hits.

The Dexter group's notion of the composite has its roots in the question of whether links are an appropriate and effective means of implementing nonnetworked structures. This chapter looks more closely at the motivation for the Dexter group's composite component and the problems with that concept. To contextualize the design discussion, we propose five cross-cutting aspects of hypermedia composites. We then consider the behavior of composite components, in particular the twin notions of computability and transience. We close with three design patterns that summarize the main issues raised by this chapter: Structuring by Reference, Computability, and Transience.

7.1   The case for linkless structures

In proposing hypermedia support for composites in his landmark "Seven Issues" paper, Frank Halasz argued against certain uses of link-based structures (Halasz 1988). In particular, he noted that complex structures formed from links are "implicit" in a problematic way. That is, the structures have no natural "head" component that can act as the destination of a link meant to connect to the structure as a whole (see figure 18). In addition, the definition of the structure is distributed through the link network, rather than accessible in any one component. Though appropriate for supporting emergent or one-off structures, links seemed artificial in cases of repeated structural patterns. In addition, such link-based structures often include system-generated links that users have trouble distinguishing from those they create explicitly.

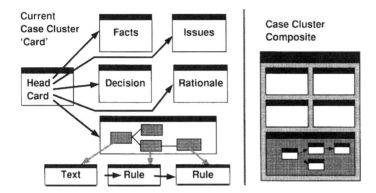

Figure 18
Halasz's example of a NoteCards link and card structure which motivated the idea of composites.

To address these problems, Halasz proposed *composites* as first-class hypermedia citizens along with atomic components and links. Composites capture nonlink-based organizations of information, making them an explicit part of hypermedia functionality. He also introduced the related notions of computed and virtual composites.

A virtual composite is represented by a description or specification that can be instantiated on demand to result in a composite component. An oft-cited example is the search composite, a query over the hyperspace that returns sets of components and links. The intent is that such composites are created and computed on demand at runtime, but not saved in the hypermedia database. In this way, they resemble computed links. For example, although the IDE templates discussed in section 6.3 were implemented using computed links in Note-Cards, they might instead have been designed as virtual composites.

Halasz was particularly critical of the browser card in NoteCards (see figure 19). At first glance, it appears to be a virtual composite. It includes a specification of a subnetwork, usually all components and links reachable from a given root component by following only links of a given type. At any time, the browser card can be recomputed to reflect changes in the hypermedia structures.

At bottom, however, the NoteCards browser is a link-based structure; "BrowserContents" links connect the browser card to the cards whose connections it graphically depicts. Such a link-based implementation makes browsers expensive to create and delete. As a composite, the structure would consist of

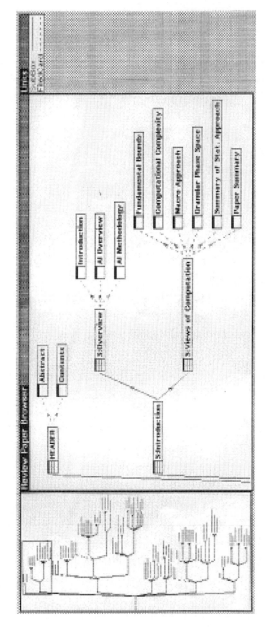

Figure 19
NoteCards graphical browser restricted to SubBox and FiledCard links.

pointers, not links, and thus would be cheaper to construct and delete.[1] On the other hand, the NoteCards browser allows users to find all browsers containing a given card (by following BrowserContents links backward), though this capability was rarely used.

7.2   The Dexter group's composite component and its limitations

Soon after Halasz's paper appeared, the Dexter group proposed a concrete realization of nonlink-based structuring. The Dexter composite was defined to be a component of equal status with link and atomic components, whose content consists of multiple instances of atomic "data."

Though a crucial first step, the Dexter composite has a variety of problems noted primarily by those who try to realize the idea in concrete systems. Lynda Hardman and her colleagues (1994) encountered problems when using composites to model the dynamic structures underlying multimedia presentations. For example, it is unclear how composite anchors can point into the contents of components (and potentially other composites) nested inside the composite. We'll return to their critique and possible solutions in chapters 10 and 11.

The primary limitations of the Dexter composite involve issues of encapsulation, reference, and containment (Grønbæk and Trigg 1994). According to the Dexter group, a composite can only contain encapsulated data objects within what were called *base components* (for example figure 11 in chapter 3). As Halasz and Schwartz (1994) noted, this kind of composite can model structures like graphical canvases, which consist of single components containing different types of data content. However, such composites cannot be used to organize and structure other hypermedia entities. The design space proposed in the next section includes composites that contain or refer to other components or component anchors.

7.3   A design space for composites

Our critique and proposed revisions of composites are based on five sets of design questions (Grønbæk 1994):

1. For example, the DHM system includes browsers constructed as composites (Grønbæk 1994) as discussed in Section 20.6.2.

Structure	Type	Location	Definition	Membership

• Unstructured collection
• Structured collection:
  - sorted list
  - keyed table
  - tree
  - ...
	• Data objects
	• Components
	  - restricted types
	  - unrestricted
	• RefSpecs
	• Combined
		• Within composite (inclusion)
		
		• Outside composite (reference)
			• Encapsulated in this composite
			
			• Globally visible
				• One-way
				
				• Two-way

Figure 20
Five aspects of composite design.

1. What kinds of structures, such as lists, tables, relations, sets, and the like, can be modeled in a composite?

2. What kinds of elements can make up a composite? In particular, should composites be able to contain full-fledged components? Could a component anchor be an element in a composite?

3. Where are the elements of a composite located? Are they refered to by the composite or contained in it? Can two composites share the same contents?

4. To what degree are the elements contained in a parent composite encapsulated? Put another way, how visible are they from the outside?

5. How is the membership relation implemented? In particular, do the member components of the composite "know" they are contained?

These issues span a design space for composites that includes five aspects: structure, type, definition, location, and membership. Figure 20 lists possible choices for each aspect.

7.3.1 Structure types

The first aspect of composite design involves the kind of structuring the composite captures. In the terminology of abstract data types, this is the *implementation* of the composite content, say, a list or set structure. A wide variety of structures have appeared in hypermedia systems over the years, including modified graphs in Trellis (Stotts and Furuta 1991) and Thoth II (Collier 1987), outline structures in Augment (Engelbart 1984a), relational composites in Aquanet (Marshall et al.

1991) and GIBIS (Conklin and Begeman 1988), and "activity spaces" in SEPIA (Streitz et al. 1992). Ideally, composites should support a standard set of structure types, which could be extended with new special-purpose data structures as discussed in chapters 10 and 11.

7.3.2 Element types

The second aspect concerns what kinds of elements the composite refers to or contains. A composite can hold data objects, other components, references into a component, or a combination of these entities. Composites that contain only data objects correspond to the original Dexter definition, which was meant to model the structures of material in third-party applications in the hypermedia system. For example, a composite that models a structured document might have data elements corresponding to chapters and sections. In that case, links from or to the composite are anchored in substructures of the document.

A composite might also contain other components or component anchors, whose types it might restrict. For example, in DHM, a link browser is a composite restricted to contain only link components. One particularly flexible kind of composite contains a structured collection of refSpecs. Using refSpecs lets the composite refer to whole components, component anchors, or arbitrary computed locations in the online material.

7.3.3 The location of elements

The third aspect of composite design involves the location of the subcomponents, in particular, whether they have an independent existence outside the composite. Frank Halasz (1988) distinguished between reference and inclusion relationships holding between a composite and its content. Composites that *reference* their components allow for the same component to be a member of several composites, whereas composites that *include* their components require that the components be included in only one composite object at a time.

We can illustrate the distinction in terms of deletion, "Does deleting affect the sub-components?", or of containment, "Does the composite actually contain the sub-components, or simply point to them?" An example is the TableTop composite, found in NoteCards and DHM, a collection of components and screen locations at which to display them (Trigg 1988). A TableTop points to the components in its collection, rather than including them directly. In these systems, deleting a TableTop has no effect on the contained components.

In contrast, let's consider a composite that represents a book with subcomponents representing each of the chapters. Unlike the composite defined in the Dexter model, the book composite consists of full-fledged components, not data elements. Because the chapters are components, they can be linked to directly from outside the composite. Unlike a TableTop's subcomponents, however, these components don't have an existence apart from the book—if the book composite is deleted, so are all the chapter components.

7.3.4 Definitional encapsulation

The fourth issue with regard to designing composites involves definitional encapsulation. The question is whether the definitions of the contained objects or components are visible outside the composite. This issue is especially important for designers implementing the hypermedia system in a block-structured, object-oriented language. This problem at the "class" level corresponds to that of location at the "instance" level. In the simplest case, the component class contained by the composite is defined globally, and thus accessible outside the composite. Global definitions do not restrict visibility, and they support the migration of subcomponents between composites.

If, on the other hand, a subcomponent's type is encapsulated within the composite's class definition, then its dependence on the parent composite is stronger than instance incapsulation; no independent existence of the subcomponent is possible. The deletion test can't distinguish inclusion from definitional encapsulation. However, the copy/move test does: an included component can be copied outside the composite, but not if its *definition* is encapsulated in that of the composite. At most, it can be copied into another instance of the same composite type.

Let's consider a structured program editor such as Sif (Mjølner 1990). The definitions of programming statements like loops and conditionals in Sif are constrained to be in the context of an overarching program, or block. Because the loop statement's type is encapsulated in the component, instances of loop statements cannot appear in isolation.

7.3.5 Membership

Finally, the membership aspect of composite design determines the relationship maintained between a composite and its member components, either one-way or two-way. In a one-way relationship, the member components don't "know" that they are members of a composite object of the given type; in a two-way relationship, it is possible, either by lookup or computation, to find the composites of which any component is a member.

7.4   Composites as hierarchical collections

Composites enable a form of hierarchy by reference embodied in such systems as KMS (Akscyn et al. 1988) and NoteCards (Halasz et al. 1987). These hierarchies are *lattices;* each frame or card may be a member of several hierarchies.[2]

Specialized composite types can restrict membership in the composite to one or more component types. For example, in a document structuring context, a ChapterComposite could be restricted to contain or reference SectionComposites only, while SectionComposites could be restricted to contain or reference SubsectionComposites and Atoms, and so forth.

7.5   Composite behavior

The Dexter group, following Halasz's recommendations, included the notion of a composite in the reference model and gave it peer status with the link. At the same time, the link was extended to include multiple endpoints. Thus both composites and links perform *grouping;* that is, they provide means of tying together multiple locations in online material. The distinction between them has two aspects: whether the grouping is more like containment or connection, and whether the behavior is more like opening or traversing. Containment and opening are suggestive of a composite while connection and traversing are suggestive of a (possibly multiheaded) link.

Another difference involves the runtime role of the construct. A link is normally moved "through"; it is rarely presented for inspection in the interface unless its definition or endpoints are being edited. At most, links are represented as line segments in a graphical browser or as link markers in an editor. In contrast, a composite is often presented for inspection and editing in the interface.

2. NoteCards also supports a weak form of physical containment, in that a card must be referenced by at least one FileBox; there is an "Orphans" FileBox in which cards that have been removed from their last FileBoxes are placed.

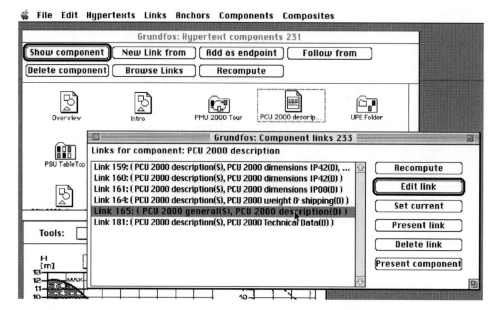

Figure 21
Examples of user interfaces for composites in the Macintosh version of Devise Hypermedia. In the background is a composite with icons representing the atomic and composite components in a HyperSpace. In the foreground is a composite containing links for a given atomic component.

There are two qualities of components bound up in Halasz's "virtual composite": computability and transience. The next two sections address some of the outstanding issues related to these qualities.

7.6   Computability

As with links, some composites include a specification that can be run at any time to recompute the content. Frank Halasz called these *virtual* composites since descriptions rather than content are stored. We prefer the terms *computed* or *recomputable,* since the composite might also store the results of previous computations and would thus behave just like a normal composite for most purposes.

For example, on the World Wide Web, URLs sometimes include a query as an argument to a search script. In such cases, one can simply save the URL in order to rerun the search at a later time. If, however, the URL points to an HTML form used to input the search parameters, then saving the URL is insufficient to recreate the search. The solution is to store the query describing the computation as an attribute or pSpec of the computable component. Then the decision as to whether to recompute at the next presentation is dictated by the component's pSpecs, although the pSpecs of the link or composite from which the user arrived at this component can also contribute to the decision.

A fascinating example of a computed, or implicit, composite that supports spatial hypermedia can be found in Cathy Marshall's (1995) VIKI system. In VIKI, composites can be computed from a spatial layout of component icons on a two-dimensional canvas, by gathering together those that are clustered in space or arranged according to perceivable patterns. Though not explicitly clustered by the user, the composite captures an implicit grouping in order to ease navigation and management of complex information. The computation behind Viki's composite takes into account the spatial grouping of component icons as well as features like color and shape.

Like *virtual composite,* the phrase *computed component* is potentially misleading. In most cases, the endpoints of the link or composite are computed rather than the entire component. For a computed link, for example, one endpoint (the source) is usually held fixed while other endpoints (destinations) are recomputed. For a computed composite, the result of a computation might be all new endpoints.

7.7 Transience

Most components in a hyperspace are created to be stored; their lifetime is expected to be longer than a single session. Some, however, like web pages containing the results of searches, are created "on the fly." Such components are increasingly common on the web, both as the results of searches and through the use of other CGI script-generated pages. The exact duration of these transient components depends on operating system settings like the size of the user's cache, but, generally, they are not saved beyond the life of a session.

Largely missing, however, is support for making such transient components permanent. In most web browsers, the user can save the transient component on a local web server. In that case, the page is indeed permanent, and its outgoing links are preserved. The problem is that any incoming links are now left dangling. In effect, the transformation of a transient page to a permanent one is equivalent to the problem discussed in chapter 8, of copying a subnetwork of a hyperspace. How do we handle the links *into* the subnetwork?

Moreover, we might want the transformation from transience to permanence to be automatic under certain circumstances. Following the strategy used for garbage collectors in operating systems, we might stipulate that a transient page should be saved as long as there is at least one link to it. In a distributed, even world-wide, hypermedia system like the WWW, however, such a requirement is a tall order indeed. As we've seen, the lists of incoming links that can be computed for web pages are at best partial and approximate.

Transience and computability typically occur together. As an example, consider a link one of whose endpoints is a computed composite. Though the link persists (along with its specification of the computation), the composite itself is transient. If a user removes the link or recomputes its endpoints, then the composite will be deleted, unless other pointers to it have been created in the interim.

7.8   Design patterns for composite structures

Three design patterns address many of the issues raised in this chapter. The Structuring by Reference pattern treats composites as structured collections of refSpecs. Such composites can easily refer to multiple types of elements: other components, anchors within components, and arbitrary computed locations in the online material. These refSpec-based composites, though flexible in terms of the elements they contain, cannot support the strict form of inclusion discussed in section 7.3.3. In the next chapter we'll introduce the hyperspace, an entity that supports strict containment.

The Computability and Transience patterns incorporate the major features of composite behavior discussed in this chapter. It's important to note that, although Halasz intended computability and transience to apply primarily to composites, both patterns are, at least in theory, applicable to any component.

Title: Structuring by Reference
Context: Online material in need of structuring.
Problem: To build hypermedia structures external to the material that offer inter-connections and organizations beyond those the material itself offers.
Solution(s): Use refSpec-based structuring entities that refer both into the material (directly or via component anchors) and to other structuring components. Both links and composites are hypermedia entities based on structured collections of such endpoint refSpecs. As we have seen, link and composite structures differ primarily with regard to their use. Because links are designed to be traversed, they include directionality attributes on their endpoints. In contrast, composites are designed to be opened and hierarchically composed. The Traversal pattern in section 9.5 concerns the behavior of structural components.

The elements the composite or link refer to are structured in some way, for example, as an ordered list, a two-dimensional table, or a relation with field names. We encourage designers to support several structure types, depending on the uses to which the composite or link will be put. If at all possible, the set of possible structuring mechanisms should be extensible.
Examples: DHM composites, Intermedia links, HyperWave collections and clusters, and Aquanet relations.
Related patterns: Depends on Wrapping Material and Local Anchoring in section 5.5. See also Traversal in section 9.5.

Title: Computation
Context: Hypermedia structures that interconnect and organize a body of heterogeneous material. Both material and structures evolve over time.
Problem: To support interconnections and structures that are virtual, or computed. The computation might be prompted by a user action or a programmed invocation.
Solution(s): Implement the structures using refSpecs that are computed at run time. That is, refSpecs that identify points in online material (and in the hypermedia structures) using the locSpecs' computable expression field. The placement defined by such a locSpec is variable, and may be different each time it is probed.

The computable and static forms of locSpec are not mutually exclusive. Both types can be used together to yield a form of error-checking redundancy, as described in the Anchor Maintenance pattern in section 14.4.
Examples: Microcosm; on the WWW, URLs that specify search; and the search language of HyTime.
Related patterns: See also Structuring by Reference in this section.

Title: Transience

Context: Hypermedia structures that interconnect and organize a body of heterogeneous material. Both material and structures evolve over time.

Problem: To build structural entities that are initially transient, but that can be made permanent as needed.

Solution(s): Provide special storage behavior for components marked as transient. Normally, components are saved—written to the storage medium—when the hyperspace is saved. However, components marked as transient are saved only if there are structures (extant refSpecs) pointing at them. Otherwise, they are garbage-collected by the runtime system. When necessary, users can also make a transient component permanent.

Examples: DHM link browsers and pages constructed on the WWW as the result of a search.

Related patterns: See also Structuring by Reference in this section.

8

Hyperspaces: Structures for Containment

This book, the 'Biblion,' the Source, the permanent Encyclopedia, the Summa, ... will constitute a systematic, complete, current registration of all the facts relating to a particular branch of knowledge. It will be formed by linking together materials and elements scattered in all relevant publications. (Paul Otlet writing in 1903, quoted in [Rayward 1994, p. 240])

If we could look in on the future at, say, the year 2000, would we see a unity, a federation, or a fragmentation? That is: would we see a single multipurpose network encompassing all applications and serving everyone? Or a more or less coherent system of intercommunicating networks? Or an incoherent assortment of isolated noncommunicating networks, most of them dedicated to single functions or serving single organizations? . . . The conclusion with respect to unification, federation, or fragmentation must be: we should strive for the kind of federation of networks that will provide coherent interconnection where needed and justified and, at the same time, provide informational privacy and security. ([Licklider and Vezza 1978], reprinted in [Greif 1988, pp. 173, 175])

The superordinate entity in the hypermedia pantheon is the hypermedia network itself, which we call a *hyperspace*.[1] Some of the oldest and most persistent questions for hypermedia research and development have been posed at this level. How big is a hyperspace? Is there one for the whole world, or a collection? Can a hyperspace contain other hyperspaces? Is a hyperspace read-only, or can users extend and modify it? Should a hyperspace stretch across several databases or Internet hosts, or should we interconnect otherwise separate hyperspaces with cross-hyperspace links? Do we also need transient sub-hyperspaces for the purpose of moving or copying? These questions have been addressed in a variety

1. In many writings in the field, the term *hypertext* or even *hypermedia* is used to refer to a particular hypermedia network. We have chosen to use a different term, *hyperspace,* to reduce confusion.

of hypermedia systems, and in each case, the answers reveal fundamental goals and assumptions about the use of hypermedia.

Underlying these design choices are two distinctive and not immediately reconcilable views of the hyperspace: as an all-encompassing information medium or as an information structuring resource for projects and workgroups. In the 1970s and 1980s, visionaries like Ted Nelson (1981) held the former view, while hypermedia system builders in research and industry took a more bottom-up approach, responding to what they saw as the practical requirements of everyday work (McCracken and Akscyn 1984). These system builders believed that small hyperspaces were the best place to invest resources and that someday, when it became practical, these hyperspaces could be linked together over wider networks.

In the early 1990s, some of the foremost researchers in the field, though agreeing in principle with a bottom-up approach, registered their concern that, without addressing issues of scale, the field would never take off (Halasz 1991; Malcolm et al. 1991). Shortly thereafter, as if in answer to their call, the World Wide Web arrived. Since the WWW developed, in great part, independently of research in the hypermedia field, it's not surprising that many felt it to be inadequate along a number of dimensions, as we've seen. Nonetheless, all agreed that it was an historical breakthrough, history's first widely available hypertext system. Almost overnight, a huge user population for hypertext appeared, an increase in scale beyond our wildest dreams.

However, even as the WWW brings to life visions of an all-encompassing hyperspace, it also affirms the need to interlink smaller hyperspaces that support various forms of access, materials, and structures. Before considering the problem of how these different stances can be integrated, let's look at three views of hyperspace that have appeared in the history of the field: the all-encompassing hyperspace, the bounded hyperspace, and the separable web. Each of these points of view has had many adherents over the years; we'll illustrate each perspective with two or three examples. Figure 22 summarizes the costs and benefits associated with the approaches.

8.1   All-encompassing hyperspaces

It may come as a surprise to learn that one of the earliest hypertext visionaries of this century was H. G. Wells, the author and influential thinker of the 1920s well

	Benefits	Problem areas
All-encompassing hyperspaces	Broad access to locally generated information	Unique (worldwide) identifiers Enforced uniformity and design to the "least common denominator" Security, privacy
Bounded hyperspaces	Private access Manageable scale	Cross-hyperspace linking Moving/copying substructure
Separable webs	Links editable apart from material	Forced separation between links and "content" Anchoring in nonmodifiable material

Figure 22
Three perspectives on hyperspaces.

known for his essays and science fiction. His notion of the "world encyclopedia," a distributed resource for international scholars, preceded Vannevar Bush's memex, a microfiche-like scholar's workstation, by 20 years.[2] Unlike Bush, Wells (1938) was primarily concerned with the accessibility of information over wide distances, rather than with the details of its use and incorporation in day-to-day scholarly work. Most important for this discussion, Wells called for a single world-straddling hyperspace, "a new world organ for the collection, indexing, summarizing, and release of knowledge" (Wells 1938). Wells echoes Paul Otlet, the author of this chapter's first epigraph, who articulated a similar vision of a unified, interlinked encyclopedia at the turn of the century.[3]

One of the best known visions of an all-encompassing hyperspace was Ted Nelson's Xanadu, first articulated in his classic book, *Computer Lib/Dream Machines* (Nelson 1974). Nelson later coined the term *docuverse* to denote a

2. Vannevar Bush is usually seen as the father of modern hypertext. Though his memex was never built, his design was remarkably detailed and well thought out (Bush 1945). For more on the memex and Bush's legacy see Kahn et al. (1991) and the "Memex and Beyond" web site at www.cs.brown.edu/memex.

3. Though not as well known among computer scientists working in hypermedia, Well's and Otlet's visions are predecessors of today's notion of the digital libary (Levy and Marshall 1995). Indeed, research on networked, digital libraries has played a significant role in library and information science for decades. See, for example, Soergel (1977).

universe of networked, interlinked documents (Nelson 1981). One of the contributions of Nelson's Xanadu project team was the invention of a technique for uniquely identifying arbitrary material stored in the docuverse. The technique employs compact representations called *tumblers* that resemble the numeric strings of the Dewey Decimal system and the IP host numbers of the Internet. The universality of this approach meant, in principle, that anything stored in the docuverse at any time could be uniquely referenced. (Tumblers could also refer to previous versions of material created in the docuverse.) Publishing in Xanadu was a matter of granting access to a portion of the docuverse previously held privately by its author. The Xanadu vision of hypertext use incorporated a free-market economic philosophy: specifically, the requirement that authors of docuverse material be financially reimbursed whenever a link to their material was constructed or followed.

Today, the best known example of an all-encompassing hyperspace is the World Wide Web. Users of the WWW have access to all pages regardless of their location,[4] thus realizing part of the Xanadu vision. The web's universal access depends on a URL addressing scheme, itself based on IP addressing that assigns unique identifiers to pages. As we will see, however, this scheme is weaker than Xanadu's in that it cannot, in general, identify points or spans of material inside a page.

Unlike Xanadu, the WWW has no financial reward structure built in, although various commercial interests are lobbying hard in that direction. It was an important lesson for the field that a large assortment of hypertext authors were willing to provide valuable material without direct compensation from their readers.

8.2 Bounded hyperspaces

More common in the hypermedia work of the last three decades have been systems that support bounded hyperspaces. Generally, these systems interlink material relevant to a single project, or to a single user or group of users. Identifiers of material for the purposes of linking have typically been unique only within the enclosing hyperspace. Only rarely do the systems' designers confront the problem of creating larger hyperspaces by linking together bounded ones.

---

4. Of course, this access is subject to speed differences based on the network configurations at the user's site and at the destination.

One of the best known hypermedia systems of this sort is Apple's HyperCard (Goodman 1987). Multimedia material able to be represented in HyperCard's extensible editor is organized and interlinked into "stacks" of "cards." As with most bounded hyperspace systems, the problem of designing universally unique identifiers can be finessed. Destinations of links are identified by means of a card number unique only within a stack. Cross-stack linking requires giving the path name for the file corresponding to the destination stack. However, these *hard-wired* pathnames often cause problems when reorganizing stack files. In fact, the same problem arises on the WWW; URLs are often invalidated when files are rearranged. Furthermore, a WWW page can have links within it; the naming of these local locations, like the destinations within a HyperCard stack, is unique only within the page.

Xerox's NoteCards system also uses a card metaphor, but includes support via fileboxes for organizing these cards hierarchically (Halasz et al. 1987). A hyper-space in NoteCards is called a *notefile*. NoteCards users organize notefiles according to projects when working collaboratively, or as single personal work-spaces when working alone (Irish and Trigg 1989; Trigg and Suchman 1989). In either case, they occasionally need to link across notefiles. Like HyperCard, NoteCards hard-wires a file path name into such cross-notefile links and experiences similar problems maintaining the links after the file organization is changed.

Unlike HyperCard, NoteCards supports copying and moving portions of a notefile, with the requirement that users temporarily demarcate the sub-notefile to be copied or moved. It was clear to the designers that links between cards in the sub-notefile should be copied or moved along with the cards, but what about links connecting to cards outside the sub-notefile? The NoteCards interface supports two basic alternatives: (1) Leave such links out of the copy/move operation, or (2) Convert the external links into cross-notefile links from the copied sub-notefile back to the cards in the original notefile. A third possibility not supported by NoteCards is to build dangling links for each external link. Once the sub-notefile is installed in its new environment (possibly in the context of other cards), the user reconnects the links as needed. Figure 23 depicts the three possibilities.

Although one can debate the design and interface choices made in NoteCards and other systems supporting subhyperspaces, confronting such problems is unavoidable (Leggett and Schnase 1994). Should we adopt (or envision) an

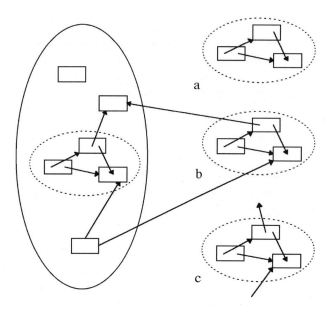

Figure 23
Three approaches to copying a subhyperspace: (a) don't copy the links out of the
subhyperspace; (b) point back into the original hyperspace using cross-hyperspace links;
(c) create "dangling" links for the user to fill in or delete.

all-encompassing hyperspace and whatever standard features and behavior it
enforces, or build smaller idiosyncratic hyperspaces and confront the infrastructure problems that arise across and between them? The position we advocate in
part III of this book is to avoid that hard choice and instead exploit both forms
of hyperspace through open, integrative system design.

8.3 Separable webs

There is a third view of the hyperspace that has played an increasingly important
role in hypermedia research and development. This view is based on the premise
that the links in a hyperspace can profitably be separated from the material, or
contents, they interconnect. The first system to realize such separability was
Intermedia, created by Norm Meyrowitz and his colleagues at Brown University
(Haan et al. 1992). An Intermedia web consists of links that are stored separately
from the material they interconnect. Students in courses at Brown University, for

example, created their own personal webs to interlink online material provided in advance for the class.

A question that arises is to what degree this separation of link authoring from contents creation actually benefited the students. As a study of Intermedia classroom use showed, the teaching assistants who constructed and found materials for the class webs rated their satisfaction with the experience of using hypermedia higher than the students who could only link what was already there (Beeman et al. 1987).

The separable web approach dovetailed in the late 1980s with the call for open systems in hypermedia and elsewhere. The Sun Link Service designed by Amy Pearl extended Intermedia's separation of web from contents by supporting a link server on a machine or address space separate from third-party applications (Pearl 1989). The Sun Link Service requires participating applications to support a protocol for link following and link creation. The Microcosm system, developed soon thereafter at Southampton University in England (Hall et al. 1996), takes web separability a step further by linking material created in arbitrary applications, including those developed independently of Microcosm.

8.4   Toward an integrated approach

It is our belief that the future will require supporting several approaches simultaneously, at least under certain conditions. The WWW may well be our future docuverse, but it needs to interlink other self-contained, encapsulated hyperspaces (such as intranets and workstation-based hyperspaces). The notion of webs that separate links from data will be useful, but will have to be flexible enough to work in multiple contexts.[5]

As is becoming rapidly clear, basing a system on the WWW does not free its designers from concern about integration. First, as the rise of intranets (Hills 1996) shows us, security concerns have forced many organizations to create bounded hyperspaces that are separated from the WWW by firewalls. Links can be followed from intranets out to the global WWW, but not in the other direction. The boundaries between intranets pose additional problems of copying and moving sub-hyperspaces from one system to another, this time across firewalls.

5. For an example of early work in this area, see the Hyper-G system (Maurer 1996).

But there is a more important problem with adoption of the WWW as a universal hypermedia substrate. It is unlikely that everyday applications like text editors and spreadsheets will migrate to the WWW in the near term. Therefore, we believe that the modern hypermedia vision should be one of linking among applications on the workstation and also between applications and the WWW. The requirement for sophisticated interchange between bounded local hyperspaces and the all-encompassing WWW is likely to persist into the foreseeable future.

The work of the Dexter group did not preclude such a hybrid vision for hypermedia. Dexter's concept of hypertext modeled a bounded address space within which the work of resolving hypermedia pointers could take place. In this sense, both all-encompassing and local hyperspaces were in principle Dexter-compliant. On the other hand, the Dexter group did not address the issue of cross-hyperspace linking, nor issues of hyperspace copying and subsetting.

Hyperspace interchange is a good example of an area that was mostly skirted by the Dexter group, and yet of critical importance in the hybrid world we envision. The Dexter group assumed that entire hyperspaces would be interchanged between remote users by rendering them as tagged SGML or possibly HyTime files. Several years after the last meeting of the Dexter group, one of its organizers, John Leggett, explored extensions to this basic notion of file interchange in order to handle copying and moving hyperspace subsets (Leggett and Schnase 1994). If we assume a future where most hyperspaces live under a WWW umbrella, however, the problem of interchange may be transformed into one of distribution and remote interoperability. In such a scenario, a part of a hyperspace might be identified rather than carved off. The distant recipient would then read and manipulate it remotely by means of a customized protocol.[6]

Part III explores related issues that are vital to the successful coevolution of the WWW with local hyperspaces living on workstations or behind firewalls. These issues include support for distribution of hypermedia entities across wide-area and local networks, asynchronous and realtime cooperative authoring of such materials, and integration of third-party applications in a way that maintains visibility across networks. For now, we present a pattern that summarizes the notion of bounded hyperspace.

---

6. A candidate for this protocol is currently under development in the World Wide Web consortium (W3C). Called WebDAV (Distibuted Authoring and Versioning), it is intended to support the management of shared collections of web resources by users distributed over the Internet (www.ics.uci.edu/~ejw/authoring).

8.5   A pattern for bounded hyperspaces

A bounded hyperspace can be thought of as a composite that contains rather than refers to other components, including, potentially, other hyperspaces. Each hyperspace has its own name space within which components are uniquely identified, just as a host server on the WWW provides a name space for local URLs.

Indeed, if the WWW is taken to be a collection of hyperspaces, one per WWW host server, then the standard URL is seen as having two parts, an identification of a hyperspace (a WWW server) and a locSpec unique in that hyperspace (the remainder of the URL). Accordingly, URLs act as cross-hyperspace pointers, but only within the limited collection of hyperspaces comprising the WWW. URLs are unable to interconnect arbitrary Internet locations with firewall-protected company intranets or non-Internet-based hypermedia systems.

The following pattern characterizes the bounded hyperspace approach as one of controlled containment.

In chapter 18, we consider how bounded hyperspaces integrate with the WWW, today's "all-encompassing" hyperspace.

Title: Structuring by Containment
Context: Hypermedia structures interconnecting and organizing a body of heterogeneous material. These structures may be distributed across multiple machines.
Problem: To provide a means of encapsulating hypermedia structures into "containers" with separate name spaces. There must also be support for references that cross the boundaries of containers.
Solution(s):   Support structural containment with the hyperspace, a kind of composite that acts as the overarching reference point for a collection of structural entities and linked material. The locating done by locSpecs in the hyperspace is relative to this collection of objects. References outside the hyperspace require some means of identifying a foreign hyperspace.
Examples: A familiar example of a bounded hyperspace is a host on the WWW. URLs specify relative locations within the scope of that host, or across servers by specifying a hostname. The cross-notefile links of NoteCards (Halasz et al. 1987) provide a pre-WWW example of interconnected bounded hyperspaces.
Related patterns: See also Structuring by Reference in chapter 8.

9

Managing Hypermedia Structures at Run Time

[T]he basic idea of [associative indexing] is a provision whereby any item may be caused at will to select immediately and automatically another. This is the essential feature of the memex. The process of tying two items together is the important thing. (Bush 1945, p. 34)

Hypertext/hypermedia has the . . . potential for making fundamental improvements to people's daily work. Like 'cut, copy, and paste,' making and following links . . . provides a powerful integrating ability and it is reasonably easy to motivate and teach to idea workers. (Meyrowitz 1989, p. 113)

Up to this point, we have largely focused on the fundamental entities of hypermedia and the means by which they structure online material. This chapter discusses the hypermedia system's runtime behavior. We start by briefly visiting the history of hypermedia runtime development before the Dexter model. We then focus on the Dexter group's vision of hypermedia run time and some of the problems it raised. We follow this discussion with closer looks at the runtime presentation of components, the entities managing runtime behavior, and the detailed work of link traversal. Finally, we close with patterns related to the work of presentation and traversal. For an excellent overview of hypermedia behavior viewed both historically and in today's context of the WWW, we refer the reader to Bieber et al. (1997).

9.1 The goal of a separate runtime environment

A primary design goal for many of the foremost hypermedia projects was to find an adequate and appropriate means of distinguishing two parts of a hypermedia system, one that stores and retrieves hypermedia material, and one through which users navigate and manipulate those structures. Unhitching run time from storage would enable collaborating users running on different platforms to share a single storage server.

At least by the early 1970s, Ted Nelson and the Xanadu team were promoting what they called a "backend/frontend" separation presaging the client-server architectures that are now so prominent (Nelson 1974). Xanadu's vision depended on the presence of frontend developers who would build hypermedia user interfaces (clients) that would communicate with Xanadu back ends (servers) via an API, possibly over a network. Xanadu assumed furthermore that the frontend developers would be building editors that were customized for Xanadu storage schemes. At that time, very few text editors supported the kind of single character addressing required by Xanadu's link endpoint addressing policy (Nelson 1981). Such constraints on applications made it difficult for the Xanadu approach to achieve widespread acceptance. (For more on the topic of client-server architectures for hypermedia, see chapter 12.)

9.2   Three-way separation in the Dexter model

In response to the call to separate run time from storage, the Dexter group went a step further, proposing a three-way separation that included a within-component layer. In part, this third layer addresses the Xanadu problem of the need for completely hypermedia-compliant editors. Three-way separation enabled the Dexter group to model the integration of existing editors in the style of the Sun Link Service (Pearl 1989). Thus the Dexter model supports client/server separations with hypermedia-compliant clients, as well as application/link-server separations in which applications are only minimally aware of hypermedia functionality.

The Dexter model includes a collection of runtime concepts meant to correspond to the storage entities. A "session" manages a storage layer hyperspace; an "instantiation," a component; and a "link marker" (more problematically as it turns out), an anchor. Crucially, these mappings are many-to-one; a single component can have multiple instantiations corresponding to different views. And in different views, a component anchor might be represented using different styles of link markers. Likewise, a hyperspace might have multiple sessions running simultaneously for different users on various platforms.

Another critical part of the Dexter runtime model is its protocol for link traversal, perhaps the most characteristic runtime behavior of a hypermedia system. Following a link requires crossing the boundaries between the runtime and storage layers, and between the runtime and within-component layers. On the one hand, Dexter's "resolver" and "accessor" operations turn specifications of link endpoints into unique component identifiers and retrieve components with those identifiers from storage. On the other hand, as we've seen, the anchor concept models link sources and destinations that are embedded in material within a component. In an integrated environment, this material might be in the province of third-party applications. Thus the Dexter approach raised thorny problems of anchor maintenance across changes to component material, issues that continue to occupy today's hypermedia developers (Davis 1995).

Finally, Dexter's notion of presentation specifications (pSpecs) helps cross the boundary between the runtime and storage layers. Pspecs offer a means of representing the parameterized behavior of anchors and components in a way that can be stored along with the object's other attributes. Thus a link endpoint might include a pSpec that influences the display of the component or anchor it designates.

9.3 The weaknesses of the Dexter model

The biggest problem with Dexter's three-layer approach is its implied division of responsibility between the runtime and within-component layers. The Dexter model assumes that the applications responsible for managing individual component types, that is, the within-component layer, make no demands on the run time. As we know today, applications take on much more than simply the storage and editing of material. They also present an interface, usually carefully crafted to fit in a particular windowing and operating system. It is naive to expect that a hypermedia system will take over complete control of the interface, at the level of either window system or application.

An open systems approach, in contrast, takes as given the existence of application environments and interfaces. This approach requires that hypermedia designers focus on the interface APIs that mark the division of labor between the hypermedia system and existing applications, window environments, and operating systems. As discussed in chapter 13, this division can be accomplished by means of a set of APIs that fit hypermedia functionality into the context of existing application interfaces or window systems. The runtime layer then has responsibility only for behavior within the hypermedia province, including navigation and link anchor presentation, and is as much as possible independent of particular application interfaces.

Another problem with the Dexter model involves the link marker concept used in the runtime layer. The model assumes a correspondence between link markers and anchors that suggests that every anchor in a system is visibly marked in its component's instantiation. As we have seen, this is not always the case. For example, some anchors are computed; that is, they correspond to arbitrary selections in an editor that could not have been marked as link endpoints prior to their selection by the user. In our view, marking the endpoints of links and composites is a complex issue, deeply dependent on the particularities of application environments and window systems.

Finally, as we've noted in chapters 3 and 6, the Dexter model's strict enforcement of rules for proper hypermedia behavior are both impossible to enforce and unreasonable in open systems contexts. The foremost example is the rule against dangling links. The Dexter model requires that the removal of a component trigger the deletion of all connected links. In a distributed environment, such a requirement is unenforceable, at least for those links living on currently inaccessible servers. Moreover, the deletion may happen outside the scope of the hypermedia system altogether. Finally, other forms of dangling link endpoints can occur as a result of editing in a component around the location of a link endpoint. Figure 24 depicts several of these situations.

Beyond the difficulties of precluding dangling links, however, is the fact that such links are actually desirable in certain situations. For example, one might create a link before its destination component, or in advance of that part of the destination's content in which the link endpoint will be anchored. Section 8.2 illustrates how dangling links can be useful in copying subnetworks of a hyperspace. Rather than outlawing such links, hypermedia systems ought to support their use, for example, by managing dangling links as reminders of work still to be done.

A lazy updating approach addresses the problem of keeping links updated when connected components are deleted or otherwise made unavailable. When the user deletes a component, the system removes it from the hyperspace, destroys its data, and sets a flag indicating the deletion. Following a link to such a deleted component, or stub, results in a dangling link exception, as described by Grønbæk and Trigg (1994).

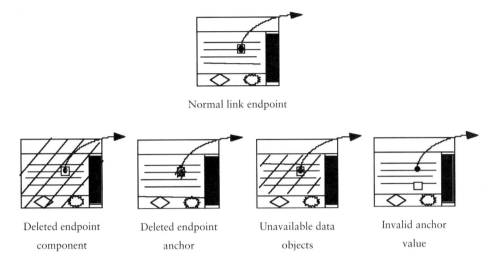

Normal link endpoint

Deleted endpoint   Deleted endpoint   Unavailable data   Invalid anchor
component   anchor   objects   value

Figure 24
Examples of dangling links.

Similarly, when presenting a composite at run time, the system can display stubs that are members of the composite using an icon signalling the deletion. The user later removes the stub from the composite manually, or invokes a cleanup operation to remove all stubs at once. Cleanup can also be performed automatically upon any presentation of a composite, ensuring that deleted components never appear in the user interface. The choice of cleanup schema should be determined by preferences the user sets.

9.4   Refining the Dexter model's runtime behavior

The remainder of this chapter extends the Dexter group's vision of runtime behavior in two areas. First, we briefly discuss the notion of the pSpec. The Dexter model described it primarily by example. Thereafter, we delve deeper into the workings of link traversal in order to incorporate the new capabilities of the hypermedia entities outlined in the preceding chapters. We start by characterizing link traversal as a five-step process. Next we give a more detailed algorithm for traversal that takes locSpecs, refSpecs, and hyperspaces into account. We then discuss traversal across hyperspaces.

9.4.1   Determining presentation behavior

The presentation specification (pSpec) is the means of capturing in the Dexter model those characterizations of runtime behavior that need to be stored with hypermedia entities like components, link endpoints, and anchors. In the best known example of their use in the Dexter model, pSpecs influence the way components are opened and how they appear in an interface. For example, section 3.3 describes how pSpecs are used in link endpoints as a means of determining in which of two modes the destination component will be opened: execute-only or editable.

The *form* of pSpecs, their syntax and structuring, was left completely open in the Dexter model, although the tendency is to implement them as lists of attribute-value pairs. An intriguing possibility is to use hypermedia itself as the medium for representing pSpecs. This approach is most natural for those cases when a pSpec in one component makes reference to another component. For example, a link might need to bring up its destination component *in context,* that is, to require that a particular enclosing composite of the destination component be opened simultaneously.

In that case, the pSpec contains a destination-context refSpec identifying a composite, or a path of nested composites down to the destination component. The same pSpec can also use attributes to specify windowing behavior. On link traversal, these attributes could direct the window system to replace the windows representing the current component with the windows of the destination component's enclosing composites.

Potentially, pSpecs can also coordinate more complex forms of runtime behavior. For example, in chapter 10, we discuss how they can help manage the synchronization of multiple streams of time-based multimedia material.

Representing pSpecs as "meta" hypermedia structures that govern the behavior of the hypermedia run time opens up advanced possibilities for user tailoring. Tailors who are already familiar with the hypermedia entities used to structure the hyperspace can use the same structuring capabilities declaratively to represent changes to the runtime behavior. In addition, as Rob Akscyn and Donald McCracken (1993) explain with regard to the KMS system, the "behavior hypermedia" is thus deeply interstructured with the "material hypermedia." Thus, for example, the structures governing the behavior of a link endpoint are attached directly to the endpoint's pSpec to which they are meant to apply.

9.4.2   Managing traversal behavior

As we've seen, the Dexter group provides three runtime entities, the session, instantiation, and link marker, for managing the runtime behavior of the hyperspace, component, and anchor entities, respectively. It is difficult, if not impossible, to develop a general model of link markers, given that they appear as embedded objects in material whose interfaces are managed by third-party applications. Furthermore, the Dexter model lacks an overarching entity to oversee the management of multiple hyperspaces.

Our recommendation is therefore to modify the Dexter runtime model slightly to use three entities that we call *session manager, session,* and *instantiation.* The session manager includes a list of *active* hyperspaces, those that are consulted during any link traversal. In section 9.4.6, we explain how new hyperspaces can be activated through the traversal of cross-hyperspace links. The second entity, the session, manages a single hyperspace. It includes operations for opening and closing components and instantiations, and for basic traversal. Finally, the instantiation manages the viewing and behavior of a single component. It includes operations for creating, deleting, and viewing anchors. Instantiations of link components can also specify the means by which traversal moves from one or more of the link's endpoints to others.

The rest of this chapter examines the work of traversal in more detail, while chapter 11 explains how that work is distributed among the operations of sessionManager, session, and instantiation.

9.4.3   Beyond simple link traversal

At its most basic level, hypermedia concerns finding, making, and following connections in online material. In open hypermedia, much of that material already exists. Furthermore, it belongs in an environment; it has a run time apart from that of the hypermedia system. The extra behavior added by an open hypermedia system involves navigation through the structures represented by links and composites. In the simplest case, the user follows links by clicking visible placements in the material of components. Alternatively, the user identifies a location in the material that is not a directly embedded placement (or *link marker* in the Dexter terminology) and the system looks for matching structure, in other words, refSpecs that resolve to that location or associate with that material. Typically, such refSpecs belong to structuring components such as links that take us elsewhere.

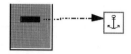

Step 1: Find or create source
anchor from selection.

RefSpec table

Step 2: Lookup matching
link endpoint refSpecs.

Link 43   Link 22

Step 3: Determine "destination"
link endpoints.

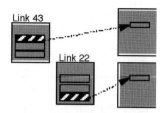

Step 4: Resolve "destination" refSpecs
to destination component locations.

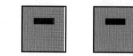

Step 5: Display destinations.

Figure 25
Steps in following a link.

Links and composites enable two kinds of navigation: traversing and opening. Both depend on the notion of mappings. In general, three components are involved: a source, a mapping component, and a destination. Each of these may in fact be multiple components, but to illustrate the basic idea, a simple case—traversing a link from a single noncomputed source anchor—will suffice. As shown in figure 25, traversal starts from a source selection in Step 1. Step 2 involves finding mapping components (in this case, links) that specify the given source anchor. In Step 3, the system chooses appropriate endpoints of the mapping components. Finally, in Steps 4 and 5 the system resolves these refSpecs and brings up the destination anchors.

The key difference between traversal and opening is that the latter starts from a mapping component rather than from a locSpec. Thus an opening operation comprises only the last three steps of figure 25. For example, opening a composite requires finding and displaying the destinations its endpoints specify. Similarly, a link component can be opened by displaying some or all of the refSpecs that comprise its endpoints.

Another variant of the simple link traversal semantics employs only the first two steps in figure 25. Let's imagine that the user wants to display all composites that refer to a given component or to a location within that component. The system could follow steps 1 and 2 to retrieve the containing composites, and then display or in some way highlight those composites. A similar scheme could display the links that refer to a particular anchor without traversing them.

9.4.4 A link traversal algorithm

Let's now look one level deeper at our scheme for link traversal. Reviewing the steps of figure 25, we start with a source locSpec (either preexisting or constructed on the fly), with which we search for matching refSpecs. Among others, they include the endpoints of links in the enclosing hyperspace that point to the material identified by the locSpec. The algorithm proceeds by traversing the links, that is, bringing up the components referred to by the links' other (usually destination) endpoints. Crucial to the process is Step 2, in which a locSpec is used to find matching refSpecs. The precise behavior of this matching or lookup process is left up to the implementation, although we have specified that it is performed by each relevant session's traversal operation.

The procedural steps that follow describe the work of traversal in a bit more detail.

1. First, identify or create a source locSpec. This can happen in one of four ways:

a. The user identifies a selection of material, say, a string of text or a graphic object. In this case, a transient locSpec is constructed on the fly based on the user's selection.

b. The user types in (or pastes or clicks) a textual representation of a locSpec. (This procedure is analogous to the use of URL strings in WWW browsers.)

c. The user identifies an anchor in some hypermedia component. In this case, the anchor's locSpec becomes the source locSpec.

d. The user identifies an entire component in a hyperspace. A transient locSpec is created, identifying the entire component (and omitting the within-component specification).

2. Identify the applicable, or active, hyperspaces. By default, they include any hyperspaces which have open components. In addition, the sessionManager can specify a default set of active hyperspaces meant to apply during any traversal operation.

3. For each hyperspace, map from the source locSpec to a collection of matching refSpecs. We call the components containing these refSpecs the *mapping compo-*

nents; that is, they are used to identify the destinations of a traversal operation. Mapping components may also belong to remote hyperspaces, as explained in the next section.

4. Traverse each mapping component, by treating the component as a map from some of its endpoints to others. This is where the directionality of the endpoint comes into play. For example, a link component might map from a source endpoint refSpec to one or more destination endpoints.[1]

5. Resolve the endpoints returned in Step 4. For each endpoint, find the relevant hyperspace. If the endpoint specifies a hyperspace ID along with its locSpec (a cross-hyperspace refSpec), then use that ID. Otherwise, use the enclosing active hyperspace. In both cases, consult the hyperspace to resolve the endpoint.

6. Finally, display or otherwise highlight the material identified as a result of resolving the endpoints. This step involves consulting the various relevant pSpecs. They include the pSpecs on the endpoints of the mapping component, as well as those on the components to be displayed. Other pSpecs might also be consulted, including any associated with the hyperspace of the destination components, as well as those on composites that contain the destination components. For more on the use of pSpecs during traversal, especially for multimedia components, see chapter 10.

As we discussed earlier, partial traversals are also possible. For example, using just the first half of the algorithm, one could find all composites pointing at a given anchor or component. Using the second half of the algorithm, one could resolve a locSpec at the endpoint of a link to its destination. Such locSpec resolution behavior is analogous to URL resolution on the WWW.

9.4.5 Traversing a link with a computed endpoint

As a simple example of link traversal, let's consider a computed link CL created in a hyperspace H1. In the style of Microcosm's "generic link" (Hall et al. 1996), CL is intended to connect any occurence of the word *gaggle* to a graphic image of a flock of geese stored in H1 and to a definition of the word in a remote dictionary hyperspace, as shown in figure 26. To achieve generality, the locSpec in CL's source refSpec specifies the string "gaggle" rather than some explicit

---

1. In the framework proposed in chapter 11, we locate the operation that performs endpoint traversal at the component's instantiation object. In addition, we might specify a general traversal algorithm (say, from source to destination endpoints) at the session level, letting individual mapping components override that algorithm as needed.

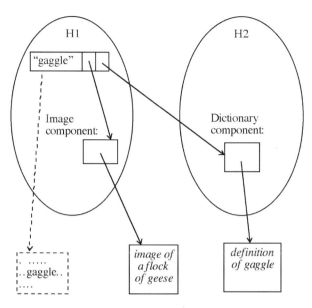

Figure 26
A link with a computed endpoint, the string "gaggle," stored in H1. The result of
following the link from a matching text string in the material, is that two destination
endpoints are brought up, an image of a flock of geese in H1, and a definition of *gaggle*
in H2.

location in H1. Assuming that the hyperspace H1 is active, when a user selects
the string "gaggle," H1's locSpecMatcher finds the matching refSpecs and the
system displays the two destinations. If H2 was not already active, it is activated
in order to access the dictionary component.

At first glance, H1's generic links seem to model the service that WWW search
engines provide today. Based on a global full-text index, the search engine's
refSpec table matches arbitrary text strings to locations anywhere on the web. In
fact, however, WWW search engines provide only partial, inaccurate refSpec
tables. Many actual matches are not recovered, and those that are may be out of
date. Nonetheless, this partiality is often good enough in practice. Indeed, one
could imagine a WWW user making an arbitrary text selection, and invoking
multiple search engines on that selection.

Let us now consider a slight variant of the generic link situation. A user whose
only active hyperspace is H2 selects the same string, "gaggle," in an H2 component. As we've explained, a session can maintain a list of active hyperspaces,
possibly specified by default according to user preferences. Furthermore, one

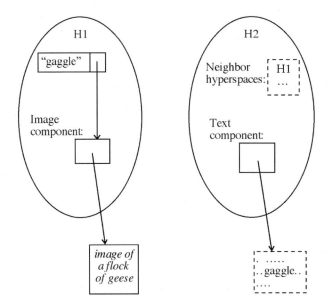

Figure 27
A link with a computed endpoint, the string "gaggle," stored in H1. Opening H2 automatically activates H1, since it is listed as a neighbor of H2. Thereafter, when a text component in H2 is opened H1's links apply to any strings selected in that component.

hyperspace can explicitly name neighbor hyperspaces that should be jointly activated. As depicted in figure 27, activating H2 causes the neighbor hyperspace H1, listed in H2, to be activated. The result is a neighborhood of active hyperspaces around H2, whose refSpec tables are consulted for any link traversal.

9.4.6   Cross-hyperspace link traversal

Ordinarily, link traversal occurs within a single hyperspace. However, the system can easily follow a cross-hyperspace link if we start from an endpoint stored in the hyperspace where the link is stored. For example, let's consider a link L constructed in hyperspace H1, connecting a source in H1 to an explicit destination in hyperspace H2, as depicted in figure 28. Because creation took place in H1, the link's definition is stored there. To follow the link *out* of H1 is the easy case. When the user selects the endpoint material managed by anchor A1 in the source component, H1's locSpecMatcher looks up the matching refSpec for L. The system traverses the link by bringing up the destination anchor found in H2.

Moving in the other direction is harder. Traversing the link L from a refSpec in H2 requires that we somehow know to activate H1. Then H1's traversal opera-

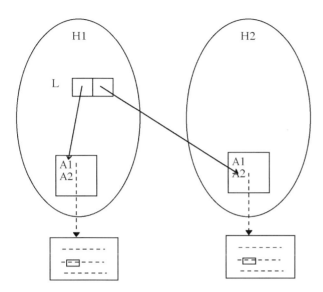

Figure 28
A link L between hyperspaces H1 and H2, stored in H1. Traversal backward through L
is not supported.

tion can be invoked, the match with L's endpoint discovered, and the link
traversed back to its H1 endpoints.

One approach is to make H1 a neighbor of H2, as illustrated in figure 27,
assuming that the creator of L has write access to H2. Another approach is to
provide explicit backpointers from a refSpec in a hyperspace to those remote
hyperspaces that point to it. In the design depicted in figure 29, cross-hyperspace
backpointers are saved in a table maintained by the session corresponding to H2.
To traverse links starting from the A2 anchor in H2, we invoke H2's traversal
operation as usual. In addition, we check the backpointers table and find the
mapping from C2.A2 to hyperspace H1. H1 is then activated, its traversal
function invoked, and L's source endpoint, an anchor in component C1,
displayed.

This approach to cross-hyperspace link traversal uses the existing within-
hyperspace link traversal mechanism, plus an extra table lookup in the remote
hyperspace. Thus L is made bidirectional (traversable in either direction) at the
cost of maintaining backpointer integrity. It's important to remember, however,
that both the backpointer and neighbor hyperspace approaches require that L's
creator have write permission in H2.

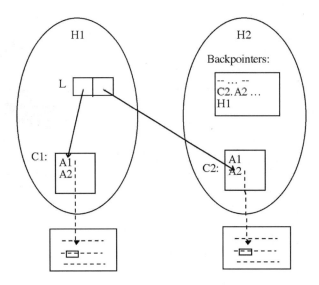

Figure 29
A link L between hyperspaces H1 and H2, stored in H1. Backward traversal along L is supported by modifying H2's refSpec table to include a backpointer to the H1 hyperspace.

In general, then, a link traversal operation checks for matching refSpecs in all active hyperspaces. Some of these lookups may result in a cross-hyperspace backpointer that activates another hyperspace for a second lookup.[2] Cross-hyperspace links with backpointers can be created whenever the author has the appropriate write permissions, and can be followed in either direction. Computed links, on the other hand, can always be defined, but apply only across a user's active hyperspaces.

9.4.7 Two patterns for hypermedia run times
In closing, we present two brief patterns addressing the goals of traversal and presentation. In chapter 10, we revisit these operations for the cases of navigation and synchronized multimedia.

2. Note, however, that chaining such indirect lookups can lead to cycles.

Title: Traversal

Context: Hypermedia structures interconnecting and organizing a body of heterogeneous material. Users of the hypermedia experience *locality,* that is, the interface positions the user at particular places in the space (or configurations of places in the case of a multiple-window interface).

Problem: To support changing locality in a user's experience of hypermedia.

Solution(s): Achieve motion through the hypermedia by bringing up the material refered to by one or more of the refSpecs of a structure that is accessible from the user's current locality. Whether the new material by default replaces the current configuration (as on the WWW) or is juxtaposed (as in DHM and NoteCards) depends on the system implementation and the needs of the user community. PSpecs can be used if this behavior needs to vary within the system.

Examples: Essentially, every hypermedia system supports some kind of traversal. Indeed, such support is often seen as the primary task of a hypermedia run time.

Related patterns: Depends on Embedded Interconnecting and Externalized Locating in section 4.8. See also Presentation in this section.

Title: Presentation

Context: Hypermedia structures interconnecting and organizing a body of heterogeneous material. The structures are made available through a run time that supports user interaction.

Problem: To visually represent each structural entity in the hypermedia system in the user interface. The representations may require modifying the appearance of the material wrapped by a component or creating a new GUI interface for a composite. The properties of such a representation depend on a variety of factors, both static and dynamic.

Solution(s): Attach presentation specifications, a pSpec, to each structural entity that is saved along with the hyperspace. A pSpec is a means of representing and storing a set of preferences for the structural entity's appearance.

Multiple pSpecs can apply in any particular case. For example, material wrapped by a component might be governed by both the component's pSpec and the pSpec of the link that was traversed to arrive at the component. Thus, implementations need to provide means of combining the effects of pSpecs and prioritizing these effects when they conflict.

Examples: Augment's link specifications, including which window to display in, how to display context around the link, and so on.

Related patterns: Depends on Wrapping Material in section 5.5 and Structuring by Reference in section 7.8.

10

Structures for Navigation and Synchronization

There is a new profession of trail blazers, those who find delight in the task of establishing useful trails through the enormous mass of the common record. (Bush 1945, p. 108)

[M]ultimedia texts are by no means the death of writing. A hypermedia display is still a text, a weaving together of elements treated symbolically. Hypermedia simply extends the principles of electronic writing into the domain of sound and image. The computer's control of structure promises to create a synaesthesia in which anything that can be seen or heard may contribute to the texture of the text. These synaesthetic texts will have the same qualities as electronic verbal texts. They too will be flexible, dynamic, and interactive; they too will blur the distinction between writer and reader. (Bolter 1991, p. 27)

Navigation in hypermedia structures is traditionally considered synonymous with link following, that is, a user invoking a follow operation on a visible link marker rendered inside some online material. However, more advanced structure-based forms of navigation have been suggested by hypermedia researchers over the years. Hypermedia pioneers dating back to Vannevar Bush have suggested structures that went beyond local links from one item of information to another. Bush himself suggested named trails as a structuring mechanism consisting of a preconstructed path through many associated information items, possibly built using links (Bush 1945).

Since then, research in hypermedia navigation has mainly focused on three areas:

· graphical, interactive representations of hypermedia sub-networks and the user's location within them (Foss 1988; Utting and Yankelovich 1989)

· the management of author-created *paths* or *guided tours* through a network (Mylonas and Heath 1990; Trigg 1991)

· various forms of automated or semi-automated traversal of hypermedia networks, including synchronized, multitrack multimedia presentations (Buchanan and Zellweger 1992; DeRose and Durand 1994)

At times, various systems have crossed the boundaries between these areas. For example, Zellweger's Scripted Documents (Zellweger 1989) were, in effect, automatable timed guided tours. Likewise, NoteCards' guided tours used the system's standard graphical network browser as an interface for creating and modifying the tours (Trigg 1988).

Today, ground-breaking research is bringing these three forms of advanced navigation to the WWW. Graphical network displays are being explored in projects like the Hyperbolic Browser (Lamping et al. 1995).[1] A simple but powerful approach to web-based guided tours is presented in Furuta et al. (1997). Finally, Java, VRML, QuickTimeVR, and RealAudio, among others, are bringing dynamic media to the web.

In this chapter, we start by presenting examples of browsers and guided tours designed as simple extensions of our basic composite. We then dive into the topic of multimedia, reviewing how the HyTime standard and the Amsterdam model have addressed problems in organizing and synchronizing the presentation of multiple tracks of dynamic material. We conclude with our own proposals that build on this previous work, summarizing them with two design patterns.

10.1   Filtered component browsing

The generic composite entity introduced in chapter 7 provides the basis for filtered component browsing over a hyperspace. Such search browsers can be used to navigate directly to components of particular types or having particular attributes or contents. What is important here, is that the search browser is itself a component in the hyperspace. Usually it is transient, but in a system like DHM, it can optionally be made permanent. Two such search browsers are shown in figure 30. Both are specialized forms of composite components in the DHM system.

1. Two further examples of WWW-based graphical browsers are WebSquirrel for bookmarks (www.eastgate.com/squirrel/welcome.html) and WebView for mapping HTML links on the WWW (www.cs.washington.edu/homes/glinden/WebView/WebView.html).

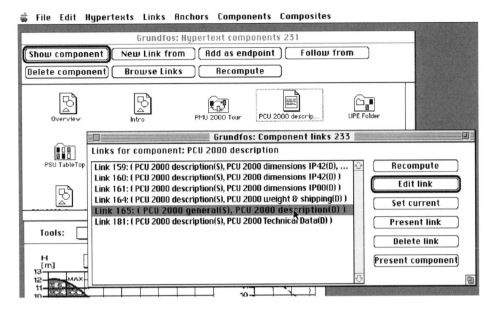

Figure 30
User interface examples from a pump documentation application. The "Hypertext components 231" browser window summarizes the atomic and composite components in the hyperspace. Folder icons with symbols are used to represent different types of composites. The "Component links 233" browser window displays all the links to and from the text component "PCU 2000 description."

The partially occluded window in the background of figure 30 is the runtime instantiation of a particular kind of search browser, a composite that includes all nonlink components, displayed using icons representing component types. Like any other component, such a search browser can be assigned transient and/or computed status. To make the composite computed, however, requires providing a computation criterion, in this case a query specifying the set of all nonlink components in the enclosing hyperspace.

The window in the foreground of figure 30 is the runtime instantiation of another kind of search browser. This one presents the set of all link components at least one of whose endpoints identifies a given component. Variants of this composite subclass can be used for a variety of browsers and queries that collect links in the network. The root component or anchor is represented in an attribute of the composite; hence the composite can recompute itself on demand.

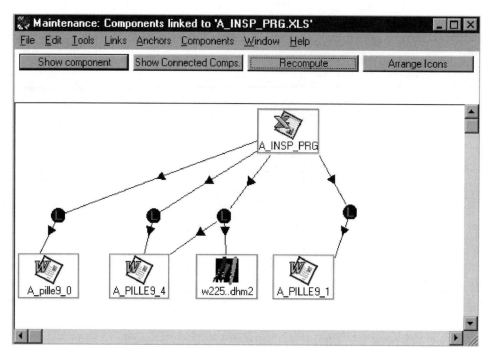

Figure 31
A local map in DHM for an Excel component.

10.2   Graphical overview browsers

The classical graphical overview browsers from hypermedia systems like Intermedia and NoteCards can also be provided by means of specialized composites. For instance, figure 31 shows a DHM composite component used to manage local map browsers in the style of Intermedia. The composite maintains a graph structure of components connected directly via links to a given root component. The functionality that manages the layout of the graph is implemented in the composite's instantiation.

10.3   Composites for tabletops and guided tours

Specialized composites can also be used to implement the trails (Bush 1945), paths (Trigg and Weiser 1986), and guided tours (Trigg 1988) that represent and communicate premapped hypermedia content and structure. These composite-

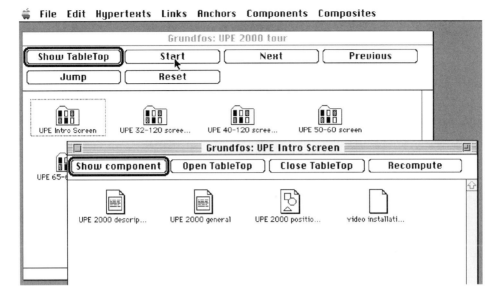

Figure 32
Example from a documentation application. The window "UPE 2000 tour" represents a nonbranching guided tour of a specific class of pumps. The order of stops on the tour is currently specified by the left-to-right sequence of icons in the tour window (a graphical interface is currently under development). The "UPE Intro Screen" window represents the first TableTop in the "UPE 2000 tour."

based structures stand in contrast to Bush's memex trails which were made up of links (Bush 1945; Trigg 1991), as are paths in the Perseus system (Mylonas and Heath 1990) and GuidedTours in NoteCards (Trigg 1988).

If we use composites to model these link-based structures, we obtain a lighter-weight design. For example, the NoteCards TableTop, a means of capturing the state of any open components on the screen, is modeled as a composite with unrestricted content, which means that it can contain any instance of the component class or its subclasses. The TableTop composite is a computed component. Its Compute procedure visits all open instantiations, adding each of their components along with location and size information to the TableTop's list. The TableTop's instantiation presents and unpresents the components referenced by the TableTop in single operations. A sample user interface is shown in figure 32.

TableTop composites illustrate the use of pSpecs in endpoints. The Dexter model anticipated the ability of links to overrule the default pSpec for a component. For example, a component might store a default window position in its pSpec to be used for presentation, but this presentation specification could be overruled by or combined with a link pSpec when the component presentation was the result of following the link. Similar functionality is also desirable for composites like TableTops, where the position and size of presentation windows are crucial (Marshall and Irish 1989). A component referenced by several Table-Tops ought to be displayable in differently positioned or sized windows for each TableTop. For this reason, we recommend providing pSpecs in composite endpoints just as we do in link endpoints.

The NoteCards GuidedTour, a traversable annotated piece of hypermedia substructure, can be implemented as a nontransient composite restricted to contain a structured collection of TableTop components, as shown in figure 32. The runtime instantiation for a GuidedTour provides support for stepping through the partially ordered collection of TableTops and presenting them one at a time. The Guided Tour instantiation adds procedures like Start, Next, Previous, Jump, and Reset to the operations of the generic component instantiation.

10.4   Contexts for arrival and departure

Navigation between composites requires us to consider the scope of presentation. If we follow a link or a guided tour to a composite, should all of the composite's children be presented? Or should we only present some graphical or textual overview of the children? Similarly, when departing from a composite, should we unpresent all the children or leave some open?

The Amsterdam Hypermedia Model (AHM) introduces a concept called *link context* to specify which components to present and unpresent when a link is followed to and from a composite (Hardman et al. 1994).[2] A link context in AHM has two parts. The *destination context* identifies the components (usually composites) to present with each destination component in order that the viewer experiences those destinations in an appropriate context. The *source context* determines which of the already presented components should be unpresented, retained or perhaps replaced with the new destination components.

Link contexts in the AHM are modelled by composites that reference the context components. These context composites have attributes determining

2. Hardman's Ph.D. dissertation was just completed at the time of this writing, and includes changes to the AHM. Thus the descriptions of the AHM in this chapter may be out of date.

whether the member components should be unpresented, retained, or replaced. The AHM, however, does not specify how this context is bound to a link object.

We believe that the link endpoint's pSpec ought to be used to represent link context. In particular, the pSpec attribute of a link endpoint can include refSpecs whose locSpecs identify components involved in the context. These components can be explicitly identified or computed from a computation criterion or structure description.

Chapter 11 proposes a framework for such an implementation. The pSpecs of the source endpoints represent the source context, and those of the destination endpoints represent the destination context. Using the endpoint's pspec for the context information lets us couple contexts with endpoints instead of using a simple context attribute for the entire link. This approach enables users following multiheaded links to present only certain endpoints, yet still benefit from the context specifications on those endpoints.

10.5   Composition and synchronization of time-based media

Support for time-based multimedia information, including video, animations, and sound, has become an essential part of modern hypermedia systems. One of the challenges for hypermedia designers involves parallel presentation or playback of such media. Composition and synchronization is required among both time- and nontime-based information resources. Moreover, support for linking in time-based media poses new problems, such as how to specify locations and how to present link markers during the playback of a piece of time-based information. In this section, we explore the central navigation problem located at the boundary between multimedia and hypermedia: composition and synchronization of chunks of time-based media.

The Dexter model was not concerned with time-based data. However, in the intervening years, the developers of AHM at CWI in the Netherlands have extended the Dexter model to address the time-based aspects of composition and synchronization (Hardman et al. 1994). For example, their model supports the presentation of synchronized multimedia in different channels on the screen, as is often done in full-screen CD-ROM applications. Their work inspired the approach to time and context that we propose in section 10.5.2.

A parallel effort within the SGML community led to the HyTime standard for hypermedia linking and synchronization of time-based media (DeRose and

Durand 1994). HyTime is an SGML-based interchange format for multimedia information and is not meant to support the design of hypermedia systems. Nonetheless, its modeling approach is relevant for anyone planning to build multimedia into a hypermedia system.

We are interested in the timing issues that arise when initially structuring a body of multimedia information and later when the information is annotated with links. For example, one might need to synchronize a sequence of pictures with speech or textual subtitles and later link the presentation to other multimedia materials. In the rest of the chapter, we review how the Amsterdam model and the HyTime standard have approached these issues and offer our own proposals for using Dexter-based structuring entities to coordinate multimedia presentations.

10.5.1 Amsterdam hypermedia model: A Dexter-based model with support for time

AHM uses composites for the course-grained structuring and synchronization of multimedia information, and the *synchronization arcs* construct for finer-grained structuring. In this section, we review both of these contributions and propose improvements based on our extended Dexter model.

Coarse-grained synchronization in AHM is expressed using hierarchical structures of composites. AHM composites, unlike the original Dexter composites, do not themselves contain data but refer to atomic components that contain the data. (This kind of composite is described in chapter 7's Structuring by Composition pattern.) The atomic components store an attribute that specifies the duration of the playback of the content.

AHM composites support a hierarchical composition of multimedia information, as figure 33 illustrates. In this example, the four composites A, B, C, and D synchronize the data contained in the seven atomic components A1, B1, ... D2. Composites order their children in a timed sequence. If two or more child components are positioned at the same starting time, the behavior depends on the type of the enclosing composite. Choice composites play only one of the components, while parallel composites play them all simultaneously. If A and B are parallel composites, and D is a choice composite, the composition in figure 33 expresses the following: The contents of atoms B1 and B2 are played in parallel with the sequence of C1 followed by C2. Then the content of atom A1 is played in parallel with either D1 or D2. In this way, structures of synchronized time-based components can be composed to form multichannel presentations.

Time   A

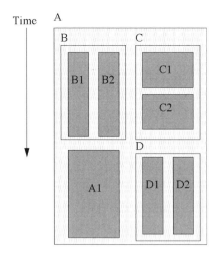

Figure 33
A hierarchical composition of multimedia information.

Hardman et al. argue that coarse-grained synchronization determined by composition is inadequate for expressing fine-grained timing relations such as the requirement in figure 25 that C2 end at the same time as B1 and B2. To support this kind of synchronization, the AHM introduces *synchronization arcs,* specifications of timing relations between pairs of components. The timing relations may be *advisory* or *hard,* and the timing may be relative to the start, end, or some offset from the start of the components data. Even though a synchronization arc is structurally similar to a link, Hardman et al. argue for a separate concept, since, from the user's point of view, synchronization arcs have nothing to do with navigation.

10.5.2 Generalized synchronization for Dexter-based hypermedia

The AHM leaves open questions such as the following. Can synchronization arcs cross composites? Can synchronization arcs have multiple "to" components synchronized with a specific "from" component? We address these questions by generalizing the AHM support for synchronization using the concepts introduced in chapters 6, 7, and 9.

Without modification, atomic components can wrap time-based data, while presentation information, such as the duration and channel of the playback, can be stored in pSpec attributes on the component. Composites that use refSpecs to reference other composite or atomic components (as described in chapter 7) are well-suited for handling coarse-grained synchronization between atomic components whose contents are time-based. We distinguish three types of synchronization composites: sequence, parallel, and choice. The components referenced in a sequence composite are played one after the other by the runtime layer. The synchronization between tracks is handled in one of two ways: for Choice composites, the runtime layer plays only one of the member components; for Parallel composites, the runtime layer plays all member components in parallel. In comparison with AHM, our sequence composite makes the sequencing specification explicit at the cost of additional structure.

The distinction between the three composites can be implemented in two ways. The first is to use the general attribute mechanism for components to introduce a semantic type attribute with one of the three values: sequence, parallel and choice. Alternatively, the composites can be implemented as subclasses of the general composite class.

In any case, the pSpecs carry the composite's behavioral characteristics. 'Parallel' composites include synchronization arcs as part of their pSpecs, as described in the next section. 'Choice' composites use the pSpec to specify how a user interface should support user choice. Finally, the composite pSpecs can shrink or expand the durations of media items to fit synchronization constraints, as proposed by Buchanan and Zellweger (1992).

In contrast to coarse-grained synchronization, fine-grained synchronization requires explicit synchronization relationships among the components in a presentation, what AHM calls synchronization arcs. Modeling synchronization arcs can be done in several ways in our conceptual framework. But given their close resemblance to links, we propose specializing the link component introduced in chapter 6 to form a Synch Link component. The timing relation information of the synch arc is stored in the Synch Link component's content or pSpecs. Thus a single Synch Link can synchronize the performance of multiple time-based components, one at each endpoint.

In chapter 9, we compared two essential behaviors associated with hypermedia structures: traversing and opening. Synch Links contribute a third; namely, coordinating. Structures for coordination can be valuable not just in multimedia settings, but anywhere that the dynamic character of one component constrains the activity of another.

10.5.3   HyTime's approach to hypermedia and time

HyTime is an ISO (International Standards Organization) standard for the interchange of hypermedia and multimedia structures (DeRose and Durand 1994). HyTime addresses composition and synchronization of time-based data by means of event scheduling. Two of its modules are relevant to the composition of time-based data, the measurement and the scheduling modules. The measurement module is used to declare finite coordinate spaces (FCS) with mutiple axes. This mechanism enables users to locate chunks of multimedia data in time and space, assuming that the units of measurement have been declared for each dimension. The measurement module also provides flexible mechanisms for transforming one unit of measurement to another.

The scheduling module is used to specify events occuring at absolute or relative locations on declared time axes. These times can be calculated using arbitrary arithmetic operations on the coordinates of the time axes. The HyTime engine also supports degradation strategies when an event is longer or shorter than the specified duration. Finally, parallel events are specified by letting the events overlap on the same timeline.

The HyTime approach is quite different from the object-oriented approach taken in this book. Events are not specified as entities with attributes and procedures for access and manipulation. More generally, the HyTime standard is not readily interpretable as a design specification for a specific hypermedia system. Nonetheless, HyTime is the first standard to address both hypermedia linking and multimedia timing issues, which makes it a promising candidate for interchange format for Dexter-based hypermedia systems.

10.6   Navigation and synchronization patterns

The patterns in this section address the design issues for advanced navigation in documents as well as in time-based multimedia information.

Title: Navigation

Context: Hypermedia structures that interconnect and organize a body of heterogeneous material. Users traverse the structures and the material.

Problem: To address what is sometimes called the "lost in hyperspace" problem. Supporting shifting localities protects users from the overwhelming complexity of the entire body of material. Unfortunately, the support that hypermedia systems provide for traversing a networked space of information can sometimes lead to a sense of dislocation, both in terms of where one *is,* and where one might be *going.*

Solution(s): Use a variety of advanced navigation tools such as those described in this chapter. Some offer overviews of the hyperspace (and even networks of hyperspaces), while others support guided navigation through localities in the hyperspace.

Examples: Graphical overviews (as in NoteCards and on the WWW), Intermedia's graphical view of local connections, and guided tours (on the WWW and in NoteCards, DHM, and Scripted Documents).

Related patterns: Depends on Traversal in chapter 9 and Structuring by Reference in section 7.8.

Title: Synchronization

Context: Hypermedia structures that interconnect and organize a body of heterogeneous material. The presentation of the structures has a dynamic or time-based aspect.

Problem: To provide a means of coordinating the time-based presentations of material.

Solution(s): Use pSpecs in combination with hypermedia structuring capabilities to manage and control coordinated presentations. A special kind of composite called a *parallel composite* presents the material identified by the locSpecs at its endpoints simultaneously, possibly in different windows on the screen. Designers control the fine-grained synchronization of these multimedia performances by adding a special form of link, called a *Synch Link,* to the parallel composite's pSpecs. Synch Links govern the relative time ordering of the material identified by the locSpecs at the Synch Link's endpoints.

Examples: The Amsterdam Hypermedia Model and HyTime.

Related patterns: Depends on Structuring by Linking in chapter 6 and Structuring by Reference in chapter 7.8.

11
Open Hypermedia Frameworks

[W]e would like to see standards develop for data models, and greater freedom preserved for users to customize interfaces to suit their preferences. Perhaps the hypermedia data model, with its potential for simplicity, can provide a basis for such standardization. If so, hypermedia may eventually replace the desktop metaphor as the reigning human-computer interaction paradigm. (Akscyn et al. 1988, p. 835)

[W]e hope to persuade the software development community that (1) application development will be most fruitful when that community at large embraces object-oriented building blocks and frameworks and (2) hypermedia will only be readily accessible when a common linking protocol is adhered to by all third-party software creators. (Yankelovich et al. 1988, p. 96)

In the preceding chapters, we introduced the basic conceptual entities of a hypermedia system, including the Dexter concepts and our proposed modifications. As we have seen, locSpecs allow us to identify points to connect. RefSpecs provide the packaging that lets us build structures out of such pointers. Components aggregate new structure with existing material in such a way that the structures appear to share the same conceptual space as the material. Some of the structures incorporated in components correspond to the groupings that are already present in the material. Other structures take the form of new aggregations of refSpecs. These structures include links, composites, collections, relations, and the like. Finally, there may be hybrid aggregates of both structure (refSpecs) and material. For example, a WWW page is a kind of hybrid component containing both material and implicit structure represented by embedded locSpecs.

We've emphasized that this book is primarily oriented to the needs of hypermedia designers. In this chapter, we use the design principles introduced earlier in part II to propose candidate frameworks for hypermedia systems. The frameworks are represented graphically using object-oriented modeling diagrams in the OMT notation (Rumbaugh et al. 1991).

In OMT, classes are represented as boxes divided vertically into three areas. The topmost area contains the name of the class, the middle area contains attributes, and the bottommost area contains operations. We explain more of the OMT notation as it arises in section 11.6.

In what follows, we first present the lowest level entities in the frameworks—locSpecs, refSpecs, anchors, and endpoints—as well as the overarching entity, the hyperspace. We then present two variants of the entities at the component level, one in which components are specialized into links, composites, and atomic components, and one in which they are consolidated into a single component entity. We then present framework diagrams that show how the entity classes are interconnected. Using examples from navigation and multimedia we show how the frameworks can be extended. Finally we present design patterns that outline two competing approaches to modeling components, specialized vs. unified.

11.1   Location specifiers

```
┌─────────────────────────────────────────┐
│ LocSpec                                   │
├─────────────────────────────────────────┤
│ WithinComponentObjectID                   │
│ WithinComponentStructureDescriptor        │
│ WithinComponentComputationSpec            │
│                                           │
│ ComponentID                               │
│ ComponentStructureDescriptor              │
│ ComponentComputationSpec                  │
├─────────────────────────────────────────┤
│                                           │
└─────────────────────────────────────────┘
```

The Location Specifier (locSpec) is the lowest-level entity defined in the framework. Unlike the rest of the hypermedia objects, locSpecs can live outside the system as human-readable text. Like URLs, they can be transported as text strings and then incorporated into a hypermedia system. Particular hypermedia implementations may either represent locSpecs as objects or traffic in the text string representation. In any case, the locSpec must be able to be represented in human-readable form.

A locSpec provides three ways of identifying a location within a component. The object ID is a named location unique within the component, for example, an anchor ID, an HTML-defined name, the ID of a persistent selection or a graphic object, or the like. A structure descriptor is a means of locating that refers to whatever structure the material in the component may have. Examples include positions or spans of text, frames in a video stream, and chapters and paragraphs in structured documents. Finally, the computation specification provides a means of embedding computation in the locSpec, which might be a query in the form of a text string or a format description, or more generally, an executable script like a Java applet.

For simple locSpecs, only one of the three means of locating are used, but specifying the same location by multiple means as described in chapter 4 is also valuable. For example, one might want to specify both a span (start and ending positions) in a text document and the corresponding text, in order to detect whether the document has been edited outside the hypermedia system's control.[1] The Anchor Maintenance pattern of chapter 14 includes practical examples of locSpecs with redundant specifications.

In addition to the three means of identifying locations within components, we include three means of identifying an enclosing component. The component ID is unique within a particular hyperspace. The structure descriptor uses cross-component structures, typically enclosing composites, to identify a component. Finally, the computation specification enables the execution of search queries, say, over component attributes like creation date as well as general scripts, in order to locate one or more components. As in the case of within-component locating, locSpecs may also use redundant specifications to locate the same component or set of components.

At most one of the component and the within-component parts of the locSpec can be empty. If the component part is blank, then the locSpec is considered applicable to any component. If the within-component part is blank, the locSpec simply identifies a component as a whole.

11.2 Reference specifiers: Anchors, endpoints, and composite references

The referenceSpecifier (refSpec) packages a locSpec together with a presentation specification (pSpec) to form a basis for anchors, and the endpoints of links and

1. Hugh Davis has argued eloquently for the use of such redundant means of locating in relation to links in Microcosm (Davis 1995).

```
┌─────────────────────────┐
│ RefSpec                 │
├─────────────────────────┤
│ ID                      │
│ locSpec                 │
│ thePSpec: PSpec         │
├─────────────────────────┤
│ EqualLocSpec( )         │
└─────────────────────────┘
```

composite references. Every refSpec includes an ID that is unique within the enclosing hyperspace. ThePSpec is a virtual slot that determines how the refSpec is to be displayed.

The basic refSpec class includes the method EqualLocSpec which accepts another locSpec as argument and determines whether it matches the locSpec belonging to this refSpec. EqualLocSpec is used during link following.

11.2.1 Anchors

```
┌─────────────────────────────┐
│ Anchor: refSpec             │
├─────────────────────────────┤
│ thePSpec: AnchorPSpec       │
├─────────────────────────────┤
│                             │
└─────────────────────────────┘
```

An anchor is a specialized refSpec that identifies a location in its enclosing component's content. The pSpec is further bound to an anchorPSpec that determines how the anchor is highlighted in the component content. Because an anchor is bound to a particular component, the anchor's locSpec, inherited from the refSpec class, explicitly names the anchor's home component using the component's ID rather than indirectly identifying it through some form of computation.

11.2.2 Endpoints

An endpoint is a refSpec associated with a particular link, composite, or other structural component. Its type specifies the directionality or structuring relationship associated with that endpoint. Examples might be Source, Destination, or Both, for link endpoints, and Substructure, Left, Right, or the like, for structural

```
┌─────────────────────────────┐
│ Endpoint: refSpec           │
├─────────────────────────────┤
│ Type: String                │
│ thePSpec: EndpointPSpec     │
├─────────────────────────────┤
│ SetType( )                  │
│ GetType( )                  │
└─────────────────────────────┘
```

components. The endpoint's locSpec can locate one or more components, as well as points within those components. The pSpec is further bound to an endpoint pSpec that determines how the endpoint is visually highlighted in the component's content.

11.2.3 A variant endpoint class that supports reuse

In the preceding description, endpoints are a specialized form of refSpec that adds a Type field. One problem with this approach is that it hinders reuse of the endpoint's locSpec across links. For locSpecs with complex search queries or scripts, for example, one might want to avoid copying the locSpec for reuse in new link endpoints. To enable such reuse, we can make a simple change to the above design. Rather than having Endpoint be a specialized refSpec, we instead make Endpoint *include* a pointer to a refSpec. The refSpec then no longer has the Type field and can thus be reused across multiple link endpoints.[2]

```
┌─────────────────────────────┐
│ Endpoint (variant)          │
├─────────────────────────────┤
│ Type: String                │
│ thePSpec: EndpointPSpec     │
│ refSpec                     │
├─────────────────────────────┤
│ SetType( )                  │
│ GetType( )                  │
└─────────────────────────────┘
```

2. We are grateful to our fellow participants at the 3.5 Open Hypermedia Systems Workshop (described on the OHSWG home page: www.csdl.tamu.edu/ohs/) in Aarhus, Denmark, September 1997, for this design of reusable endpoints.

Though this design supports reuse, it incurs a potential cost. For certain kinds of endpoints, namely, those that do not identify an anchor, the variant endpoint requires one more object than the first approach. However, if reuse is important or if most endpoints point at anchor refSpecs, the slight extra cost may be worth incuring.

11.3   Hyperspaces

HyperSpace
refSpecs components
AddRefSpec( ) RemoveRefSpec( ) AddComponent( ) RemoveComponent( ) SearchComponent( )

The hyperspace can be thought of as providing strict containment in a hypermedia system; that is, each of our persistent entities, refSpecs and components, belongs to exactly one hyperspace. Moreover, the hyperspace provides a bounded *name space* that restricts the scope of addressing possible in locSpecs. Resolving a locSpec reference is always performed in relation to one or more active hyperspaces. Any explicit references to components in another hyperspace (cross-hyperspace pointers) must include an identifier of that hyperspace, as we discussed in chapter 9.

At run time, a hyperspace is managed by a session. Components and refSpecs are created and deleted through calls to the session, which in turn invokes the respective hyperspace operations, AddComponent, RemoveComponent, Add-RefSpec, and RemoveRefSpec. As described in section 11.7.2, the session also manages the work of structure traversal.

Given that hyperspaces embody a kind of containment, one might be led to consider implementing the hyperspace as a specialization of the composite class. This would allow hyperspaces to be elements in the structures of other hyperspaces; for example, one could link to a hyperspace. The notion of nested hyperspaces follows logically from such a composite-based implementation.

We have chosen not to propose such a design variant, for two reasons. First, it leads to confusing hybrids of composite-hyperspace, for example, hyperspaces with endpoints and anchors. More important, this choice of design has an inherent infinite regress. The fact that every component belongs to a hyperspace implies that every hyperspace belongs to another hyperspace. To which hyperspace does the largest enclosing hyperspace belong?

Instead of having hyperspace inherit from the composite class, we use a separate class that contains a set of components (and refSpecs). To nest one hyperspace in another, we package the first hyperspace as the content of a special component in the second hyperspace. This approach is analogous to the way pages on the WWW provide the interfaces to other hidden systems, such as databases.

In the next two sections, we present alternative ways to model the component within our frameworks.

11.4   Components as specialized structures

Our first variant definition of the component makes use of an overarching entity that is specialized for each of the basic forms of structuring: atomic components, links and composites.

Component
ID thePSpec: PSpec Anchors Content
AddAnchor( ) RemoveAnchor( )

The component is the basic hypermedia entity; it can be instantiated directly to create the atomic component we introduced in chapter 5. At the same time, the component serves as the superclass for structuring entities like links and composites. Components are identified by an ID that is unique within its enclosing hyperspace.[3] The component's pSpec consists of attribute-value pairs governing default presentation features and is consulted when the component is opened. If the opening results from following a link (or opening a composite), then the component's pSpec is combined with the pSpec of the link's (or composite's) endpoint and that of the destination anchor, if any.

All components (including links and composites) include a structured collection of anchors as well as the content, which is either a data object or a reference to a data object stored separately. Components include two operations for adding and removing anchors, AddAnchor and RemoveAnchor.

Link
Endpoints
AddEndpoint( ) RemoveEndpoint( )

Composite
Endpoints
AddEndpoint( ) RemoveEndpoint( )

Links and composites are specialized components that include structured collections of endpoints as well as operations for adding, and removing endpoints.

Though links and composites are nearly identical with regard to implementation (apart from the directionality of the endpoints), the runtime behavior can be quite different. Composites, when opened, bring up the components their endpoints point at, whereas links are traversed from and to one or more endpoints.

As we explained in chapter 7, a component can be transient and/or computed. We propose that the attribute-value list associated with all hypermedia entities be used to implement such "virtual composites," as Frank Halasz called them. Rather than restricting "virtualness" to composites, we provide support at the level of generic components. Any component in a hypermedia system can be made transient by setting an attribute, in which case the component is usually not

---

3. We have chosen not to require globally unique component identifiers. Uniqueness within the containing hyperspace is usually sufficient, assuming that the hyperspace itself can be uniquely identified. The choice of identifier scope depends in part on whether and how the system is intended to support copying, moving, and sharing components across hyperspaces.

saved in the database. The transient component will be saved, however, if a link or other component references it. Transient components resemble objects in a dynamic programming environment; if they are not referenced, garbage collection reclaims them.

Any composite can be the result of a computation, or it can be manually created by the user. A typical example of a computed composite is one created by executing a query. An attribute contains the information used to perform the computation. The composite's content can later be recomputed, either on demand or automatically.

Using attributes, the component class provides transience and computedness without requiring subclassing. Thus a user can start from a query that by default produces a computed, transient component, and later convert it into a static, nontransient component.

11.5   Components as unified structures

Separate classes for component, link, and composite make sense when the distinctions among the three entities are clear and unchanging. Under certain conditions, however, users may need to move smoothly between component types. For example, after adding numerous endpoints to what was originally a two-headed link, a user may feel that a composite (with its opening behavior) is a more appropriate construct. In addition, certain applications may require hybrid structural components some of whose endpoints are traversable, like link endpoints, while others have the hierarchical character of composite endpoints. In such situations, a hypermedia designer may choose to consolidate the forms of hypermedia structuring supported by the various component types. Toward this end, we offer an alternative version of the component that contains a list of endpoints in addition to its list of anchors. Such a component can be the source or destination of a link or subcomponent of a composite, as well as a mapping component, that is, it can itself be opened or traversed.

Like a WWW page, this consolidated structural component can be used to aggregate any material in a hypermedia system. It contains content, anchors *and* endpoints. With this variant, a composite is not a separate class, but rather a structural component whose endpoints are exclusively hierarchical. Similarly, a link is a structural component all of whose endpoints have directionality. In any case, all components can gain or lose endpoints over time as appropriate.

```
┌────────────────────────────┐
│ Component                  │
├────────────────────────────┤
│ ID                         │
│ thePSpec: PSpec            │
│ RefSpecs:                  │
│ Content:                   │
├────────────────────────────┤
│ AddAnchor( )               │
│ RemoveAnchor( )            │
│ AddEndpoint( )             │
│ RemoveEndpoint( )          │
│                            │
└────────────────────────────┘
```

One advantage of a consolidated approach to components is illustrated by the WWW's concept of a page. A user of the web does not have to determine what kind of page is required for each bit of material. One simply creates a page and adds links and content as appropriate. (In HTML, however, one's ability to add any structure at all is constrained, as we have seen.) Similarly, a user constructing new components in a hypermedia system based on our framework may want to put off or avoid altogether decisions about whether a particular component is more like a link or a composite (Monty and Moran 1986).

We should emphasize that in this variant, although the concepts of composite and link are not implemented as separate classes, they can nonetheless be made available as reified categories. For example, a consolidated component could include an attribute indicating whether the component's endpoints are all hierarchical, that is, whether it is exclusively viewable as a composite. In other cases, the attributes at a given moment would allow searches over a hyperspace to return only pure links and composites. Such an attribute could be maintained automatically as endpoints are added and deleted. A different attribute could indicate the user's intention that the component be interpretable as a composite regardless of whether it has hierarchical endpoints. Such an attribute would be maintained manually.

11.6   Two alternative frameworks

The two object-oriented design diagrams depicted in figure 34 and figure 35 illustrate the component variants described in the preceding two sections.

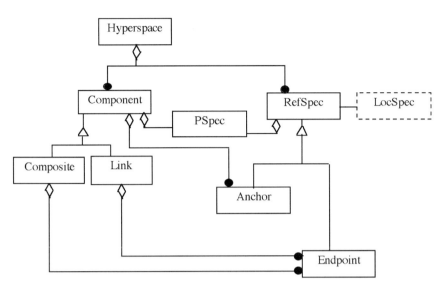

Figure 34
The structural framework variant, where the subclasses of the component class are composite and link. Endpoints belong to links and composites, while anchors belong to components.

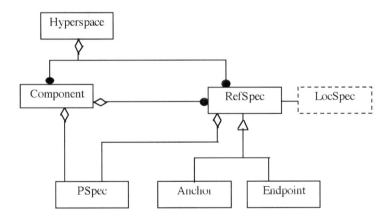

Figure 35
The unified structuring framework variant, where the single consolidated component class has both anchors and endpoints.

The diagrams use standard OMT notations that reflect the interrelationships among the concepts, as follows.

Inheritance. Lines with triangles indicate inheritance relations. For example, Component is a superclass of Composite and Link in the top framework. In addition, the diagrams show that endpoints and anchors are specializations of refSpecs as discussed in chapter 4.

Aggregation. Lines with circles and diamonds denote aggregation relations. For example, a link object includes zero or more endpoints. This reflects our belief, explained in chapter 6, that so-called dangling links, those with fewer than two endpoints, ought to be perfectly legal.

Association. Lines with only circles or no circles denote associations, that is, a looser relation between objects than one of aggregation. For example, a refSpec is associated with a single locSpec. Other locSpecs may, however, be "free-floating," that is, having no associations with refSpecs. Alternatively, locSpecs can be shared by multiple anchors. The dashed box around locSpec indicates that it can be implemented as a full-fledged object in the system, or as an ASCII string, like a URL.

11.7   Runtime entities

As presented in chapter 9, the management of hypermedia behavior at run time is the province of three entities: session manager, session, and instantiation. The session manager is the overarching runtime object that manages multiple sessions, each in control of a single hyperspace. Within a session are instantiations that manage the viewing and editing of particular components.

11.7.1   Session managers

The session manager is the primary runtime interface. It includes a list of sessions, as well as operations to create new sessions and delete existing ones. DefaultHyperspaces is a list of hyperspaces that are activated when the session manager starts. The session manager's Traverse operation invokes the Traverse operations of each of its sessions on a given set of refSpecs and combines the results. Links crossing between active hyperspaces can thus easily be traversed. In addition, as described in chapter 9, link traversal can cause the activation of new

```
┌──────────────────────────────┐
│ SessionManager               │
├──────────────────────────────┤
│ sessions                     │
│ defaultHyperspaces           │
├──────────────────────────────┤
│ Traverse(refSpecs)           │
│ CreateSession (hyperspace)   │
│ DeleteSession ( )            │
│ CreateHyperspace ( )         │
│ DeleteHyperspace ( )         │
│ ParentHyperspace(refSpec)    │
│ ParentHyperspace(component)  │
│                              │
└──────────────────────────────┘
```

hyperspaces. In such cases, the session manager invokes its CreateSession and CreateHyperspace operations. Finally, ParentHyperspace maps a refSpec or component to its enclosing hyperspace.

11.7.2 Sessions

```
┌──────────────────────────────┐
│                              │
│ Session                      │
├──────────────────────────────┤
│ hyperspace                   │
│ instantiations               │
│ refSpecTable                 │
├──────────────────────────────┤
│ Traverse(refSpecs)           │
│ CreateComponent ( )          │
│ DeleteComponent ( )          │
│ SearchRefSpecs ( )           │
│ SearchComponents ( )         │
│ CreateInstantiation ( )      │
│ RemoveInstantiation ( )      │
└──────────────────────────────┘
```

The session is the runtime entity that manages the activity surrounding a particular hyperspace. It contains a list of instantiations that manage the runtime behavior of the components in its hyperspace. Components and instantiations can be created and deleted using the CreateComponent, DeleteComponent, CreateInstantiation, and RemoveInstantiation operations. SearchRefSpecs and SearchComponents provide means of accessing the refSpecs and components that belong to the hyperspace.

The Session includes the Traverse operation used during structure traversal. Given a set of locSpecs, Traverse returns refSpecs that correspond to the destination endpoints of any applicable links, that is, those with an endpoint matching one of the given locSpecs. There are multiple implementations of Traverse depending on the conditions of the environment. The following is a sketch of several suboperations suited to the two variants of Endpoint discussed in sections 11.2.2 and 11.2.3.

We first consider the case where Endpoint is a specialization of refSpec. The first operation, LocSpecsToRefSpecs, takes one or more locSpecs (usually corresponding to a user selection in the content of a component) and returns all the refSpecs in the hyperspace that match at least one of them. Some of these refSpecs might be anchors; others might be refSpecs for endpoints of links or composites. For those corresponding to anchors, the operation AnchorRefSpecsToEndpointRefSpecs maps these anchors to the endpoints that resolve to them.

Once endpoint refSpecs matching the original locSpecs have been found, the next step is to traverse the links to which these endpoints belong. TraverseRefSpecs takes a list of endpoint refSpecs and returns other refSpecs obtained by mapping across the links (and possibly also composites, as discussed in chapter 9) that contain the endpoints. These destination refSpecs can then be brought up in the contexts of their enclosing components and composites, possibly after filtering by the user.

In systems implemented according to the refSpec reuse variant described in section 11.2.3, a single refSpec might be shared by multiple endpoints. After LocSpecsToRefSpecs has obtained a set of refSpecs, the RefSpecsToEndpoints operation maps each anchor refSpec to the set of endpoints whose locSpec identifies it.

11.7.3 Instantiations

An instantiation is the runtime manager of a component. Instantiations include operations for building and searching the list of anchors associated with the component: CreateAnchor, DeleteAnchor, and SearchAnchors. The other two operations are Open, which brings up the component positioned at particular anchors, and Traverse, which maps from one set of endpoints to another.

```
┌─────────────────────────────┐
│  Instantiation              │
├─────────────────────────────┤
│  component                  │
├─────────────────────────────┤
│  Traverse(refSpecs)         │
│  Open(refSpecs)             │
│  CreateAnchor ( )           │
│  DeleteAnchor ( )           │
│  SearchAnchors ( )          │
└─────────────────────────────┘
```

To manage the behavior of member components of a composite without full-fledged instantiations, we propose a light-weight instantiation class called SubInst. Unlike an ordinary instantiation, a subInst does not invoke an application to present the component's content. Rather it provides an interface for accessing component attributes and for invoking a real instantiation when needed. A subInst typically appears in the user interface as an icon in the composite's viewer window. The icon allows the user to view and query the components belonging to a composite in the graphical interface, without having to invoke their editors.

11.8   Composites and structuring

The examples in this section suggest that our frameworks can model a rich variety of composite components, including those that support advanced structuring and navigation.

11.8.1   Composites containing data objects

As we have seen, the Content slot of the generic Component class can hold an arbitrary collection of data objects. The Dexter group's original composite concept of the composite is thus a special case of our component class. For example, to implement a composite that contains both a graphical and a textual data object, we can specify a specialization of the generic component class, as shown in figure 36.

In this case, the virtual attribute, "content," in the Component superclass is used to encapsulate aggregate content. In fact, this approach can be combined with the use of endpoints to create hybrid composites that compose both by inclusion and by reference.

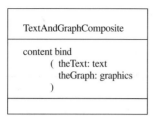

TextAndGraphComposite

content bind
    (theText: text
       theGraph: graphics
)

Figure 36
A component that contains two different types of data objects.

11.8.2 Composites referencing components

The TableTop is a hypermedia composite that captures configurations of components to be presented together on the screen (Trigg 1988). According to our frameworks, the Tabletop is simply a specialization of the general composite class whose endpoints can refer to components of arbitrary type (including links and other composites). It does not directly contain or wrap any data objects.

Another example is the search component, which appears in systems such as Intermedia, NoteCards, and the WWW. Such components can be modeled by a SearchComposite, shown in figure 37, which again is a simple specialization of the general composite class. In this case, the composite endpoints point to components of arbitrary type resulting from a query over the components in a given hyperspace.

Relational hypertext provides a third example. An Aquanet relation (Marshall et al. 1991) is an example of a hypermedia composite with structured content. It resembles a multiheaded link with named endpoints. We suggest implementing such a relation as a composite containing a keyed table of endpoints, as shown in figure 38. The relation composite can refer to basic objects, such as atomic components, as well as to other relations.

11.8.3 Anchoring in composites

The original Dexter model did not adequately support anchoring in composites, especially in the case of collection composites that point at other components in the hyperspace. In our object-oriented frameworks, every composite includes a set of anchors. However, it is unclear how the composite's anchors point into the content of the member components.

Using our object-oriented extensible framework, we introduce the CompositeAnchor, a specialized anchor that contains a list of locSpecs, as shown in

Figure 37
A search composite that collects the results of a query.

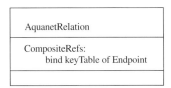

Figure 38
A composite that models Aquanet relations.

figure 39. Each locSpec identifies an anchor in one of the composite's member components.

The CompositeAnchor fulfills needs such as those described in chapter 10, to link to an anchor that locates objects in multiple tracks. Indeed, (Hardman et al. 1994) propose just such aggregate anchors for their composites in the AHM, but the idea is also valuable for non-runtime based composites.

11.8.4 Synchronization within composites

In chapter 10 we proposed using a specialized link object to model the Amsterdam hypermedia model's concept of synchronization arcs. To model such synchLink objects, we can extend our object-oriented framework with two new classes, as shown in figure 40. The timing relation information is represented as a separate object so that it can be reused across multiple synchLinks.

11.9 Framework design patterns

This chapter concludes with two patterns that arise directly from our framework design considerations. They outline the two approaches to implementing the

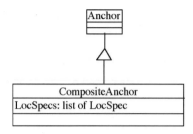

Figure 39
A specialized anchor for composites.

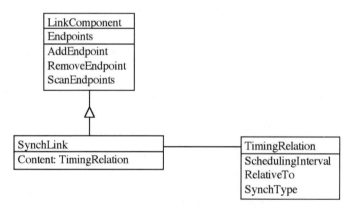

Figure 40
SynchLink—an alternative to synchronization arcs.

Component class depicted in figures 34 and 35: as one combined structuring component, or as several specialized components that include atomic components, links, and composites.

Equipped with frameworks of hypermedia entities and an understanding of the basic forms of hypermedia runtime behavior, we can now explore some of the most pressing issues faced by today's designers of open hypermedia systems.

Title: Unified Structuring
Context: Hypermedia structures that interconnect and organize a body of heterogeneous material.
Problem: To design structures that users can dynamically redesign over time. For example, as endpoints are added to a link over time, the user might decide that it is more reasonable to begin treating the link as a composite. Or a single structure might have both directional and hierarchical endpoints, which would allow the structure to be both traversed and opened.
Solution(s): Use a single structuring component that has the features of both links and composites. It can be both opened hierarchically and traversed.
Examples: In KMS, the single unified component type, the frame, supports hierarchical structuring. HyperCard and HTML both have single component types (the card and page, respectively), but no real support for hierarchy.
Related patterns: Depends on Externalized Locating in chapter 4. See also Structuring by Reference in section 7.8.

Title: Specialized Structuring
Context: Hypermedia structures that interconnect and organize a body of heterogeneous material.
Problem: To design simple structures with clearly identified roles and capabilities.
Solution(s): Use a different component type for each functional role. For example, links and composites are implemented as separate types due to their distinctive roles as traversable interconnections and hierarchical structures, respectively.
Examples: NoteCards and DHM.
Related patterns: See structuring by Linking in chapter 6 and structuring by Reference in chapter 7.

III

Implementing Open Hypermedia Systems

In part II we introduced principles for designing extensible object-oriented frameworks for open hypermedia data structures and behavior. Part III focuses on implementing open hypermedia systems that provide these structures and behaviors for users. In chapter 12, we discuss the design of architectures for open hypermedia systems. Chapter 13 takes up issues related to tailorability and customization. Chapter 14 applies our approaches to architecture and tailorability to the problem of integrating users' applications with open hypermedia services. Chapter 15 describes an open protocol that supports cross-platform communication between applications and hypermedia services. Chapters 16 and 17 take up the topics of collaboration and distribution support. Finally, in chapter 18, we discuss how open hypermedia services and collaboration support can be applied to the World Wide Web.

Each of these six chapters includes a brief review of relevant foundational research. As in part II, our approach to addressing outstanding issues is outlined at the end of each chapter in one or more design patterns. These patterns encapsulate the principles that we believe should inform the design and development of any open hypermedia system. The patterns for part III appear in figure 41. Although many of their names reflect general computer science issues, in the context of this book they relate specifically to "open hypermedia."

The examples that appear in the patterns for part III are drawn primarily from the same set of systems used in part II. For short descriptions of each system and selected references, see appendix A.

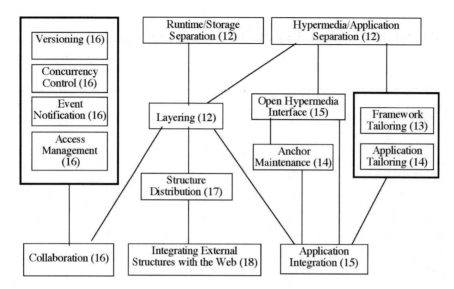

Figure 41
Design patterns in part III. Chapter numbers appear in parentheses.

12

Open Hypermedia Architectures

[A]n infrastructure occurs when local practices are afforded by a larger-scale technology, which can then be used in a natural, ready-to-hand fashion. (Star and Ruhleder 1996, p. 114)

At the screen of your computer you explore what is stored, change it, add to it. The service we propose takes care of putting it away and sending you whatever part you ask for as fast as possible. That is the back end. What computer you watch it through, and how *that* machine is programmed, is your 'front end'—a separate problem. (Nelson 1981, p. 2/6)

Chapter 11 applied the principles proposed in part II to the design and use of frameworks for open hypermedia; in this chapter we focus on the design of hypermedia system architectures that take advantage of those same design principles. We discuss how to apply concepts from part II in the context of system architecture. The chapter starts with a historical overview of hypermedia architectures, followed by discussions of layering, databases, operating systems, and platforms. The chapter concludes with four design patterns that address the range of architectural choices.

12.1 Layered architectures

In the area of operating systems, layering is frequently used as a way to separate concerns in architecture design (Tanenbaum 1992). For the same reason, many of the hypermedia architectures found in the literature adopt a layered form. In this section, we review several of them to set the stage for the contemporary proposals for open hypermedia architectures that follow.

12.1.1 Conceptual and physical layers

Architectural discussions employ both conceptual and physical notions of layers. On the one hand, layers are used to make conceptual distinctions among groups of concepts, classes, or capabilities of a system. Such conceptual layers can map to physical layers of a running system that consist of modules used to implement a system or a process. The conceptual layers can also map to layers of processes communicating through specified protocols. On the other hand, the mapping is typically not one-to-one; often a physical layer, such as a process, corresponds to several conceptual layers or vice versa. In the discussions that follow, we consider architectures that exhibit both kinds of layering.

12.1.2 Two-layered architectures: Separating front end and back end

Early hypermedia systems were typically designed as two-layered architectures based on a special purpose database, called the *back end,* and one or more interface programs, called the *front ends.* Examples include Xanadu (Nelson 1981), HAM (Campbell and Goodman 1988), Intermedia (Yankelovich et al. 1988), and Augment (Engelbart 1984a). Figure 42 illustrates such an architecture. The frontend/backend distinction is typically a physical layering based on a client/server solution, where the back end constitutes a server for one or more frontend client applications.

These early hypermedia architectures were based on the assumption that the backend database is responsible for storing both structure and content of the hyperspaces. Similarly the frontend applications provided user interfaces for editing both structure and content. The main architectural design decisions concerned the division of labor between front end and back end, and the protocol between them. The next three sections illustrate the use of this two-layered architectural model in three different systems.

Xanadu One design option is to support openness at the back end, so that a particular back end is usable by different frontend applications. For instance, the back end of the Xanadu system (Nelson 1981) was designed to support a variety of frontend applications developed and marketed by third-party vendors. This openness required that back end and front end communicate using a standard protocol; in the Xanadu system it is called a FEBE (FrontEndBackEnd) protocol. Openness in this kind of architecture also requires support for distribution, by which the backend processes are able to gain access to objects residing on remote

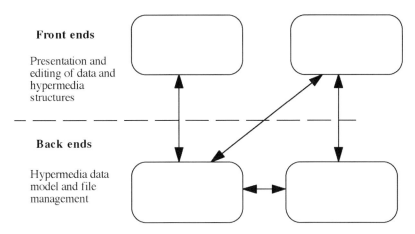

Front ends

Presentation and
editing of data and
hypermedia
structures

Back ends

Hypermedia data
model and file
management

Figure 42
A traditional two-layered hypermedia architecture.

backend servers; in Xanadu a BEBE (BackEndBackEnd) protocol provides this
support.

The World Wide Web   Another system based on a two-layered architecture and
a close coupling of content and structure is the World Wide Web (Berners-Lee
et al. 1992a; Berners-Lee et al. 1992b). On the WWW, described in chapter 18,
structures are built into the content of pages. The web employs a frontend/back-
end architecture similar to Xanadu's; however, there is no explicit hypermedia
database in the back end of the WWW. The back end consists of a process
serving an ordinary hierarchical file system and a gateway to call arbitrary
programs on the server machine. On the WWW, fronts ends and back ends
communicate using the hypertext transport protocol (HTTP).

Thus the frontend applications—browsers like Mosaic, Netscape Navigator,
and Internet Explorer—are responsible for presenting both content and structure
to the end-user. In some cases, external plug-in modules or helper applications
are used to display specific data formats not directly supported by the browsers.
Recently, some of these browsers have made built-in editors available for the
textual parts of content and structure.

IRIS Intermedia   Hypermedia systems that adopt a physical frontend/backend
architecture can be designed with conceptual layers that model the structure of

the front end and the back end respectively. An example is the IRIS Hypermedia service (Haan et al. 1992), which uses an approach based on object-oriented application frameworks.

The physical layering is embodied by two communicating processes: the Intermedia process and the link server process. The link server process in turn has two conceptual layers: a link server layer that communicates with the Intermedia Process and a link database layer responsible for storage.

The Intermedia process is a specialized object-oriented application framework (Meyrowitz 1986), a collection of generic classes that model the core behavior of a system. The framework supports the application developer in specializing the behavior by overriding or further binding virtual procedures that the generic classes automatically call. The Intermedia process itself is based on such an application framework, MacApp (Wilson et al. 1990), and has four conceptual layers of classes: the MacApp layer, which supports basic user interface functionality; the Intermedia layer, which provides basic hypermedia classes; the building blocks layer, which includes basic word processing and graphics editing classes; and finally, the editor layer, which contains the end-user editors such as Inter-Word.

IRIS Intermedia was the first hypermedia system built with a framework approach, and served as an inspiration for our Open Dexter framework. The difference between the Open Dexter framework and the IRIS Intermedia framework is that the latter focuses mainly on the construction of editors from generic classes, whereas the Open Dexter framework separates applications and editors from its framework in order to focus on hypermedia structures and behaviors.

The limitations of a two-layered architecture The simple backend/frontend architecture is powerful for hypermedia systems that manage the storing and editing of data formats for both hypermedia structure and content. But our goal of building open hypermedia services that are integrated with the users' favorite applications and that enable users to create content and structure dynamically while they browse hypermedia material requires a more elaborate architecture. The applications or editors must be separated conceptually and physically from the hypermedia service. The Intermedia designers also recognized this need for more layers. In the Intermedia memorial paper (Haan et al. 1992), they write that such an open hypermedia service requires an intermediary process which they call a link hub to manage link creation, browsing, and so on, by providing APIs

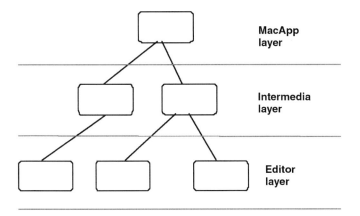

Figure 43
The conceptual layers of the Intermedia framework.

that the individual applications integrate. The need to separate the applications and the hypermedia system is summarized as a general design pattern at the end of this chapter. But first, in what follows, we review several architectural proposals that support such separation. They include the original Dexter model architecture, as well as recent proposals for open hypermedia architectures.

12.1.3 The Dexter model's original three layers

The Dexter hypertext reference model (Halasz and Schwartz 1990; Halasz and Schwartz 1994) represents a step toward a hypermedia model that supports the separation of content and structure and thus indirectly, the separation of applications from the hypermedia system. As mentioned in chapter 3, a fundamental feature of the original model is the separation between its three conceptual layers, runtime, storage and within-component. To distinguish these conceptual layers from physical ones, we describe them horizontally, as shown in figure 44.

These three layers can be embodied in a Dexter-based hypermedia system as shown in figure 45. Figures 44 and 45 suggest a division of labor between the three layers: The runtime layer is responsible for the presentation of the hypermedia structure, the user interaction, and the hypermedia behavior. The storage layer is a database that contains a network of structural nodes and links. The within-component layer is responsible for the content inside the nodes. As discussed in chapter 3, the model suggests that the interface between the runtime

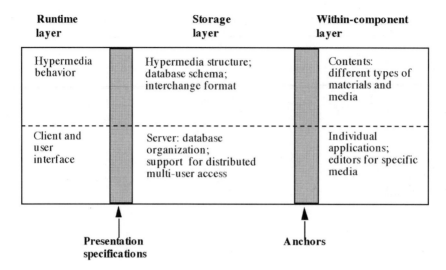

Figure 44
A horizontal description of the Dexter model's layers.

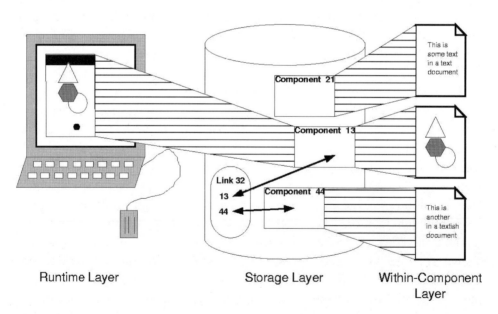

Figure 45
An illustration of the role of the three Dexter layers in a concrete system.[1]

1. Thanks to Frank Halasz for permission to use this figure from a talk he gave on the Dexter model.

and storage layers is managed by presentation specifications; and the interface between the storage and within-component layers, by anchors.

Figure 44 seems to suggest that presentation specifications and anchors are sufficient to constitute a full interface between the respective layers. Actually, communication protocols between the layers are needed. For example, in communications between the storage layer and the within-component layer, the identification of the content file for a component is as important as the anchor values. Moreover, it is unreasonable to place the applications that manage the content of nodes in an architectural layer below the storage layer, because the applications' behavioral aspects have to communicate with the runtime layer. Although the layers are probably best viewed as purely conceptual, we can use the model's distinction between runtime environment and storage in our architectural considerations, as the next section shows.

12.1.4 A Dexter-based open hypermedia architecture

This section proposes a hypermedia architecture that maps the conceptual layers of the Dexter model to a physical architecture. This mapping, in turn, suggests where the elements of the framework should be physically implemented in an open hypermedia system.

Our Devise Hypermedia framework (Grønbæk and Trigg 1994) first introduced a mapping of the conceptual layers of the original Dexter model to a physical open hypermedia architecture. This mapping, depicted in figure 46, views the applications and editors that manage the content of components as part of the within-component layer rather than of the hypermedia system client and user interface, as the Dexter model suggests. This change makes sense in an open hypermedia service where the applications that manage the content are just as important as the format of the data. In fact, the hypermedia system rarely confronts the actual data format of the content of a component. For example, an open hypermedia system supporting links within spreadsheets never sees the spreadsheet data structure. Rather, it uses Microsoft Excel or a similar application with an API, a communication protocol, and a user interface, to manage the spreadsheet data and links within it. We can no longer expect a hypermedia system to take over the user interface to the content, nor even to be responsible for the entire hypermedia-specific user interface.

This recognition of the importance of applications in an open hypermedia environment is one reason for the Open Dexter architecture's radical reorganization of the Dexter model's conceptual layers. The within-component layer,

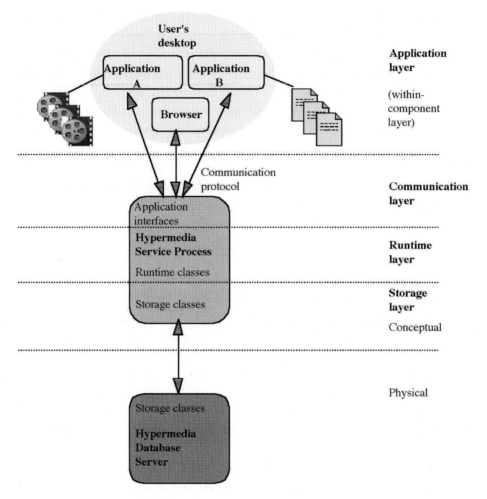

Figure 46
A proposed general Open Dexter architecture.

instead of being at the bottom and hidden from users behind the hypermedia system, moves to the top and is renamed the application layer. Moreover, a new, fourth conceptual layer, the communication layer, models the communication between applications and the hypermedia service. The conceptual layers are mapped to three physical layers of communicating processes, as shown in figure 46. However, this physical architecture is not fixed, variants are possible. For instance, the hypermedia database (HDB) may consist of several separate servers or simply a library that is included in the single hypermedia service process (HSP). The browser user interface may be either a plug-in to a third-party application, an integral part of the HSP, or a separate process. Finally, the distribution of the processes among server hosts and user workstations may differ, as we discuss in chapter 17.

Application processes   Application processes integrate end-user applications with the hypermedia service, including media such as text, graphics and video, as well as browsers over hypermedia structures. Applications manage specific types of data objects, for example, text corresponding to the content of text components or CAD drawings corresponding to CAD components.

The data objects are typically stored by the applications themselves in separate files outside the HDB, but the applications may also take advantage of the HDB's storage facility to store data objects in the same database as the hypermedia structures. The data objects manipulated by these applications belong to the Dexter within-component layer. However, our interpretation of the conceptual within-component layer is somewhat broader than that of the original model, since it is not limited to passive data.

We view the internal manipulations of data objects as operations on the data objects, but mediated by dedicated applications. Thus, in the Open Dexter framework, an application's functionality belongs to the application layer, not the runtime layer, as proposed in the original Dexter model. The applications' hypermedia functionality depends on the communication with the corresponding Instantiation object in the runtime layer. An application represents the content for a specific type of component by supporting a protocol for communication with the HSP. This also holds for the hypermedia browsers, which are implemented by means of composites, as described in chapter 7. Thus a browser edits the within-component objects of composites. Applications communicate anchor locSpecs to storage objects (through an HSP), and they interpret pSpecs provided by an HSP.

Below the conceptual application layer is the layer that is responsible for communication between the hypermedia service process and the applications of the application layer: the communication layer. This layer implements the Open Dexter-based hypermedia protocol (ODHP) by means of the inter-application communication facility on a given platform. The ODHP is discussed in further detail in chapter 15. The communication layer is physically realized in two places: through macros or plug-in modules in the application processes and as classes and objects in the hypermedia service processes.

The Hypermedia Service Process   Below the communication layer is the runtime layer, which implements the core hypermedia behavior specified by the generic classes of the runtime layer, described in section 11.7. The runtime classes are physically implemented within the hypermedia service process (HSP).

An HSP provides the hypermedia service for a set of application processes employed by a user. The HSP is responsible for handling links, anchors, and components at run time, and for interfacing with the applications on the one hand and the HDB server on the other. The HSP creates instances of the generic and specific classes that implement the Dexter runtime layer concepts, and provides application-independent operations for creating and manipulating component and link objects that implement the Dexter storage layer concepts. The HSPs resemble the tool integrators proposed in the HyperForm architecture (Wiil and Leggett 1992) and the link hub proposed in the IRIS Hypermedia Services (Haan et al. 1992). A typical architecture would include an HSP running on each workstation managing the user's interaction with the hypermedia database, including link creation and browsing. However, the HSP might also run on a host shared by several users, as proposed in chapter 18, which concerns Open Dexter support for the WWW.

The lowest conceptual layer of the Open Dexter architecture is the storage layer, consisting of two elements, the database schema, which implements the Open Dexter storage classes and the physical hypermedia database (HDB) system, which stores the objects. The storage layer resembles the communication layer in that it is physically located in two places in an implemented system.

The Hypermedia database server process   The hypermedia database (HDB) server provides persistent physical storage for the hypermedia objects. The stored objects are instances of specializations of the generic classes that implement the Dexter storage layer concepts. Depending on the type of database chosen, the storage layer classes can be represented in several ways. Let's asssume that the HSP is an object-oriented program and the HDB is a tailored relational database; then the storage data is represented as objects in the HSP and as relations in the HDB. If both the HSP and the HDB are object-oriented, the schema, that is, the classes, may physically be declared in either of the two places, and used by both types of processes.[2] Issues that arise in choosing or designing HDBs are discussed further in section 12.3.

12.2 Proposals for open hypermedia architectures

Currently, the open hypermedia systems (OHS) community is working on proposals to standardize architectures and communication protocols for open hypermedia (Wiil 1997). The next two sections review two of these proposals for the shim architecture and the Common Reference Architecture.

12.2.1 The shim architecture

Davis et al. (1996) propose an architecture that supports reuse of third-party application extension modules across multiple open hypermedia systems. Each application is extended to communicate with a hypermedia service by means of a standardized protocol called OHP (open hypermedia protocol). The shims are processes that map the standardized OHP to proprietary protocols implemented by, say, DHM and Microcosm. This approach frees the OHS community from writing nearly identical extension modules for the applications to be integrated with each open hypermedia system. Instead, one shim is written for each system. This proposal focuses exclusively on the relationship between the application processes and the hypermedia service processes in the Open Dexter architecture described in the preceding section. The idea is illustrated in figure 47.

The shim architecture proposal does a nice job of supporting multiple protocols without attempting to cover the rest of the hypermedia system architecture, for example, database interfaces and the like. An implementation of OHP shims for the existing open hypermedia systems would significantly improve interoperability between open hypermedia systems and tailored applications.

Shims offer an intermediate solution until an OHP is standardized. When all open hypermedia systems use a single OHP, there will be no need for the extra overhead involved in developing a shim module and translating from standardized OHP to a proprietary protocol. The shim approach, however, may still

---

2. For example, in the Mjølner Beta System's OODB, used in DEVISE Hypermedia, the conceptual schema is defined in the client processes, that is, in the HSP. There may be several HDB servers running at the same time; in a future version, the OODB distribution facilities will make it possible to link between hyperspaces stored on different HDB servers.

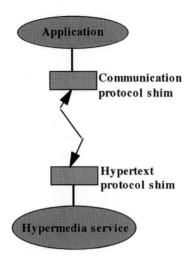

Figure 47
The Shim architecture.

be necessary in situations where an open hypermedia system supports multiple carrier communication protocols such as TCP/IP, DDE, and AppleEvents. In such situations, the shim could translate from the abstract OHP to the actual carrier communication protocol on each platform. It may also be the case that an application or open hypermedia system on one platform needs to use several carrier protocols at once, for instance, TCP/IP and DDE on Microsoft Windows.

12.2.2   A common reference architecture for open hypermedia

This section reviews Grønbæk and Wiil's (1997) survey of 1997 of current open hypermedia architectures, focusing on their proposals for a common terminology and a common reference architecture.

Common terminology   The survey revealed a huge diversity in the terminology in spite of similarities in the proposed architecture. Grønbæk and Wiil propose the following generic terms to encompass the architectural elements and terms appearing in the literature.

Despite the diverse terminology, there is enough commonality in the functionality of the different elements across open hypermedia systems to justify the synthesis into the five basic architectural elements presented in table 6. Grønbæk and Wiil go on to propose a common reference architecture for open hypermedia

Name	Intention	Other names
Content handler	A program used to view and edit the date or content of the hypermedia structures	Viewers, third-party applications, participating applications, editors, applications, and tools
Hypermedia service	A process that manages the hypermedia structures at runtime	Link service, run time, tool integrator, session manager, and hypermedia service
Interfaces	A connection between the hypermedia service and other architectural elements	Shim, protocol, wrapper, gateway, proxy, shell, and communication translator
Hypermedia database	A database that provides persistent storage of hypermedia structures	Storage, link service, structure server, filter, OODB, HBMS, hyperbase, hyperbase system, workspace, data model manager, and collaboration server
Document manager	A process that provides unique identification of data objects and documents independently of the physical file system location	Document manager, docuverse, and storage manager

Figure 48
Terminology of open hypermedia systems.

(CoReArc) that synthesizes important features of the architectures and reference models they examined.

The CoReArc proposal is based on a layered architecture like the Open Dexter architecture proposed in the preceding section, but the CoReArc has been simplified by eliminating the communication layer, as shown in figure 49. Since communication potentially takes place in multiple places in the architecture, it is not isolated in a layer but instead represented by a symbol that indicates a connection between different architectural elements, a line with a double bar across it. These interfaces are analogous to CORBA IDL interfaces and to suites in the AppleEvent terminology.[3] The interfaces represent peer-to-peer communi-

3. CORBA (Mowbray and Zahavi 1995) is a general object-oriented distribution framework which enables objects programmed in different programming languages and running on different platforms to communicate. The communication interfaces are specified in a special interface definition language called IDL. AppleEvents (Apple Computer 1991) is the inter-program communication protocol on the Apple Macintosh platform.

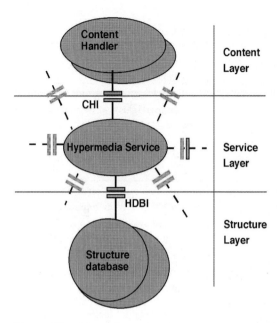

Figure 49
A diagrammatic view of CoReArc.

cation. The notation does not specify whether the bars are implemented as shims or as interface modules in the hypermedia service or content handlers.

Common Interfaces   The CoReArc architecture includes two main interfaces: a content handler interface (CHI) and a hypermedia database interface (HDBI). New types of services that emerge in the future will prompt the creation of additional interfaces, as indicated in figure 49 by the dashed double bars not connected to architectural elements. The multiple conceptual protocols serve to analytically distinguish the different types of communication. The actual implementation of the protocols should resemble that of topics in DDE for Microsoft Windows or suites in AppleEvents. The proposed conceptual protocols can be further divided into subsuites; for example, the CHP might have a core suite to handle linking and more advanced suites to handle composites (Grønbæk 1994; Halasz 1988) and collaboration. The subsuites can be folded into a single physical protocol with common methods for initialization, error handling, and the like.

Many existing open hypermedia systems, such as DHM, HyperDisco, and Microcosm, can be mapped to the CoReArc conceptual architecture. Although the different systems are often broken down into more detailed module configurations, at a conceptual level the modules can be categorized as belonging to one or more of our architectural elements. CoReArc is thus a point of reference for analyzing the differences between existing systems and for identifying interfaces or protocols on which to standardize. But CoReArc can also be used as a general design pattern for open hypermedia architectures, one which refers to existing architectures as examples.

12.3   Hypermedia databases

Storage of hypermedia objects has always been a concern in the hypermedia research community. The pioneering systems like Xanadu, NLS/Augment, Intemedia, and NoteCards all relied on a special purpose database to store the objects derived from the system's data model. The databases were typically an integrated and optimized part of the system.

12.3.1   The hypertext abstract machine

In the mid 1980s, Campbell and Goodman (1988) proposed the idea of a generic back end that could service many different hypermedia systems. This back end, called a hypertext abstract machine (HAM), was a general purpose hypermedia database intended for the architectural context depicted in figure 50.

The HAM layer includes a generic hypermedia data model consisting of graph, context, node, link, and attribute objects. Campbell and Goodman (1988) used the HAM to model systems like Guide (Brown 1987), Intermedia (Yankelovich et al. 1988), and NoteCards (Halasz et al. 1987). Thus the HAM can serve as a back end for such systems. In addition to the generic data model, the HAM provides a transaction mechanism to manage multiuser access, version history, filtering, and security.

One problem with the HAM approach is that it provides a single fixed hypermedia data model to which hypermedia designers must then map their systems. In contrast, newer hypermedia databases such as HyperForm (Wiil and Leggett 1992) support multiple data models. The HAM also lacks collaboration support facilities, which have become common in recent hypermedia databases.

12.3.2   Hyperbases

The HAM was the first of what are today called *hyperbases,* generic hypermedia databases that provide abstract data models and general database functionality,

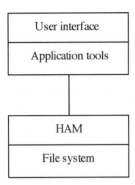

Figure 50
The architecture of a HAM-based system.

(Leggett and Schnase 1994; Wiil 1991). Like the HAM, the TAMU HB1–3 (Leggett and Schnase 1994; Wiil 1991) and the Aalborg hyperbase (Wiil 1991) provide a single abstract data model.

In contrast, HyperForm (Wiil and Leggett 1992) is an open hypermedia database that supports multiple hypermedia data models. Database features such as locking and notification are supported by generic classes such as concurrency control (CC) and notification control (NC). When implementing a specific data model, classes that support notification and locking inherit from the NC and the CC classes, respectively. Using HyperForm, a hypermedia designer can provide a specific data model and include the database behavior needed for each class in the model.

12.3.3 General object-oriented databases

The emergence of object-oriented database (OODB) systems suggests taking the idea of a data model-independent hyperbase (Wiil and Leggett 1992) a step further. With a general OODB, database features such as locking and notification are metaproperties that one need not specify when designing a data model.

Several hypermedia systems, such as Hyper-G (Andrews et al. 1995; Maurer 1996), Multicard (Amann et al. 1994; Rizk and Sauter 1992), and Devise Hypermedia (Grønbæk et al. 1994), use object-oriented database technology. For example, the OODB used in the Devise Hypermedia system was designed in part to meet hypermedia requirements. Nonetheless, it is a general OODB in the sense that it supports locking and notification for all types of objects independently of whether they are hypermedia objects or, say, CAD objects. Designers do not have to predict which objects or classes of objects will need support for locking and event notification. Instead, applications can be tailored at any stage to subscribe to notifications on events for arbitrary objects or classes that are stored in the database. Because locking and event notification are completely independent of the declarations of the objects stored in the OODB, a system can be developed to use a large existing database and to subscribe to notifications on events not anticipated by the original conceptual schema for the stored objects.

12.4   Hypermedia support in operating systems

Meyrowitz (Meyrowitz 1989) argued in his legendary "Missing link" paper (1989) that most hypermedia systems developed up to the end of the 1980s were monolithic in that they required that the user adopt editors implemented within the hypermedia system. Maintaining that this monolithic approach was a failure, Meyrowitz proposed instead to move hypermedia functionality to the operating system level and make link creation and traversal as generally available as cut, copy, and paste.

12.4.1   Linking in the operating system

Some operating systems support linking. For example, in GOs PenPoint (Meyrowitz 1991), all applications support link creation and traversal with simple pen-based gestures. The Microsoft Windows operating system also provides linking, through the object linking and embedding (OLE) protocol soon to be integrated in all Windows applications. OLE depends on a compound document model that enables embedded document representations, as figure 51 illustrates.

OLE propagates to Doc 1 any changes made to the linked document, Doc2, either on request or automatically. Moreover, double-clicking the embedded representation in Doc1 shifts the user into an editor for the target document, Doc2. From a hypermedia point of view these OLE links resemble Ted Nelson's transclusions, in that they constitute a channel for maintaining a copy of data from one document in another document. They do not support the construction of associative relationships among documents. In general, current operating system links only provide a fraction of normal hypermedia functionality. However, the general OLE protocol (Brockschmidt 1995) includes mechanisms with the potential for supporting more extensive hypermedia linking for OLE-compatible applications.

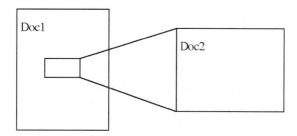

Figure 51
OLE linking. Doc2 is linked into Doc1; the content of Doc2 becomes part of Doc1's content.

12.4.2 Hypermedia operating systems

Nürnberg et al. (1996) have taken up the ideas of Meyrowitz and propose building a new generation of operating systems. Their proposed hypermedia operating system architecture (HOSS) offers hypermedia functionality at the operating system level. It is too early to assess the potential of HOSS, but the idea shares one of the drawbacks of the Sun Link service: application developers have to be convinced that they will benefit from porting their applications to the HOSS and modifying their applications to take advantage of its hypermedia support.

12.5 Platform independence

In chapter 2 we described real-world experiences of hypermedia use in the domain of bridge engineering. Our scenarios showed how engineering work depends on heterogeneous hardware and software platforms. To meet the challenges of providing open hypermedia support for such complex technical and organizational contexts, solutions must be as platform-independent as possible.

12.5.1 Availability on multiple platforms

The goal of platform independence is partly met by the WWW, through its use of widely supported data formats such as ASCII text and GIF pictures. With open hypermedia services, however, the goal is to provide support for the users' favorite applications and not to impose new data formats on them. Rather than supporting a specific data format on a new platform, the goal is to provide a portable framework on which to construct hypermedia services that communicate with applications on different platforms.

In the Open Dexter framework, the core framework classes of the storage, runtime, and communication layers can be ported between platforms without modification. Only the window system usage, the private methods of the Communication layer and the HSP/HDB communication vary from platform to platform. Utilizing abstract classes to wrap communication and user interface objects, in our experience more than 50% of the code of an Open Dexter based system can be ported without modification.

12.5.2   Cross platform support

The hypermedia service's portability is one aspect of platform independence; another is the ability for an open hypermedia system to work across platforms. Once the HSP is ported to multiple platforms, it must manage the applications and document types on the different platforms in a consistent manner. Different byte orderings and carriage-return/line-feed differences are among the issues that make such cross-platform support difficult to implement at a low level.

Nonetheless, the Open Dexter architecture permits such cross-platform distribution. The HDB servers and the HSPs can run on different platforms, supporting peer-to-peer communication in a distributed environment. For example, the HSPs might run on Macintoshes and PCs, while the HDB server runs on a UNIX or Windows NT host. It is thus possible to share hyperspaces among client programs running on different hardware platforms. The HDB supports sharing of hypermedia structures, but requires multiplatform applications that permit the same document to be opened on several platforms in a shared file system.

The Open Dexter framework can be implemented in a layered architecture in a distributed multiplatform environment. However, the ability to distribute access to particular documents depends on the operating systems and applications used. Emerging operating system facilities and distribution standards make distributed cross-platform implementations more feasible in the near future. Chapters 14 and 17 discuss openness and distribution in more detail, as well as problems and prospects for achieving full-fledged distributed open hypermedia systems.

12.6   Open hypermedia architecture patterns

This section addresses the design issues related to hypermedia architectures with four design patterns: Hypermedia/Application Separation, Storage/Runtime Separation, Layering, and Platform Independence.

Title: Hypermedia/Application Separation
Context: Open hypermedia systems that can integrate heterogeneous applications, be distributed, and support collaboration.
Problem: To implement hypermedia functionality for the users' favorite applications.
Solution(s): Keep applications and editors separate from the hypermedia system. Use application tailoring facilities to establish communication between application and hypermedia system, and use communication facilities to communicate location information and operations to invoke.
Examples: Microcosm, Devise Hypermedia, and Chimera.
Related patterns: Depends on Locating in chapter 4.

Title: Storage/Runtime Separation
Context: Open hypermedia systems that can integrate heterogeneous applications, be distributed, and support collaboration. Hypermedia structures are maintained as objects apart from the content.
Problem: To implement an architecture that allows hypermedia structures to be shared and distributed among many users and clients.
Solution(s): Develop two separate architectural modules: a hypermedia database module, a database designed, specialized, or configured to handle hypermedia data structures; and a hypermedia service module, a program that can instantiate and manipulate stored hypermedia objects as well as create new ones. This separation can be accomplished in three ways.

· Implement hypermedia databases and hypermedia services as separate intercommunicating processes.
· Provide interfaces that allow multiple hypermedia service processes to connect to multiple distributed hypermedia databases.
· Provide interfaces that allow multiple users to share the same hypermedia structures through a common hypermedia service process; that is both processes should be able distinguish among several users. See figure 49.

Examples: Devise Hypermedia, Hyperform and HyperDisco, and HOSS.
Related patterns: See also Hypermedia/Application Separation in this section.

Title: Layering
Context: Open hypermedia systems that can integrate heterogeneous applications, be distributed, and support collaboration.
Problem: To design a platform-independent process and module architecture for open hypermedia.
Solution(s): Implement an architecture that includes the following three main layers:

Content handler layer. The applications, viewers, and editors responsible for displaying and manipulating the multimedia content.
Service layer. The processes that provide hypermedia services to content handlers, manage sessions, and coordinate collaboration over shared hypermedia structures.
Storage layer. The data structures and database processes that maintain hypermedia structures persistently.

Publish well-defined protocols between the layers.
Examples: The Dexter model, Devise Hypermedia framework, Hyperform and HyperDisco, and HOSS.
Related patterns: Depends on Storage/Runtime Separation and Hypermedia/Application Separation in this section.

Title: Platform Independence
Context: Open hypermedia systems that can integrate heterogeneous applications, be distributed, and support collaboration. Hypermedia structures are maintained as objects apart from the content.
Problem: To provide open hypermedia services that run on multiple platforms.
Solution(s): Use one of the following approaches to achieve platform independence:

· Develop hypermedia services as system components in programming languages and libraries supported on multiple platforms.
· Encapsulate user interface and communication mechanisms in replaceable system components.
· Utilize de-facto standard communication protocols such as HTTP and TCP/IP for communication between system components.
· Utilize object distribution mechanisms such as CORBA (Mowbray and Zahavi 1995), Java BEANS/RMI (Microsystems 1997), and Mjølner BETA distribution (Brandt and Madsen 1993) with cross-platform support.

Examples: WWW, Devise Hypermedia Framework.
Related patterns: N/A.

13

Framework Tailorability

[The] generic nature of hypermedia systems is both a blessing and a curse. It is a blessing because it allows hypermedia to be useful in a wide variety of task domains and user populations. It is a curse because generic hypermedia is not particularly well suited to any specific task or style of use. (Halasz 1988, p. 850)

Trigg, Moran, and Halasz (1987) introduced the term *tailorability* for the domain of hypermedia. They deem a system tailorable if it lets users change the system, by building accelerators, specializing behavior, adding functionality, and so on. As an example, they describe how advanced users tailored the behavior of the NoteCards system using an application programmer's interface (API), and added new media types by means of the NoteCards card type mechanism. Tailoring thus involved adding to and modifying an already delivered system at the source-code level; this was possible because NoteCards was built in the Interlisp environment (Masinter 1981), in which system functions are accessible and modifiable at any time.

In contrast, the Intermedia (Meyrowitz 1986) system was built as an extensible hypermedia framework, specialized from the general MacApp application framework (Schmucker 1986; Wilson et al. 1990). The Intermedia framework provided support for hypermedia designers to construct their own variants of the system by adding new media types as specializations of framework classes (Catlin et al. 1989). However, since MacApp was written in Object Pascal, adding extensions required access to the Intermedia source code as well as a compiler, to perform the necessary recompilation.

This chapter discusses how to provide an open hypermedia service whose framework can be easily modified, or tailored, to support completely new types of hypermedia-based applications.[1] We start by presenting a collection of tailoring techniques that range from selecting configuration options from a preference sheet, to modifying and recompiling part of the system's source code. We discuss the use of these techniques in two kinds of tailoring: of the user interface, and of the underlying data and process modules. We then step through a typical advanced tailoring task adding a new media type to an existing hypermedia system. We conclude with brief discussions of other forms of advanced tailoring and an existing tailorable Dexter-based framework, along with a design pattern outlining two approaches to supporting framework tailoring. Chapters 14 and 15 address the tailoring of applications and of the communication interface, respectively.

13.1   Tailoring techniques

Both NoteCards and Intermedia are highly tailorable hypermedia systems. However, the tailoring support assumes that the tailor has the same access to the entire development environment as the original developer. Other forms of tailorability make fewer demands on the expertise and resources available to tailors. In general, the tailorability literature (Kiczales et al. 1991; MacLean et al. 1990; Trigg et al. 1987) and commercially available systems feature a number of such techniques. The most common are

· Using preference sheets over a fixed set of options to configure the systems' appearance and behavior
· Writing macros in application-oriented programming languages
· Controlling an application remotely by sending remote procedure call (RPC), dynamic data exchange (DDE) or AppleEvent commands from other applications
· Using open points for plug-in modules such as those web browsers use to render specific data types, or for scripts such as those executed on hypermedia objects in MultiCard (Nørmark 1992; Pree 1997)
· Programming using an embedded source code interpreter, as in Lisp- and Smalltalk-based systems

1. In the literature, authors use terms like adaptability, customizability, and extensibility, to describe a system that offers users the ability to change it. We have chosen the term tailorability to encompass them all.

· Performing dynamic link and load of source-code modifications
· Editing and compiling source code after making modifications and extensions

These general purpose tailoring techniques are relevant to two broad aspects of open hypermedia service: 1) user interface and appearance, and 2) underlying hypermedia data and process models. Figure 52 indicates which category characterizes the major role of each technique.

The first three techniques are mainly applicable when tailoring the user interface and changing the appearance of existing functionality. An example of preference sheet tailoring is the specification of which Microcosm filters to apply and in which sequence (Hall et al. 1996). Macro languages are also used to extend the hypermedia process model. For example, in MultiCard (Rizk and Sauter 1992), hypermedia objects such as links, nodes, and anchors can be associated with scripts that alter or extend their default behavior.

The other techniques add extensibility to the data and process models by parametrizing, extending, and specializing generic classes of the hypermedia framework. For example, open points and an embedded interpreter were used in an experimental version of the Devise Hypermedia system (Grønbæk and Malhotra 1994) to enable source code extensions for new media types not originally included in the framework.

An example of the technique of editing and recompiling appeared in the Intermedia system (Meyrowitz 1986). Tailors integrated their extensions into

Tailoring technique	User interface and appearance	Data and process model
Configuring preference sheets	X	
Writing macros	X	X
Communication between applications	X	
Using open points		X
Programming using an embedded interpreter		X
Dynamic linking and loading		X
Editing and recompiling	X	X

Figure 52
Primary roles of tailoring techniques for open hypermedia systems.

new versions of the system by recompiling and linking the entire system, including the extension classes.

In a Dexter-based architecture, the user interface to the hypermedia service typically appears as an application in the application layer communicating with the hypermedia service process by means of a communication protocol, as shown in figure 53. Whereas tailoring the user interface and appearance involves the hypermedia client application, tailoring the data and process models involves the hypermedia service process and database schema.

In the rest of the chapter, we briefly consider the issues involved in tailoring the user interface and appearance, and then take up the problem of tailoring the data and process models.

13.2   Tailoring the user interface and appearance

With respect to the user interface and appearance of an open hypermedia system we recommend supporting two radically different kinds of tailoring: configuring the delivered client application and building an alternative or supplementary user interface.

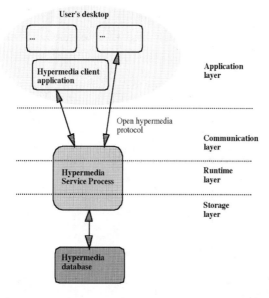

Figure 53
The relationship between the user interface and the hypermedia service.

13.2.1 Configuring a client application

The user interfaces of modern applications are typically tailored by specifying preferred options for predefined aspects, including toolbars, fonts, and the like. For open hypermedia this often involves choosing among predefined media types and editors. Users select from existing component, instantiation, and communication object types to support particular kinds of information and applications.

For example, for users to be able to choose between two CAD systems that behave and communicate slightly differently, the user interface of the client application as well as the communication protocol of the hypermedia service must support unregistering the instantiation and communication classes for the first CAD system and registering the corresponding classes for the second. The ability to support reregistration assumes that the hypermedia service already has code for the media types in question. Section 13.4 discusses how to tailor the hypermedia service to include different sets of media types.

13.2.2 Building a new user interface

Tailors construct a new user interface for the hypermedia service by building a new hypermedia client application using the standard communication protocol of the hypermedia service. Users can then access the same hypermedia service through several different interfaces. For example, chapter 18 discusses the case of a Dexter-based hypermedia service whose separate hypermedia client application is replaced by a new interface written as a JAVA applet. This is accomplished without tailoring the data and process model of the hypermedia service. However, if the new or alternative user interface imposes requirements for extended functionality, then the hypermedia service—the general data and process model—must be extended accordingly.

13.3 Tailoring the data and process models

The purpose of our Dexter-based framework is to support the rapid construction of open hypermedia services for different application domains. The generic framework classes provide general-purpose hypermedia functionality. Tailoring the hypermedia service generally requires specializing these framework classes to suit specific domains. The next five sections illustrate some of the extensions possible with a Dexter-based framework.

13.3.1   Building a new atomic component type

Integrating a new media type sometimes requires developing an atomic component class that models the new type with specific pSpec, anchor, locSpec, and content attributes. The new class specializes an existing component type and may include code copied from other types. Such new media types may also require a new instantiation type to enable additional behaviors.

13.3.2   Building a new composite component type

A tailor may construct a new composite type in order to integrate a new media type that has a composite nature, such as video with multiple tracks, or build a new type of structure browser, such as a guided tour or map, not supported by the framework. In such cases, the tailor creates a new specialization of the Composite class. Generally, doing so requires the creation of a new instantiation type, a specialization of CompositeInst.

13.3.3   Building a new link component type

Tailors may want to provide new kinds of links that cannot be modeled directly with standard multiheaded bidirectional links, for example, a Dexter-based version of Microcosm's generic links (Davis et al. 1992). In that case, the tailor specializes the link component to register its source endpoint in a new hash table using the endpoint locSpec's computation specifier as a key. Section 9.4.5 discusses the modeling of generic links in more detail. Since the behavior of link traversal does not involve instantiations, tailors normally do not build an additional link instantiation type.

13.3.4   Building new instantiation types

New instantiations are typically built for one of two reasons. First, they may be part of an entirely new component/instantiation/communication set for some new media type, such as video. The new video component can maintain locations within video data, the new communication object manages the video application, and the new instantiation manages link traversal and anchoring in video.

Second, instantiations provide new behavior for existing components and/or communication objects. A new instantiation might, for example, manage a new communication type that interacts with a remote database lookup facility. The database query might be modeled with an existing component type, say, by storing textual queries in the content of a text component. However, the runtime behavior of the instantiation needs to be distinctive; instead of displaying the text in an editor, the instantiation should use the content to invoke a database query. Thus the new communication object managing the database lookup requires a new instantiation class, even though it uses an existing text component type.

13.3.5 Building a new communication type

Open hypermedia systems often already have appropriate component and instantiation types for the information managed by new applications—the work is in creating new communication classes that interact with the applications. Let's suppose that we want to support a new kind of text application that communicates with an existing text instantiation. To do so, we can write a new communication class that manages the communication, perhaps reusing the code of an existing communication class by specialization or cloning.

In some cases, communication classes for already integrated applications need to be modified following a new release of the application. The new release might include changes to macro languages or APIs that affect communication with the hypermedia service. In such cases, changes to the communication class should not affect the rest of the framework.

13.3.6 Porting the framework to a new platform

When porting a framework to another operating system platform one usually has to consider the set of programming languages the platform supports, the inter-application communication facility, and the windowing system. If the framework is written in an object-oriented language, code reuse requires that the new platform include a compiler for the language in which the framework is implemented. In that case, the runtime and storage modules can be directly copied and recompiled, although communication modules may need to be rewritten to support the interapplication communication facility and the applications available on the new platform. However, if the same applications exist on both platforms, the communication classes can be largely reused. In any case, the hypermedia client implementing the user interface must be ported to the new window system.

The next section describes a framework tailoring exercise that involves several of these forms of tailoring.

13.4   Adding a new media type

Our framework is organized so that a hypermedia designer can introduce a new media type by providing an application and building specialized classes for each of the storage, runtime and communication layers. Integrating the application into a system developed from the Open Dexter framework requires tailoring both the framework and the application. The effort required to tailor the application is typically considerably larger than that required for the framework, possibly days or weeks, depending on the degree of openness the application supports.

In this section, we consider the task of integrating a new application called DrawEditor. We start by describing the tailoring work required at each of our architectural levels. We then discuss a tailoring infrastructure based on meta-classes and how it can be used to implement DrawEditor.

Let's consider the task of integrating a new application called DrawEditor. If it is an entirely new kind of application, we must add a specialized class for each of the three conceptual layers—storage, runtime, and communication. In addition, we need to tailor DrawEditor itself to communicate with the new communication object.

13.4.1   Tailoring at the storage layer

Assuming that DrawEditor manages simple drawings with no internal hierarchical organization, we can model DrawEditor documents with a specialized atomic component called DrawComponent. If, as is common in open hypermedia, DrawEditor documents are stored apart from the HDB, the content of Draw-Component might simply be a file identifier. To support object drawing, DrawEditor could maintain unique IDs for individual drawing objects. In that case, the anchor locSpecs would be object IDs. Further tailoring might involve the DrawComponent's pSpec, say, in order to capture a zoom level at which the hypermedia service could display the document.

13.4.2   Tailoring at the runtime layer

If DrawEditor requires special behavior of its components at run time, we can define a DrawInstantiation class. One example of runtime-specific behavior might be a special check of component attributes to be performed before certain communication methods are called. Another might involve checking the compo-

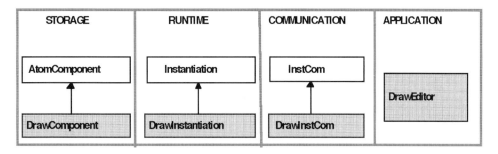

Figure 54
Classes involved in adding a drawing media type to the hypermedia system.

nent's pSpec information at presentation time, possibly combining it with pSpec information supplied by a link's endpoint pSpec. This information would then be used in calls to present the component.

13.4.3   Tailoring at the communication layer

The HSP and DrawEditor communicate by means of a specialization of the abstract Communication class called DrawInstCom. The brunt of the tailor's work consists of implementing the standard open hypermedia protocol operations as API calls to DrawEditor using the platform's inter-application communication facility. This is the difficult part of HSP tailoring, since applications' APIs and communication suites can vary significantly. For example, some applications allow external calls with parameters, while others require the parameters to be stored in shared memory before a parameterless method is called.

13.4.4   Tailoring at the application layer

At the application layer, tailoring involves augmenting the DrawEditor user interface with access to the hypermedia functionality and then establishing communication with the HSP DrawInstCom objects. The details of integrating external applications appear in chapters 14 and 15.

Now that we have declared the specialized classes, they need to be compiled or interpreted and then loaded into a running HSP. How best to accomplish this depends on the development language and the environment in which we develop the framework. The next section discusses a general technique using typeInfo classes that is useful regardless of the choice of development environment.

13.4.5 Meta-information: Defining typeInfo classes

To enable a Dexter-based system to process information about the component, instantiation, and communication classes available in a given configuration of a system, metaclasses containing information about a particular class, which we call typeInfo classes, can be introduced. They are defined in parallel inheritance hierarchies. For example, figure 55 shows how the drawComponent's typeInfo class specializes the atomComponent's typeInfo class. Each typeInfo class contains an attribute table consisting of pairs of entities identified by name and value together with a general procedural interface for manipulating the table. This structure makes all typeInfo objects similar from the perspective of the session manager; only the actual registration of attributes varies across the inheritance hierarchy.

The values of attributes in a typeInfo object are usually set during initialization, but they can also be modified dynamically at any time. An example of initializing the typeInfo object for DrawComponent, called DrawCompType-

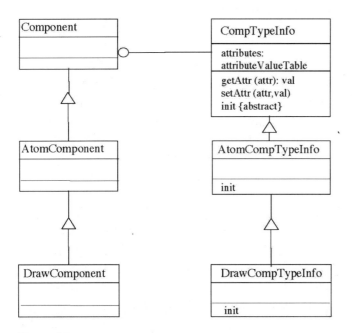

Figure 55
A typeInfo subclass hierarchy and its relationship to component classes. The "init" operation is marked with {abstract} which means that the actual implementation is found in the operation of the same name in the relevant subclass.

```
DrawCompTypeInfo: Class AtomCompTypeInfo
.
init
{
    ('Name','DrawComponent') -> setAttr;
    ('Class',<ref>DrawComponent) -> setAttr;
    ('PrefInstTypeName','DrawInstantiation')   -> setAttr;
    ...

  ;
}
```

Figure 56
Example of the initialization of a DrawCompTypeInfo object declared in an abstract object-oriented language syntax.[2]

Info, is shown in figure 56. In particular, the name, component class, and instantiation class are registered in the attribute table.

TypeInfo objects can also be viewed as meta-objects (Kiczales et al. 1991) and their interface as a meta-object protocol. This style of constructing a tailorable system is in keeping with Kiczales's call for open (non-black-box) abstractions (Kiczales 1992).

Some object-oriented environments support classes as first-class objects in a program;[3] in which case the typeInfo objects can point directly at the classes they describe. A table of typeInfo objects could then serve as a database of registered types, which could be queried for information related to the classes. The table could also be used to dynamically construct menu items, and to create instantiation and communication objects of the right types for a given type of component.

13.4.6   Registering an extension

To add the drawing media type to a system based on the Open Dexter framework, a hypermedia tailor provides the specialized classes shaded in gray in figure 54 along with a typeInfo object for each of the classes. Once the classes are completed, the tailor registers the corresponding typeInfo objects with the

2. The syntax is inspired by the Mjølner BETA language, in which a version of the Open Dexter framework was implemented as a basis for developing the DHM system.

3. For instance, the Mjølner BETA language, which has been used for the implementation of the DHM system, provides dynamic references to classes.

session manager's typeInfoTable using a session-level registration operation. At this point, the drawing application is installed in the hypermedia system, and the user can access the drawing component through, say, a New Components menu.

13.5 Tailoring applications for existing media types

The examples of tailorability described in this chapter involve the addition of new media. Similar tailoring is possible for the addition of new component types, such as specialized composites, that manage structures within the scope of a hyperspace object. The critical aspect of an open hypermedia service with respect to tailoring, however, is its openness to integration of new media types. Issues concerning how to tailor for more flexibility remain for hypermedia designers to resolve.

Adding a new trio of classes each time one adds a new media type may seem a little cumbersome, especially when the new classes share properties. Minimizing the number of situations that necessitate rebuilding the system or adding new classes can help. One approach is to classify the typical categories of applications to be integrated, for instance, in terms of their need for anchor locSpecs and pSpecs. Then a small number of generic AtomComponent classes can serve to model the different categories.

To integrate a new application then requires picking the right category and registering the application as an instance of the given category with the HSP. The TypeInfo classes are dynamically extensible attribute-value tables; hence they can serve as registration objects specified at run time. With each application category possessing its own trio of specialized classes, we can associate typeInfo objects that provide exact specifications of applications in that category. Suppose, for example, that we have identified a category for CAD applications. We then develop a trio of classes to model generic CAD applications. For each CAD system—such as AutoCAD, MiniCAD, and Microstation—we provide a parametrized typeInfo class, by means of which the framework can distinguish the icons, registry names, and the like that belong to the specific CAD system.

This approach is currently used to tailor the DHM system. However, due to variations in the applications' communication interfaces, the applications are difficult to group into general categories. This inconsistency limits the degree to which runtime integration can be supported, at least for the communication layer.

13.6 An example of a tailorable Dexter-based framework

Grønbæk and Malhotra (1994) describe the tailoring architecture for the Devise Hypermedia (DHM) system, which is based on a tailorable Dexter-based framework. In the framework, tailors add new media types by registering the required classes and rebuilding an executable system. The rebuilding process requires writing source code to register the new classes, and compiling or interpreting the additional code and the new classes. The new executable system can be built using an edit-compile-link process or an edit-compile-dynamic link, or with the help of a built-in interpreter.

Grønbæk and Malhotra (1994) advocate the latter approach, which takes advantage of an implemented version of the framework that includes an interpreter for the Beta language (Malhotra 1993; Malhotra 1994), in which the system is implemented. The embedded interpreter can dynamically incorporate new classes into an executing hypermedia system. The dynamically tailorable DHM system uses the interpreter to load the classes for a new media type and then registers them with the session manager's typeInfoTable. Thus, the conceptual extensibility that is available at the framework level is also available in a runtime-tailorable version of the DHM system.

13.7 A pattern for framework tailorability

Our recommendations for tailorable open hypermedia services are outlined in the following pattern.

Title: Framework Tailoring

Context: An open hypermedia system and an increasing set of open applications that manage various types of multimedia data.

Problem: To configure the hypermedia system in order to communicate with and model new applications.

Solution(s): Base the hypermedia system on an object-oriented application framework. There are two approaches to tailoring such a framework:

• Object-oriented specialization of the generic component, instantiation, and communication classes of the framework. This solution typically requires compiling or interpreting source code extensions.

• Configuration of generic component and instantiation types. This solution assumes that the designer can anticipate the main categories of integratable applications and model them by unifying components and instantiations. In that case, new applications can be integrated on the fly at run time, through parametrization. Communication interfaces remain specific to applications; thus tailored communication classes usually still have to be provided in the form of the preceding solution.

Examples: HOSS is an example of the first solution. Intermedia, DHM, and HyperDisco are examples of the second solution.

Related patterns: Depends on Open Hypermedia Interface in chapter 15. See also Application Tailoring in chapter 14.

14

Hypermedia and Application Openness

[H]ypertext/hypermedia will only catch on as a fundamentally integrating paradigm when . . . incorporated, as a fundamental advance in application integration, into the heart of the standard computing toolboxes . . . —and application developers must be provided with the tools that enable applications to 'link up' in a standard manner. Only when the paradigm is positioned as an integrating factor for all third-party applications, and not as a special attribute of a limited few, will knowledge workers accept and integrate hypertext and hypermedia into their daily work process. (Meyrowitz 1989, p. 113)

As discussed in chapter 1, the notion of hypermedia structuring offers new possibilities for more efficient information management in application domains like engineering, office work, and case handling (DeYoung 1989; Grønbæk et al. 1993; Malcolm et al. 1991). Nonetheless, users don't want to give up their favorite word processor, spreadsheet, or CAD system to get hypermedia capabilities Grønbæk et al. (1993).

This may explain why there has been so little diffusion of hypermedia technology into information management in organizations. Many of the early hypermedia systems were closed monolithic entities with their own editors for all media types, their own internal data formats, and their own processing models. This is still the case with the WWW. Although web browser plug-ins can render a variety of data formats, there are still few professional applications whose WWW integrations allow the user to create hypermedia links from locations in the data while editing or annotating.

In this chapter, we begin by reviewing hypermedia research aimed at moving beyond monolithic systems and toward the integration of third-party applications. Next, we survey common means of supporting tailorability and inter-application communication, and propose several degrees of application openness relevant to hypermedia integration. We then consider in some detail one of the hardest problems encountered in application integration: how to maintain consistency between application documents and the hypermedia structures that refer into them. We close with two patterns that address design issues relevant to application tailoring and anchor maintenance.

14.1   Transcending monolithic hypermedia

The last two decades of research have resulted in at least three approaches to the development of nonmonolithic hypermedia, each of which has distinct problems and prospects.

14.1.1   Hypermedia at the operating system level

In his classic "Missing link" paper, Norm Meyrowitz (1989) argued that the monolithic approach to hypermedia was a failure and proposed moving hypermedia functionality to the operating system. Indeed, several subsequent operating systems support linking. Two examples are GO's PenPoint (Meyrowitz 1991) and Microsoft Windows, with its object linking and embedding (OLE) protocol. OLE will soon be an integrated feature of all Windows applications, enabling the user to create a representation of any document and embed it in any other document. Thereafter, invoking an operation on the embedded representation brings up the target document. However, seen from the point of view of a hypermedia designer, these operating system links are no more than embedded jump addresses. An OLE link is not a first-class object expressing a relationship between two information chunks, nor is it stored in an independent link database that allows users to create a map of their links or inspect individual links without opening the documents that contain them. Current operating system-level links thus only partially support hypermedia functionality.

Recently, Nürnberg et al. (1996) presented an approach to providing hypermedia support at the operating system level they call HOSS (Hypermedia Operating System Services). Developers of new applications use HOSS interfaces to add hypermedia services to the applications. HOSS databases store structures and behaviors separately from the data of the applications. Thus, this approach resembles the concept of open hypermedia services proposed in this book.

14.1.2   Link services to be integrated during application development

Amy Pearl (1989), in developing the Sun Link service, took a first step beyond monolithic hypermedia on a specific platform. Her idea was to build a link server database that any application developed for the Sun platform could use. The only requirement was that the application include a set of hypermedia library routines and integrate the link service protocol at development time. For this approach to succeed, application developers for the Sun platform needed to compile the hypermedia libraries into their applications and perform the necessary source code integration. A similar link service, called LinkWorks (Clark 1992), was developed for the DEC platform. Unfortunately, it has proved difficult to convince application developers to include such hypermedia access libraries in their applications.

Chimera (Anderson et al. 1994) is a recent example of an open hypermedia service that, in addition to integrating third-party applications, also resembles the Sun Link Service by providing libraries for application integration at the source code level.

14.1.3 Open hypermedia services

Open hypermedia services offer a third means of bringing hypermedia to the users' favorite applications. These services can, in principle, be integrated with any third-party application, depending on the degree of its openness (though launch-only integration is always possible). Hypermedia systems that adopt such an open hypermedia approach include Microcosm (Davis et al. 1994), Devise Hypermedia (DHM) (Grønbæk and Malhotra 1994; Grønbæk and Trigg 1994), Chimera (Anderson et al. 1994), and MultiCard (Rizk and Sauter 1992). These systems provide a communication protocol and/or an API integration facility that enables third-party applications to support hypermedia linking for portions of their data. For instance, Microscosm and DHM are both integrated by means of the Windows DDE communication facility with Microsoft Excel and Word on the Windows platform. Each of these applications provides a macro language that allows the addition of menus and buttons as well as the invocation of DDE routines in other applications, in this case, the open hypermedia services. The main difference between Microcosm and DHM with respect to integration is that Microcosm's primary goal is to support generic links. These links are defined using text string templates stored in a separate link database. The same generic link can be invoked from matching text strings in multiple applications. (See chapter 6 for an introduction to generic links.) DHM's primary goal is to support links from specific selected locations in arbitrary media.

Figure 57 illustrates how the functionality of an open hypermedia service can appear to users as small additions to the familiar office and CAD application

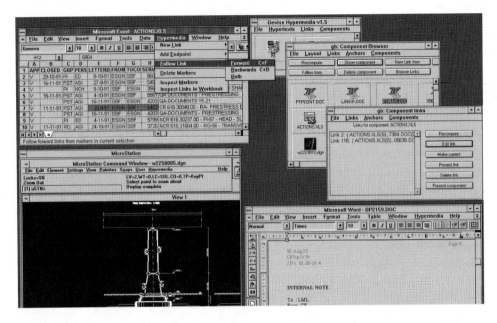

Figure 57
Applications integrated with Devise Hypermedia on the Microsoft Windows platform.
Microsoft Excel and Word, and Bentley's Microstation were each extended using their
own macro languages with menu items or toolbar buttons that communicate data and
requests to the Devise Hypermedia service.

interfaces. The remainder of this chapter discusses general issues that arise with
regard to integrating an open hypermedia service with second or third-party
applications.

14.2   Application support for communication and tailoring

The goal of designing open hypermedia systems is to smoothly integrate heterogeneous applications using shared hypermedia structures. The work of integrating includes identifying and locating parts of material managed by the
applications as anchors for hypermedia structures. The open hypermedia architecture described in chapter 12 is expressly designed to provide such an open
hypermedia service that interoperates with the applications available to users on
the given platform.

To achieve this goal, it is not sufficient just to design the hypermedia service.
Applications and operating systems also need to fulfil special requirements.

· The operating system should support asynchronous peer-to-peer communication between applications. Client/server support is insufficient since the open hypermedia service needs to invoke operations in applications. Such operations might, for example, present particular link endpoints.

· The applications should be able to send and receive messages through this communication facility.

· The applications should be tailorable and should provide facilities to address portions of the material they manage.

These ideal requirements are only partly met by today's operating systems and applications. Nonetheless, it is possible to provide extensive hypermedia support in such environments.

14.2.1 Interapplication communication in modern operating systems

A prerequisite for open hypermedia service is the ability for both the operating system platform and the applications to support inter-application communication. The operating system should support peer-to-peer communication (asynchronous or synchronous), while the applications should be modified to take advantage of that communication.

Most modern operating systems support interapplication communication including symmetric peer-to-peer communication between applications. However, not all open applications support two-way communication. For example, some applications support sending messages but not receiving, or vice versa. This section briefly describes inter-application communication facilities for the three most common operating systems.

UNIX: TCP/IP and sockets   The UNIX operating system supports communication between processes by means of TCP/IP and sockets (Tanenbaum 1992). Applications support communication using specific data formats on sockets assigned to agreed-upon port addresses. Applications typically allocate an active socket for sending data and a passive socket for listening to incoming data events. Communication in a UNIX application can take different forms, depending on which abstractions are built using the basic socket facility.

Apple MacOS: AppleEvent and AppleScript   On the Apple Macintosh platform, communication between applications is supported by several toolbox managers, including the AppleEvent and AppleScript managers. An application supporting AppleEvents and AppleScript sends a message to an application using its registered name. MacOS then directs the message to the appropriate running application. Applications need to have set up an AppleEvent handler that catches communication events from the keyboard or mouse. The applications usually include a suite of operations and data structures that are invoked and accessed using standard mechanisms.

Microsoft Windows: DDE/OLE Microsoft Windows supports two types of communication between applications. The original communication facility is the convenient Dynamic Data Exchange (DDE). It allows one application to call up a second application with a given DDE name and invoke one of its advertised operations. As in the MacOS, applications publish suites of operations and data structures that can be invoked and accessed.

The newer facility, object linking and embedding (OLE), supports DDE-like communication, embedded data objects interlinked across applications, and distributed object communication. To be certified, Windows 95 applications must support a large part of OLE. In the future, most Windows applications will allow communication as well as the linking and embedding of central data objects. Since OLE has also been implemented for the MacOS, Windows/OLE applications ported to the MacOS can support OLE communication with other OLE-compatible applications. However, as yet, only a few applications support full OLE communication.

14.2.2 Platform dependence
Because platforms like UNIX, MacOS, and Windows provide their own communication facilities, it is difficult to develop a platform-independent open hypermedia service. For the time being, the communication layer of a Dexter-based architecture still has to be implemented in a platform-dependent way, unless the open hypermedia service is restricted to only OLE-compatible applications. Fortunately, greater commonality in communication support is on the way. The Internet protocol TCP/IP is currently supported on most platforms, and emerging research in object distribution standards promises further cross-platform support.

TCP/IP TCP/IP was first developed for the UNIX operating system. Now, however, both MS Windows and Apple's MacOS offer TCP/IP support; on MS

Windows, through the WinSocket library and on the MacOS, through the Open Transport protocol. However, TCP/IP on these platforms is mainly used for communication over the Internet rather than for inter-application communication. Platform-internal communication still uses proprietary communication protocols.

Object distribution Object distribution has been an active research area for several years. The goal of the research is to enable developers to write object-oriented programs without considering whether the objects being manipulated are local to the application or live within the scope of another application. Many of today's distributed object systems appear in application frameworks for end-user applications. Two of the most prominent compound document frameworks are OLE and OpenDoc, based on the distributed object models COM (Brockschmidt 1995) and OMG CORBA (Mowbray and Zahavi 1995), respectively. Unlike COM, CORBA is platform-independent; if OpenDoc has a commercial breakthrough, new platform-independent hypermedia services that can communicate with applications and their data objects will emerge. Moreover, CORBA support will be available for the popular Java language, although JavaSoft is also promoting its own object distribution protocol, RMI (remote method invocation),[1] which will only support Java to Java communication. In any case, object distribution is not yet widespread enough to serve as a standard platform for the integration of third-party applications. Perhaps the development of object-oriented applications for the WWW will lead to such a breakthrough.

14.2.3 Levels of openness in applications
Existing and newly developed applications do not all support the same degree of open communication and access to data objects. Few applications support two-way communication, allow access to data structures or window selections, and enable tailoring of the user interface. This lack of openness limits the extent of hypermedia support that an open hypermedia service can provide for an application.

The following sections survey different kinds of application openness and the potential for open hypermedia support. This overview covers some of the same territory as the Microcosm group's discussion of "hypermedia-aware" applications, which they designate as "fully aware," "semi-aware," and "unaware"

---

1. http://www.javasoft.com/marketing/collateral/rmi_ds.html

(Hall et al. 1996). For Microcosm, a fully aware application is one that has been developed or tailored to communicate with the open Microcosm hypermedia service. In contrast, when we talk about a fully open application, we mean an application that as is, has the potential to support extensive hypermedia integration.

Our categories of applications do not cover every variant of open applications, but they do constitute a spectrum of openness relevant to the task of integrating with open hypermedia services.

Closed applications   Closed applications are those that support no inter-application communication and no tailoring. The only possibility for interacting with such an application is to launch it on a file of the right type and use built-in functionality.

Open hypermedia potential   A document managed by a closed application can serve as the content of an atomic component, although anchors located within the document cannot be supported. The document can only be the endpoint of a whole component link. It is generally not possible to invoke hypermedia functionality from the user interface of closed applications. Closed applications can, however, be "cheated" open by means of window system programming that attaches popup menus in the titlebar and catches selections. Examples of closed application integration include the Microcosm Universal viewer (Davis et al. 1994) and the experimental Netscape integration discussed by Grønbæk et al. (1997a).

Communication about selections, without tailoring   Applications in this category support a communication interface, but the user interface is not modifiable or extensible. Such applications present a suite of operations and data structures that other applications can invoke and access.

Open hypermedia potential   The communication suite for such an application provides access to user-specified selections and lets programs set the selection as well as scroll it into view in the window. A user can make a selection with the application, use the hypermedia service to establish an anchor with a locSpec for the selection, and then build links to that anchor. Links can then be followed to and from such selections. Invoking operations on selections in the application documents always requires a shift to the hypermedia service. Even though the applications may allow local anchoring in documents, they are usually not able to update the hypermedia service when a user makes changes to the documents.

Communication about selections, with tailoring   Applications in this category allow the user interface and communication from the application to be tailored by means of an application programmers interface (API) or macro language.

Open hypermedia potential   These applications add to the preceding category the ability to make hypermedia functionality available from within the application as menubar and/or toolbar extensions. Certain object-based graphics editors offer this kind of integration, which gives users the feeling of a fully integrated hypermedia application. Anchor locSpecs in such an application may be as simple as a graphical object ID; the application only has to notify the hypermedia system upon deletion of the object, since no other edits can affect the anchor locSpec information.

Communication, tailoring, and persistent selections   Applications in this category extend the preceding category to include an internal facility for storing information about persistent selections (Leggett and Schnase 1994; Meyrowitz 1989). These selections act as bookmarks for pieces of document data. Such functionality is becoming more common in office applications.

Open hypermedia potentials   Applications in this category can be fully integrated with the hypermedia system; the anchor locSpecs simply identify persistent selections supported by the application. Such applications can be used to create link anchors that "stick" to a certain piece of document data while the document is being edited.

Object distribution, tailoring, and persistent selections   Applications in this category give external applications the further ability to obtain a reference to an object inside the application or its data. Applications built using the compound document models OLE and OpenDoc can present parts of their inner data or behavior objects as distributed objects that users can manipulate directly from external applications.

Open hypermedia potentials   The data objects of such applications can be accessed directly using object references, allowing component content and anchor locSpecs to be distributed. This capability allows hypermedia services

direct access to unique references for data objects and thus reduces the need
to write application-specific code to lookup data objects based on locSpec
attributes.

14.2.4   The problem of user interface consistency

In an open hypermedia system, the hypermedia operations, object representations, and system feedback should be provided through the interface of the
integrated applications whenever possible. In this way the hypermedia functionality can be ready-to-hand in the applications with which the users are familiar.
The risk, however, is that the diversity of tailoring possibilities among the
applications may lead to inconsistent interfaces to the shared hypermedia
functionality.

Examples of inconsistencies that can occur in the hypermedia user interfaces of
tailorable third-party applications are:

· Missing support for hierarchical menus. Some applications support the tailor
in making hierarchical menus and some do not. Thus a hypermedia menu may
appear differently in two integrated applications.

· Keyboard shortcut conflicts. It is generally not possible to provide the same
keyboard shortcuts for hypermedia operations across all applications.

· Link marker highlighting. The possibilities for marking a link endpoint may
differ. For example, some applications support colors, while others do not.

There are, however, approaches that offer hope for a consistent user interface.
For example, the Microscosm universal viewer (Davis et al. 1994), attaches the
same "parasite" window system program to all applications to provide a consistent interface. However, the limited control this gives over the application led
Microcosm also to provide application-specific macros and plug-ins where
possible.

Another approach to enhancing consistency is development-time tailoring like
that provided by Sun Link Service (Pearl 1989), LinkWorks (Clark 1992), and
Chimera (Anderson et al. 1994). These systems require that application developers support a specific hypermedia service library. The library may enforce a
standardized user interface, which requires the application designer to revise
initial design decisions, for example, to avoid conflicts among keyboard short
cuts.

14.3 Keeping application data and hypermedia structures consistent

A central goal of open hypermedia is to maintain a stable and consistent relationship between material managed by dedicated applications and hypermedia structures in a separate database. In this section, we discuss problems of consistency and how they can be addressed.

14.3.1 Linking in documents with changing access rights

The access modes of documents raise issues of consistency between documents and the open hypermedia service structures.

On the one hand, maintaining links inside documents that are writable and that can be dynamically changed is a challenge for open hypermedia designers, because anchors must be kept up to date with changes to the content. A location approach based on persistent selections like bookmarks and defined names in spreadsheets can support the maintenance of links in such dynamically changing documents.

On the other hand, linking into read-only documents precludes the use of objects, such as bookmarks and defined names, that are stored with the document. A location approach based on structural information or search criteria can support linking in read-only material.

Finally, documents may change access mode over time, say, in a collaborative setting where authors take turns editing documents. Such cases require both persistent selection and structured search approaches.

In a Dexter-based framework this problem is addressed by the use of redundant locSpec information, as discussed in chapter 4. A runtime mechanism determines, on the basis of access rights, which location approach should be applied.

Here is one approach to linking in documents with changing access rights that supports seamless transitions:

1. When a document is read-only, fill in only the structure descriptor and the computation criteria of anchor locSpecs.

2. When a document is writable, create persistent selections and fill in all attributes of the anchor locSpecs, including the Object IDs for persistent selections.

3. When a read-only document becomes writable, direct the application to create persistent selections for all "read-only" locSpecs before any edits take place.

4. When a writable document becomes read-only, switch to the generation of "read-only" locSpecs with an Object ID attributes.

This approach has been implemented in the DHM system to support integration with Microsoft Word and other applications (Grønbæk and Mogensen 1997).

14.3.2   Inconsistent anchors and dangling links

Inconsistencies between documents or objects and hypermedia structures may arise when documents can be moved, renamed, or deleted in the operating system "behind the back" of the open hypermedia service. Furthermore, the documents may be opened and edited by versions of applications that are not integrated with the open hypermedia service. Consequently, the changes made to objects and locations inside the documents are not communicated to the hypermedia service, which, in turn, leads to the inconsistencies.

These same inconsistencies appeared in the dangling link discussion of chapter 6. There we identified four dangling link situations arising in an integrated Dexter-based hypermedia system.

· An endpoint's component is deleted.
· An endpoint's anchor is deleted.
· Data objects referred to by the component's content are unavailable.
· An anchor locSpec is invalid.

The first two cases can be handled by strategies within the hypermedia service, as discussed in chapter 6. The third and fourth cases are most relevant for this discussion because they usually result from actions outside the control of the hypermedia service. Data objects making up a component's content can become unavailable, for example, if the content is a file identifier, and the file is moved or deleted independently of the hypermedia system. In this case, the followLink operation should catch the file system exception and pass it along to the user. Component attributes and file system information can inform the user about what went wrong.

The last case arises when the data location specified by the anchor locSpec becomes invalid, usually because a component's content is modified by an application that is not in communication with the hypermedia service. For example, imagine a user who brings a spreadsheet from her office workstation to her home machine where the hypermedia service isn't installed. She modifies the spreadsheet document on the home machine, brings it to the office workstation, and overwrites the original file, which was consistent with the hypermedia service application. This situation is hard to address in general; however, the next section describes heuristics that can help.

14.3.3 Detecting and repairing inconsistencies

Hall et al. (1996) propose heuristics to detect and repair link and anchor inconsistencies. For example, the hypermedia service can store modification date and time, in order to inform the user if a document changes after the anchor information was last updated. The other heuristics invoke storing redundant information that helps the user repair the inconsistency. These and other heuristics can be supported within a Dexter-based framework. The first approach involves maintaining a component attribute that records modification dates. The redundancy heuristic is directly supported by the locSpec design.

Using modification dates to detect inconsistencies A strategy for detecting inconsistencies is to store each component's last modification date in an attribute. Generally, this date is the same or later than the modification date of the document corresponding to the component's content. If not, we can conclude that the document was updated since the last communication with the open hypermedia service, indicating a possible inconsistency with the external structures in the hypermedia database.

However, the fact that the modification date of the component is the same or later than that of the document does not guarantee that the document and the hypermedia structures are consistent. Let's consider the situation in which a user modifies a document and makes new links and anchors, but quits the application without saving changes. Because changes to the component's anchor list were saved, its modification date is later than that of the document, but the two are nonetheless inconsistent because of the unsaved changes to the document. Fortunately, inconsistencies created in this situation can usually be detected using the heuristics based on locSpecs described in the next section.

Detecting and repairing inconsistencies using locSpecs As described in chapter 4, locSpecs use three attributes to hold information about locations inside a component's content:

· Object ID
· Structure Descriptor
· Computation Descriptor

In most cases *one* of these attributes is sufficient to determine a location inside a component's content. But to detect and propose repairs of inconsistencies between a document and its hypermedia service representation, we can take advantage of redundant location specification. For example, a span of text in a word processor that supports bookmarks is uniquely identified by a locSpec whose object ID is set equal to the text span's bookmark ID. However, if the user, without communicating to the hypermedia service, deletes the bookmark from the document, then the locSpec can no longer be used to locate the span of text.

Repairing the inconsistency is possible, however, if the hypermedia service requests sufficient information to fill in all the attributes of the locSpec (Davis 1995; Hall et al. 1996). The span of text in the example can be redundantly identified with a locSpec of the following form:

· Object ID: a bookmark ID
· Structure Descriptor: a position, such as start position, and length of span
· Computation Descriptor: the text of the span to search for

With such redundant information the hypermedia service can detect and repair a variety of inconsistent situations. In the following two situations, modification dates cannot detect the inconsistency; rather, it is discovered upon following a link on a composite reference to an anchor.

A user accidentally deletes a bookmark referred to by a locSpec.

A system error or power failure causes the application to shut down without saving modifications to the document.

In such situations, the open hypermedia service can trigger the following repair actions:

1. If the anchor locSpec's referred bookmark is missing in the document, notify the user that the bookmark with the given ID no longer exists.

2. Direct the word processor to highlight the span of text corresponding to the locSpec's structure descriptor, and tell the user that the old bookmark represented this span.

3. If the span corresponding to the structure descriptor is identical with the stored text string in the locSpec's computation descriptor, ask the user to confirm the updating of the anchor with a new bookmark.

4. If the span corresponding to the structure descriptor is not consistent with the stored text string in the computation descriptor, notify the user and ask whether she wishes to perform a search for a nearby occurrence of the text string.

5. If the search is successful, ask the user whether she wishes to update the anchor to locate the span of text in this new position.

The third situation can be detected by checking modification dates.

A user edits a document while disconnected from the open hypermedia service.

In this situation, the open hypermedia service can perform steps 2–5 of the preceding procedure for *every* anchor locSpec registered for the document. In most cases such strategies enable the user to re-establish links anchored in documents that have become inconsistent with the hypermedia structures. However, if none of the three locSpec attributes captures the intended location of the link endpoint, the endpoint needs to be removed or rebuilt from scratch.

14.3.4 LocSpecs for various media

Different media use different location characteristics that call for new approaches to repair inconsistencies. For example, media types that support only one or two location methods can fill only one or two locSpec attributes and thus cannot fully employ the heuristics described in the previous section.

In what follows, we propose locSpec attributes for some common media types; similar proposals were made by Hall et al. (1996).

Text: The locSpec attributes for a span of text that can be marked as a persistent selection are as described in the previous section:

· Object ID: a bookmark ID
· Structure descriptor: a position, such as the start position, and length of a span
· Computation: the text of the span to search for

Object drawings: Individual objects in, say, CAD drawings, usually possess a unique identifier that the application uses to locate the object within internally maintained coordinate spaces. Since object IDs are usually unique and unaffected by edits related to other parts of a drawing, no redundant information is necessary to ensure link consistency. The locSpec simply consists of:

· Object ID: ID of a built-in graphical object

Bitmaps: Anchors corresponding to rectangular areas of bitmaps can be represented in a locSpec using coordinates, for instance, the upper left and lower right corners. Some bitmap editors, however, support placement of objects in a layer on top of the bitmap. If these objects possess identifiers, they can be used as locSpec Object IDs as follows:

· Object ID: ID of a graphical object in a transparent layer
· Structure descriptor: coordinates of selected regions

Video/sound: In time-based data, segments of video or sound are the typical units for anchoring. They are usually represented using an offset from the start of the segment and a duration time. For video, another option is to overlay graphical objects on the running video at certain positions within the dimensions of the frame. Again, an identifier of the objects serves as the object ID attribute in the locSpec as follows:

· Object ID: ID of a graphical object in a transparent layer
· Structure descriptor: a segment specified, for example, by its start time and length

Database records: An anchor in a relational database table can locate a span of several records, just as an anchor in text can span several lines or paragraphs. The actual query used to find particular records can also be used as the location method. In a locSpec, a query is a form of computation descriptor. Hence, we have the following two location attributes for database records:

· Object ID: key values for the records
· Computation: text of a query to find the records

14.3.5 Document management and file systems

Consistency problems arise when the content of components are stored in file systems and managed by separate applications. For example, users moving or deleting files in the file system without notifying the hypermedia service can cause link consistency problems. These problems cannot be addressed without cooperation between the file system and the hypermedia service.

Document management systems based on databases are being introduced in many organizations to handle document storage, retrieval, versioning, and the like. Such document management systems function as a layer on top of the file system, representing files with identifiers that are independent of physical location. A document management system in conjunction with an open hypermedia service can thus avoid file address inconsistencies. Moreover, the document management system can post notifications when invoking particular operations, in order to inform the hypermedia service about file deletions and updates.

14.4 Patterns for integrating applications

The patterns in this section address the work of application tailoring and the problem of keeping hypermedia structures consistent with application documents.

Title: Application Tailoring
Context: An open hypermedia system and an ever-changing set of open applications to handle various types of multimedia data.
Problem: To configure the hypermedia system to communicate with and model the new applications.
Solution(s): The application should support or be made to support at least one of the following: plug-ins, macro language programming, or a window system-based API.

Using one or more of those tools, tailor the application by building:

· User interface extensions such as a menu, a tool bar or a command interface to access hypermedia functionality
· A communication module that implements the integration protocol interface
· Support for mapping between selections and locSpecs
· A highlighting operation that uses locSpec information
· The ability to display and undisplay markers

Examples: The integration of Microcosm with Microsoft Word, Devise Hypermedia with Microsoft Word and Excel, HyperDisco with Xemacs, and Chimera with Framemaker.
Related patterns: Depends on Open Hypermedia Interface in chapter 15. See also Framework Tailoring in chapter 13.

Title: Anchor Maintenance

Context: The implementation of open hypermedia systems that can integrate heterogeneous nonhypermedia applications. Some applications may not be able to maintain persistent selections by themselves.

Problem: To keep anchor locSpecs consistent with the documents that constitute the content of components, particularly when document content change outside the control of the open hypermedia service.

Solution(s): Use heuristics based on stored modification dates and redundant locSpec attributes to detect and repair inconsistencies. Generally, an inconsistent situation is a case in which at least one of the following holds:

· The modification date of the content document is later than the date stored in the component.

· At least two of the three locSpec attributes (object id, structure descriptor, and computation) exist but identify different parts of the content.

· One or more attributes have values that correspond to invalid parts of the content.

Heuristic detection and repair can be performed if the application and the hyper-media service can implement the following kinds of actions:

· Detect when a document has been modified later than the corresponding hyper-media component.

· Notify the user that a persistent selection with a given ID is missing in a document.

· Direct the application to highlight the selection given by the structure descriptor.

· Compare the persistent selection represented by the object ID with the content represented by the structure and computation attributes.

· Compare the structure descriptor selection to the content represented by the computation attribute.

· Perform a search for the content represented by the computation attribute.

· Iteratively check the consistency of *every* anchor locSpec registered for a document.

· Let the user update an individual anchor to match a new location found by the structure- or computation-based relocating methods.

· Let the user delete and rebuild an anchor when it is impossible to relocate it.

Combinations of these primitives can handle some of the inconsistencies that commonly arise in working with open hypermedia.

Examples: Microcosm and the Devise Hypermedia framework

Related patterns: Depends on Locating in Material in chapter 4, Local Anchoring in chapter 5, and Open Hypermedia Interface in chapter 15.

15

Open Hypermedia Communication Design

All the things of the universe and all those of man would be registered from afar as they were created. Thus the moving image of the world would be established–its memory, its true duplicate. From afar anyone would be able to read any passage, expanded or limited to the desired subject, that would be projected onto his individual screen. Thus in his armchair, anyone would be able to contemplate the whole of creation or particular parts of it (Paul Otlet writing in 1903, quoted in [Feenberg 1995, pp. 390–391])

Crucial to open hypermedia design is deciding how applications and the hypermedia service communicate to each other. Recently, the Open Hypermedia Systems (OHS) Working Group was established to standardize the format of such communications. Hugh Davis et al. (1996) proposed an open hypermedia protocol (OHP) based on experiences with Microcosm (Davis et al. 1994) and Multicard (Rizk and Sauter 1992). This proposal prompted the working group to discuss questions of format and operations, among others. For example, a recent question has been whether to formulate open hypermedia communication in terms of a text-based protocol or by using interface definitions with data structures and operations.

In our work with the Devise Hypermedia framework, we have developed open hypermedia communication support for third-party applications that uses a text-based protocol. Since our framework is Dexter-based, this protocol supports most of the extended Dexter concepts introduced in this book. This chapter's proposal for a Dexter-based open hypermedia protocol (ODHP), is derived from that framework and its protocol. This chapter begins by outlining the format of the protocol and presenting examples of operations relevant to linking, browsing and structure management, and multiuser coordination. We illustrate the protocol's use in integrating third-party applications, such as Microsoft Word. We

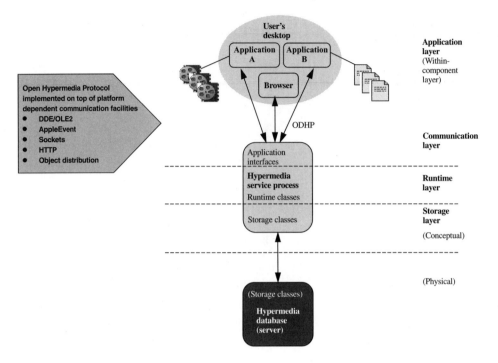

Figure 58
Locating an open hypermedia protocol in a Dexter-based architecture.

close with two design patterns related to the format of communication interfaces and the steps required to integrate a new application.

15.1   The role of the open hypermedia protocol

In a Dexter-based architecture, the open hypermedia protocol is located in the communication layer, which manages interactions between the hypermedia services process (HSP) and applications on the users' desktops, as the diagram in figure 58 shows.

The communication layer specifies a generic protocol and interface that we call the open Dexter-based hypermedia protocol (ODHP). This protocol can be implemented on different carrier protocols, such as TCP/IP, Microsoft DDE/OLE, and Apple's AppleEvents.

As depicted in figure 58, hypermedia browsers are considered part of the application layer; thus a full-blown ODHP supports browser facilities and general user interfaces for the open hypermedia service. In the next section, we focus on how the ODHP is organized to support communication with applications that manage component content.

15.2 The communication layer

The communication layer and its ODHP protocol facilitate two-way communication between the runtime and application layers. The communication can be either synchronous or asynchronous, depending on the methods supported by the protocol for carrier communication.

The generic class hierarchy of the communication layer, following the runtime class hierarchy described in section 11.7, provides protocols at the levels of the session manager and the instantiation. The session manager protocol supports alternative hypermedia user interfaces running as separate processes. In this way, a Dexter-based hypermedia system can be controlled by alternate user interfaces or macros written in a third-party application. The instantiation protocol performs an essential kind of integration, that of new media types managed by separately running applications. This part of the protocol is discussed in detail in the next section.

The communication layer also manages the platform-dependent parts of the framework; in particular, the interface to the actual carrier protocol is encapsulated in implementation files behind the abstract, platform-independent protocol interface. Whereas all modules of the runtime and storage layers are easily portable from one platform to another (assuming that the platforms support the programming language used in the implementation), only the interface modules of the communication layer can be ported. The implementation modules of the communication layer generally have to be rewritten for each platform. For example, an editor like Microsoft Excel on the Macintosh needs communication objects that use AppleEvents to interact with the open instantiations managing the contents of components displayed with Excel. Porting such a communication module to Excel under Microsoft Windows would require rewriting to use Dynamic Data Exchange (DDE) rather than AppleEvents.

Finally, the communication protocols are extensible in that new procedures can be added by specializing the Communication class hierarchies. The next section discusses the protocols in more detail.

15.3   An open hypermedia protocol for applications

The protocol at the instantiation level of the ODHP, is designed to support communication with applications that manage component content. The sections that follow describe the format of communication and operations, giving a few examples. Appendix B more comprehensively describes the ODHP, including its operations for browsing and multiuser support.

15.3.1   The format of the instantiation protocol

The ODHP is a peer-to-peer communication protocol: both the HSP and the external application can send and receive messages. A simple implementation of the ODHP uses a textual encoding that can be exchanged via a communication facility and that can be interpreted by both the HSP and the applications to be integrated.

In the text-based protocol, messages are composed of commands and lists of parameters. For example, Davis et al.'s (1996) proposed OHP uses a verbatim set of commands in a LaTex-like syntax. The DHM system uses a more compact encoding consisting of operation codes and parameters.

For this presentation, we describe each ODHP command abstractly and provide examples of usage in the format of the DHM system. Since the protocol is to be used in peer-to-peer communication, we distinguish messages sent from the HSP to applications, from those sent from applications to the HSP.

The exact format of messages sent from the HSP to an external application depends on the application in question. Some of the examples in the next three sections are messages sent to Emacs on a UNIX platform. Emacs receives the text string and unpacks the commands and parameters. However, in Word and Excel on the Windows platform, messages take the form of direct calls from the hypermedia service to Word and Excel Visual Basic macros. The opcodes are irrelevant in such cases.

The general form of a message sent from hypermedia-extended applications to the hypermedia service is as follows: "UserName,ApplicationID,opCode, . . .". The unnamed arguments contain, e.g., locSpec and pSpec information. In contrast to messages sent in the other direction, the messages to the HSP have the same format for every application. The messages sent from applications are encoded with user name and host identifier, in order to identify the proper user and session in the hypermedia service handling the request, and to facilitate addressing a reply to the application.

Figure 59 summarizes the types of parameters encoded in the message.

Parameter	Explanation
userName	the login name of the user
ApplicationID	an identifier that uniquely identifies the running instance of an application, e.g. a DDE name in Windows or a four letter signature on a Macintosh
hyperSpaceID	a unique identifier for a hyperspace object, here encoded as a pair of integers. Hyperspaces are usually also assigned a human readable name, HyperSpace Name.
compID	a unique identifier for a component object, here encoded as a pair of integers.
opCode	an integer encoding of the command in question
accessCode	a code that determines the access and availability rights for a given object
N	an integer used to tell the HSP/application that a list of parameters of a certain length is at the end of the message
nodeSpec	a unique identification of the content for a component. Typically this is a document identifier, e.g. a full file name and path or a document management system ID.
docType	a MIME-type for a document
locSpec	an application-specific specification of a location inside a document
pSpec	an application-specific encoding of information relevant to the presentation of a given document or an anchor inside a document
direction	an integer determining the direction of the endpoint to be either SOURCE, DESTINATION, BOTH or NONE.
linkType	a number encoding the type of link in question
lockValue	a number encoding the lock type on a component, e.g. read, write
responseCode	a number encoding the result of an operation, where 1 = success, 0 = failure, and numbers preceeded by '-' refer to specific messages describing the status of the operation

Figure 59
Parameters appearing in the protocol.

15.3.2   The basic linking protocol

The basic linking protocol supports the creation, traversal, and deletion of links anchored to parts of material managed by hypermedia-extended applications.

Messages from the HSP to hypermedia-extended applications   The two operations that follow are examples of essential messages sent from the hypermedia service to applications.

The HSP sends the PresentSelection operation upon resolving a link in order to present the set of endpoints in a given application. Each call to PresentSelection presents a single endpoint. The operation code and an example of usage follow:

```
PresentSelection:    13
Usage: Used to present an anchor within a given document.
Format: Application,opCode,nodeSpec,locSpec,pSpec
Response: (ResponseCode)
Example: emacs,13,/users/kgronbak/DHM/docs/interface.tex,1,,
```

The HSP issues the SendAnchorlist operation to make external application display markers for all the anchors registered for the document. The operation is specified as follows:

```
SendAnchorList:    807
Usage: Used to send the anchorList for a given component/document to
the external application.
Format: ApplicationID,opCode, nodeSpec, N,{locSpec}*
Response: (ResponseCode)
Example: emacs,807,/users/kgronbak/DHM/docs/interface.tex,1,0#836#852
```

A more comprehensive set of messages from the hypermedia service to applications appears in appendix B.

Messages from hypermedia-extended applications to the HSP   The three operations that follow are examples of essential messages sent from applications to the hypermedia service. The applications invokes these operations on the current selection in an open document.

The application invokes the NewLink operation to create a link with a source endpoint that corresponds to the locSpec representing the user's selection:

```
NewLink:          0
Usage: Creates a new link of a given type with a number of endpoints
determined by the given sets of (nodeSpec,locSpec,direction).
Format: UserName,ApplicationID,opCode,NoOfEndpoints,{nodeSpec, loc-
Spec,direction}*,linkType,NoOfHyperSpaces,{HyperSpaceId}*

Response: (LinkId,{EndPointId}*)
Example: kgronbak@daimi.aau.dk,WebBrowser,0,1,
("http://www.daimi.aau.dk/~devise/front.html"),("Devise Homepage
http://www.daimi.aau.dk/~devise/ MainFrame ""DEVISE
""0""0""0""0""0"),3,2,1,1,888855764
```

Assuming that the hypermedia service holds a current active link for the user, the application can invoke the AddEndPoint operation to create a new source or destination endpoint, again providing the locSpec representing the user's selection:

```
AddEndpoint:    100
Usage: Adds a number of endpoints to the link determined by LinkId.
Format: UserName,ApplicationID,opCode,NoOfEndpoints, {nodeSpec,loc-
Spec,direction}*,NoOfHyperSpaces,{HyperSpaceId}*,LinkId
Response: ({EndPointId}*)
Example: kgronbak@daimi.aau.dk,WebBrowser,100,1,
("http://www.cit.dk/Coconut/introduction.html"),("Project introduc-
tion http://www.cit.dk/Coconut/ display ""Coconut: Collaboration and
Components, (inter)Net-based Ubiquitous Telework-
ing""0""0""0""0""0"),3,1,1,888855764,13
```

The application invokes the FollowLink operation to follow a link from the anchor that corresponds to the locSpec being sent. The operation traverses the link in the direction specified:

```
FollowLink:    200
Usage: Follow links in the given direction from the specified loc-
Specs.
Format: UserName,ApplicationID,opCode,nodeSpec,noOfLocSpecs, {loc-
Spec}*,direction
Response: (ResponseCode,N,{nodeSpec,locSpec,endpointName}*)
Example: kgronbak@daimi.aau.dk,WinWord,200,("C:\My Docu-
ments\Doc1.doc"),1,("HMB_4#75:82"""""0""0""0""0""0"),1
```

A similar operation follows links from destination to source endpoints, while a third traverses the link independently of the directionality of the endpoint associated with the current selection. (See appendix B for the descriptions of these operations.)

15.3.3 The browsing and management protocol

The browsing and management protocol is optional. It provides access to browsers and commands that manipulate hypermedia structures directly from the user interface of hypermedia-extended applications. This protocol includes no extra messages from the HSP to the application; the new messages are responses to requests for information from the HSP.

Messages from the HSP to hypermedia-extended applications It is generally not necessary for the HSP to communicate with the applications in order to support browsing and management. A notable exception is the need to update browsers to reflect changes that occur in the database. This need is addressed by the ChangedOnServer notification, as we'll see in section 15.3.4 on the multiuser protocol.

Messages from hypermedia-extended applications to the HSP The two operations that follow are examples of browsing and management messages sent from applications to the hypermedia service. Operations like the first are invoked with documents and selections as arguments. Those like the second operate on the hypermedia databases and structures themselves.

Applications invoke the InspectCompLinks operation on a document in order to gain an overview of the links to and from the document:

```
InspectCompLinks:    450
Usage: Show information about the links with anchors in the given
document.
Format: UserName,ApplicationID,opCode,nodeSpec
Response: (ResponseCode)
Example: kgronbak@daimi.aau.dk,emacs,450, /users/kgronbak/DHM/docs/
interface.tex
```

Applications invoke the OpenHyperSpace operation with the name of a HyperSpace object to add the hyperspace to the scope of subsequent FollowLink operations:

```
OpenHyperSpace:    600
Usage: Used to open a hyperspace on the server with a given ID (pair
of integers).
Format: UserName,ApplicationID,opCode,N,{HyperSpaceId,LockValue}*
Response: (N,{ResponseCode,HyperSpaceId,Lock}*)
Example: kgronbak@daimi.aau.dk,Webbrowser,600,1,1,875045420,2
```

15.3.4 The multiuser protocol

The ODHP includes several operations that coordinate collaboration among several users of the same hyperspaces.

Messages from the HSP to hypermedia-extended applications   The changedOn-Server operation is an example of a multiuser protocol message sent from the hypermedia service to the application. It informs the application that the component corresponding to the given document has changed on the server, perhaps because of edits another user has made:

```
ChangedOnServer:    803
Usage: Used to inform the external application that a given component
has been changed by another hypermedia client.
Format: ApplicationID,opCode,nodeSpec
Response: (ResponseCode)
Example: emacs,803,/users/kgronbak/DHM/docs/interface.tex
```

Messages from hypermedia-extended applications to the HSP   The two operations that follow are examples of multiuser protocol messages sent from applications to the hypermedia service. The operations typically are invoked with documents as arguments, but they may also operate on the hypermedia databases and structures themselves.

The RefetchComps operation is invoked to retrieve the most recent versions of components and the corresponding documents from the hypermedia service:

```
RefetchComps:       503
Usage: Refetch the components corresponding to the listed documents
from the database.
Format: UserName,ApplicationID,opCode,N,{nodeSpec}*
Response: (ResponseCode)
Example: kgronbak@daimi.aau.dk,emacs,503,2, /users/kgron-
bak/DHM/docs/interface.tex, /users/kgronbak/DHM/docs/protocol.tex
```

Applications invoke the SubscribeDoc operation on a document to cause notifications to be sent to the client whenever a specified event such as locking or updating is performed on the component in the hypermedia database corresponding to the document:

```
SubscribeComps:     504
Usage: Subscribe to specific notifications for components correspond-
ing to the given set of documents.
Format: UserName,ApplicationID,opCode,N,{nodeSpec}*
Response: (ResponseCode)
Example: kgronbak@daimi.aau.dk,emacs,504,1, /users/kgron-
bak/DHM/docs/interface.tex
```

15.4   Tailoring the application layer

Ideally, before a second- or third-party application uses the ODHP, it should be customized to present hypermedia operations in the user interface and to communicate ODHP messages to the open hypermedia service. For second-party

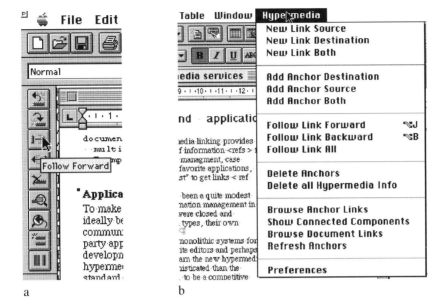

Figure 60
The Devise Hypermedia toolbar and menu added to Microsoft Word. (Word, unlike Excel, does not allow hierarchical menus.) *(a)* Toolbar extension for Word; *(b)* Word's menu extension.

applications, tailors can modify the source code at development time. But for third-party applications developed without hypermedia integration in mind, the tailoring requires the use of programming interfaces the applications might provide, in the form of APIs or macro languages.

15.4.1   Tailoring Microsoft Word

In this section we briefly illustrate how a third-party application, Microsoft Word, was tailored to provide Dexter-based hypermedia in the user interface and to support ODHP communication with the Devise Hypermedia system. Figure 60 shows how the tailored version of Microsoft Word appears to the user. Both the toolbar and the menu have been added to the application using Word's built-in macro language.

Each of the operations available on the toolbar or the menu invokes ODHP operations with DDE as the carrier protocol. Figure 61 illustrates how the NewLink operation is implemented in Word Basic.

```
Sub newLink
Print "Making new Source Link..."
Call WordToHM.sendWithOpCode("0000")
Print ""
End Sub


Sub sendWithOpCode(opcode$)
.
channel = connectToHM
If channel <> 0 Then
    item$ = "DocLockStatus,WinWord,800," + FileName$()",0"
    LockStatus$ = DDERequest$(channel, item$)
    Call menuEnabling.enableMenus(LockStatus$)
Else
    Goto endOnError
End If
.
opc = Val(opcode$)
REM Handle Newlink and AddAnchor (Source, Destination, Both) operations
Select Case opc
Case 0 To 2, 100 To 102
REM Check whether the current HyperSpace is open with write access
    If LockStatus$ = "1" Then Goto endOnError

    BMString$ = selIsBookmark$
    PosString$ = getPosition$
    If BMString$ = ""Then
        REM Compose LocSpec information depending on the
        REM access mode of this document
        If GetDocumentVar$("HMB_ReadOnly") = "Yes" Then
                BMString$ = getNewBookmark$("PositionMark")
        Else
                BMString$ = getNewBookmark$("BookmarkMark")
        End If
        EditBookmark .Name = BMString$, .Add
        RealSavedStatus = 1
    End If
    REM Compose argument string with bookmark ID and position
    ArgumentString$ = ",1," + BMString$ + PosString$
    Call myLib.ColorSelection
.
REM  Compose the command string and send it to DHM
cmdString$ = "WinWord," + opcode$ + "," + FileName$() + ArgumentString$
DDEExecute channel, cmdString$

endOnError:
DDETerminateAll
End Sub'********** End of sendWithOpCode
```

Figure 61
Excerpts from the newLink macro in Microsoft Word Basic.

The macro examples show how Microsoft Word composes ODHP command strings and sends them to the Devise Hypermedia service. Microsoft Word is only one of several applications that we have integrated with Devise Hypermedia. The three examples that follow posed even greater challenges.

15.4.2   Tailoring UNIX VI

Because the UNIX VI text editor does not support direct communication, we used a workaround. From VI to DHM we wrote simple VI macros that perform ODHP operations by executing shell scripts. The shell scripts invoke C programs to communicate via sockets to the DHM service. From DHM to VI we used X Windows-based communication to emulate keyboard input to VI. We used embedded text IDs to act as the object IDs of locSpecs.

15.4.3   Tailoring Microsoft EXCEL 4.0 for the Macintosh

Early versions of our Excel integration used remote control; rather than extending the interface of Excel with menus, we used AppleEvents to request and set selections in spreadsheets. Unfortunately, this meant that a two-part interaction was necessary to create or follow a link. After making the selection in MS Excel, the user switched to the hypermedia service application to invoke the appropriate action. In a later Windows integration, we used macros in the same way that we described for Word in section 15.4.1.

15.4.4   Tailoring Netscape for Windows

Netscape does not provide a macro language for tailoring the user interface. We were thus forced to use Windows low-level routines, as illustrated by the following examples:

· We attached the DHM menu to the menubar in Netscape using standard window and menu functions.

· Using Windows hooks, we caught the events generated when users selected items in the DHM menu.

· We used Netscape's implementation of the Software Development Interface API defined by Spyglass, Inc. to fetch and present URLs.

These examples show that hypermedia integration is still possible for applications that are less open than the extensively tailorable Word and Excel.

15.4.5 The challenges of application tailoring

Devise Hypermedia has taken significant steps toward providing an extensible Dexter-based hypermedia service to third-party applications. We now believe that integration through anchor-based linking can be realized on most platforms and with many application types.

But there are still a number of open issues. How can we more effectively avoid or detect invalid anchor values in third-party applications? How can we provide cross-platform hypermedia support for external files and third-party applications? For example, can the integrity of links in an MS Word document be preserved regardless of whether it is edited on a Mac or a PC? Finally, it is not clear how to support *cooperative* use of hypermedia for single-user tools like those that make up most office and CAD applications. How might we develop a hypermedia-based cooperative authoring environment based on MS Word, WordPerfect, or the like? Though these questions have no easy answers, we are confident that recent work on component-based software and distributed objects will begin to address some of the underlying issues.

15.5 Patterns for integrating third-party applications

This section presents two design patterns that address part of the work of integrating open hypermedia with third-party applications. The first pattern involves the form of the communication interface, while the second outlines the steps required to integrate an application.

Title: Open Hypermedia Interface
Context: Implementing open hypermedia systems that can integrate heterogeneous applications. The applications can be custom-made or developed by third-party developers. The applications and the hypermedia system may also run on different platforms.
Problem: To design a format and a set of operations for communicating between applications and a hypermedia system.
Solution(s): Define a logical interface to be supported by applications or wrappers. The interface can be specified in either of two ways:

· As a protocol with a specified textual message format
· As an object-oriented communication interface, together with the definitions of objects to be communicated

In both cases, the interfaces should be logically independent of the carrier protocols such as TCP/IP, CORBA, COM, DDE, and AppleEvents.
Examples: M2000, OHP, and the Devise Hyermedia protocol.
Related patterns: Depends on Hypermedia/Application Separation in chapter 12.

Title: Application Integration
Context: The implementation of open hypermedia systems that can integrate heterogeneous applications, be distributed, and support collaboration. Hypermedia structures are maintained as objects apart from the content.
Problem: To develop a versatile method of integrating new types of applications with a hypermedia service.
Solution(s): Fully integrate a hypermedia service with a new application by following these steps:

· Augment the hypermedia service with support for objects that model the new application as described in the Framework Tailoring pattern in chapter 13.
· Use the application's own tailoring mechanisms (such as API or scripting language) to enable communication through the open hypermedia interface to the hypermedia service process.
· Use the Application Tailoring pattern of chapter 14 to define the locSpecs to be communicated, including the information needed for ensuring anchor consistency as described in the Anchor Maintenance pattern in chapter 14.
· Use a persistent selection referenced by the object ID part of the locSpec whenever possible. A persistent selection, such as a Microsoft Word bookmark, is maintained by the application during editing.

Examples: Microcosm, Devise Hypermedia, and Chimera.
Related patterns: Depends on Layering (chapter 12), Framework Tailoring (chapter 13), Application Tailoring (chapter 24), Open Hypermedia Interface (chapter 14), and Anchor Maintenance (chapter 14).

16

Collaborative Hypermedia

> The next generation of hypermedia needs to drastically improve support for collaborative work in these two disparate but interrelated areas: the mechanics of simultaneous multiuser access to a common network, and the social interactions involved in collaboratively using a shared network. Supporting the mechanics of multiuser access involves extending the standard technologies for shared databases (e.g., transactions, concurrency control, and change notification) to handle the special requirements engendered by hypermedia. (Halasz 1988, p. 849)

The goal of providing support for collaboration was articulated by several of the early researchers in the hypermedia field. Engelbart (1984a; 1984b) was the first to develop a computer supported cooperative work (CSCW) system, NLS/Augment, that supported both asynchronous and synchronous cooperation on hypermedia material. Users could edit Augment statements in parallel, and even start a desktop conference, sharing a window between several workstations. KMS (Akscyn et al. 1988) features similar multiuser editing of frames based on an optimistic concurrency control mechanism; that is, KMS detects conflicts that users then resolve manually.

Intermedia (Garrett et al. 1986) was another pre-WWW system that provided support for multiple users cooperating on shared materials. Intermedia introduced the idea of superimposing external hypermedia structures, or webs, on a set of documents. Users created multiple public, group, and private webs that used the same documents. Intermedia also introduced the notion of annotation access as an addition to read and write access. Annotation access allows users to create links in documents for which they do not possess write access. Around the same time, the Notecards system (Trigg and Suchman 1989) was tailored with new card types, called *collaborator* and *history* cards, that trace changes and support coordination between authors taking turns on the same notefile.

Halasz, in his "Seven Issues" paper (1988), issued a call to hypermedia designers to support collaboration and versioning. He argued for long-term transactions, flexible locking mechanisms including interruptable locks, and event notifications for critical changes to shared structures. He also pointed out that certain aspects of cooperation cannot be supported technically, but must be handled by social conventions and coordination outside the scope of the hypermedia system.

During the late 1980s and the 1990s, hypermedia researchers built several prototypes and systems incorporating Halasz's ideas. For example, SEPIA (Streitz et al. 1992), EHTS (Wiil 1991), and Devise Hypermedia (Grønbæk et al. 1994) support event notifications and flexible locking for long-term transactions. SEPIA and EHTS are built on specialized hyperbases. In contrast, DHM applies general object-oriented database technology. These systems only support small-scale structures, typically using a file system shared over a local area network (LAN).

The WWW represents a move away from hypermedia structures that can be dynamically edited and annotated. However, there have been a number of systems that attempt to support cooperation on the web, including Futplex (Holtman 1996), BSCW (Bentley et al. 1997a), and ComMentor (Röscheisen et al. 1994). These systems are less sophisticated than the LAN-based systems mentioned above in that the web support consists mainly of form-based annotations and modifications to pages at given open points. Transactions and event notifications are not supported, nor are editing and linking capabilities adequate to meet the goals of researchers in the field.

Providing efficient and scalable support for cooperative hypermedia structuring is still a major challenge for the field of open hypermedia. Before discussing the potential of a Dexter-based framework and architecture in this area, we briefly review the major issues related to hypermedia support for collaborative work.

16.1   Collaborative work and hypermedia support

Engineering, architecture, system design, case handling, administration, and authoring are examples of application domains characterized by collaborative work among individuals who contribute to a shared overall task and often produce large bodies of documentation. Such work involves explicit communica-

	Same place	Different place
Same time (Synchronous)		
Different time (Asynchronous)		

Figure 62
The classic framework for classifying groupware systems.

tion and coordination, as well as implicit coordination through shared materials (Sørgaard 1987). Moreover, the collaborating users are often separated in time and space. Indeed, the classical framework for characterizing computer support within CSCW and groupware is the time/space matrix depicted in figure 62 (Ellis et al. 1991).

However, this framework is better suited to classifying the features of existing types of systems than to framing a design discussion for a specific type of system. The fact that the same hypermedia system might appear in all four cells tells us little about *how* the system supports a collaborative work practice on shared materials.

In discussing collaborative hypermedia in this chapter, we assume that the shared materials are accessible through an open hypermedia service, and organized as a collection of hyperspaces. The hyperspaces are in turn organized hierarchically into nested hyperspaces or other composites and, ultimately, into individual components. In this context, modes of cooperation support can be characterized according to how users coordinate work on shared materials at the level of hyperspace or component:

1. Divide and conquer.   The shared material is divided into disjoint parts, each managed by one user. The cooperation is loose and consists mainly of one user employing materials developed by others.

2. Turn taking.   Material circulates among a group of users. At most one user at a time is allowed to modify a given piece of material. Such a user typically holds a long-term lock that excludes others from modifying the given material.

3. Interleaving.   Users dynamically exchange write access during a session. Suppose, for example, that one user, A, wants to modify material currently locked by another user, B. A asks B to transfer the lock to A for some period of time, after which it is returned to B.

4. Simultaneous linking and structuring. Users can create and modify hyper-media structures for shared material simultaneously, but the material itself is locked according to one of the other modes. The hypermedia structures them-selves are either shared or private.

5. Alternative versions. Different users develop alternate versions of the same material. Users coordinate their contributions by merging the versions at a later time.

6. Mutual sessions. Two or more users work on the same material at the same time, that is synchronously, through a direct communication channel. Each operation immediately updates a shared copy of the material. Later, the users jointly invoke an operation to update the material in the hypermedia database. In a variant of this mode, a user's changes can be undone before other users see them.

7. Fully synchronous sessions. Users work synchronously as they do in mutual sessions, except that the material is visible and editable through a shared win-dow. In this mode, all users have exactly the same view of the material.

In real work situations, these modes are typically combined. In the rest of this section, we keep them separate to simplify the discussion of goals for open cooperative hypermedia services.

Collaborative hypermedia primarily addresses asynchronous cooperation on shared materials, as represented by the first four modes. These modes require support for awareness among users about who is doing what in the shared body of materials. To the degree that the material is structured by links and compos-ites, cooperation can take place through linked annotations to materials devel-oped by others. Linking in multiuser contexts is enabled by flexible locking mechanisms in the underlying hypermedia database.

The alternative version approach, mode 5, is also an asynchronous mode of cooperation that is appropriate for sharing, say, ASCII text (Magnusson et al. 1993). The need to merge versions, however, makes this approach difficult to support for general hypermedia structures. Efficient versioning and merging algorithms, developed primarily for ASCII text, have been difficult to apply to objects in a hypermedia database.

Modes 6 and 7, which support synchronous sessions, correspond to the tightly coupled cooperation modes introduced by (Streitz et al. 1992). The main differ-ence between mutual and fully synchronous sessions lies in whether a shared view is maintained. In a mutual session several users can edit the same component in the hyperspace without maintaining a single view, whereas in a synchronous session, all users have the same view of the hypermedia structures and content being edited. Both modes require extensions to the hypermedia system to support shared commitment of changes to the hypermedia database, as well as integration with shared window and computer conferencing systems.

In the next section, we discuss how a hypermedia architecture can support asynchronous modes of cooperation.

16.2   A Dexter-based collaborative hypermedia architecture

Our proposal for a collaborative hypermedia architecture extends the Dexter-based architecture presented in chapter 12. Cooperative editing of Dexter-based structures requires that the hypermedia database (HDB) support concurrency control through long-term transactions, locking, and event notification, as called for by Halasz (1988). Moreover, the HDB server should support peer-to-peer communication with the client processes, the hypermedia service processes (HSPs). Server to client communication is needed in order to distribute event notifications to the HSPs. The HDB can be either a special purpose hyperbase or a general object-oriented database (OODB) that physically stores objects in the storage layer.

The HDB usually only provides storage and concurrency control for those hypermedia objects that are stored explicitly in the database. In order to provide an open collaborative hypermedia service in which documents being edited and structured are stored apart from the HDB, we need mechanisms for concurrency control for the documents themselves. These mechanisms can be achieved either by extending the HDB, or by integrating the hypermedia service with a general document management system that manages both storage and access.

Figure 63 shows a version of the architecture presented in chapter 12, in which we have duplicated the HSPs and applications to run on multiple users' workstations. In this case, the documents of the application layer are handled by a shared document management system. The HSPs use a special purpose protocol to communicate with the document management system, in order to manage document locations and locks.

In the architecture shown in figure 63, the document management system conceptually belongs to the application layer, since it manages the content of

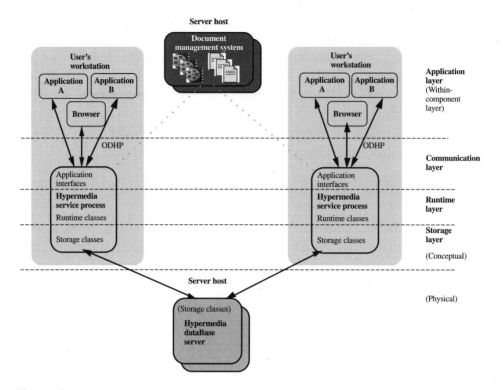

Figure 63
A collaborative hypermedia process architecture that includes a document management system.

hypermedia components. However, the document management system and the HDB can run on the same server host.

The HSPs are responsible for distributing event notifications received from the HDB server to the editors at the runtime layer, as discussed in section 16.3.3. If a document management system is employed, the HSP also has to communicate with it using a special purpose protocol different from the open data hypermedia protocol (ODHP).

The HDB server maintains information about its clients. In part, this is because the HDB is responsible for detecting changes to objects in the database and for notifying clients that have implicitly or explicitly subscribed to notifications about such events.

The collaborative hypermedia architecture proposed in this chapter is similar to the HyperForm (Wiil and Leggett 1992) and HyperDisco (Wiil and Leggett

1997) architectures, in which the tool integrators take on many of the same responsibilities as the HSPs. The main difference between the HyperForm/HyperDisco and Dexter-based architectures is the division of labor among the clients and servers. The Dexter-based architecture allocates responsibility for most structural management to the HSP level; the HyperForm/HyperDisco architecture, to the HDB level.

16.3 Support for collaboration at the storage layer

This section describes four storage-layer facilities, access management, concurrency control, event notification, and versioning, and relates them to the hypermedia structures defined by the Dexter-based framework. We are particularly interested in the range of granularities at which these facilities can be supported for Dexter-based hypermedia structures.

16.3.1 Access management

Supporting shared hypermedia structures requires managing access rights, that is, who may create, modify, and delete objects in the structures. In particular, we can assign attributes to hyperspaces, components, and refSpecs in the Dexter-based framework, indicating whether the objects are public or belong to a group or a specific user, and what access rights each category of user possesses. Such attributes might be in the form of UNIX file access rights. They could also be extended to provide the access for annotation proposed for Intermedia (Yankelovich et al. 1988), which allows users to create links and other structures without modifying the content. Figure 64 shows a possible framework for availability and access rights. The attributes it lists allow a session for a shared hyperspace to present only those objects for which the current user has access permission.

As in file systems, hypermedia objects should include attributes that indicate who is the owner, who was the last modifier, when the object was last modified, and so on.

16.3.2 Concurrency control

Specifying availability and access rights is not sufficient for the runtime management of objects that can be modified by multiple users. The hypermedia database needs concurrency control to coordinate users' work on the shared modifiable objects. For hypermedia databases, Halasz advocated long-term transactions as

	Access	Read	Write	Annotate
Availability				
Public				
Group				
User				

Figure 64
Possible combinations of availability and access rights for hypermedia structures.

a means for users to check out a piece of structure and content and work on it for a period of time (Halasz 1988). Such long-term transactions are supported by various explicit locking mechanisms.

The lock assigned to an object dictates the legal forms of access other users may have to the object over the course of a transaction. The database literature discusses a variety of lock types (Ahmed et al. 1991). Ideally hypermedia databases should support at least the following basic lock types for hypermedia objects.

· A *read lock* grants read access to the holder of the lock.
· An *exclusive read lock* restricts read access to the holder of the lock.
· A *write lock* grants write access to the holder of the lock.
· An *exclusive write lock* restricts read and write access to the holder of the lock.
· A *soft lock* allows the lock to be taken by other users under special conditions.

In the context of the Open Dexter framework, such locks allow coarse- and fine-grained locking at the following levels:

· Entire hyperspaces
· Individual components
· The content of a component[1]
· The anchors in a component
· Individual refSpec objects
· The pSpec in a component
· Attributes of a component

1. At the HSP level, locking the content of a component should be accompanied by a request to lock the corresponding document in the document management system.

Locking can support both short- and long-term transactions. The content lock is usually associated with a long-term transaction, for example, when the component is to be modified over an extended period of hours, days, or weeks. In contrast, the anchor lock is typically used for a short-term transaction, so that multiple users can create links and anchors in the component, in effect, simultaneously.

Systems like KMS (Akscyn et al. 1988) use a different method, optimistic concurrency control, to manage transactions and locks. With this method, all objects can be edited at any time; conflicting updates are detected only when the user commits changes to the hyperbase. In the case of a conflict, the second user to commit saves a copy of the component in question and usually merges her changes with those of the previous user. Optimistic concurrency control is most applicable for systems with small components, like KMS. Components with content of arbitrarily large size require more work to recover from editing conflicts, thus reducing the effectiveness of the approach.

16.3.3 Event notification

Event notifications are messages sent to users' client programs that signal the occurrence of events in the HDB. First proposed by Halasz (1988), hypermedia event notifications have been implemented in systems like EHTS (Wiil 1991) and Devise Hypermedia (Grønbæk et al. 1994).

An HDB's event notification mechanism signals such higher-level events on shared hyperspaces as

· Starting, committing, and aborting transactions
· Creating, deleting, and updating hyperspaces
· Creating, deleting, and updating components (atomic, link, or composite) within a hyperspace
· Creating, deleting, and updating refSpecs
· Changing the attributes of components
· Changing locks for hyperspaces and components

Receiving notifications of such events helps a user maintain an awareness of colleagues' work on relevant shared structures and contents.

Event notification mechanisms are typically accompanied by some means of filtering, so that users of shared hypermedia structures are not overloaded with irrelevant notifications. Users or their client programs stipulate to the hypermedia service which kinds of notifications they will receive using a subscription mechanism. Typically, users subscribe to notifications through a preference sheet or dialog box. Hypermedia client programs that must receive certain event notifications can perform automatic subscription.

16.3.4 Versioning

Versioning is the process of maintaining histories of changes to online documents and structures. Users employ versions to inspect and sometimes recover work from an earlier session. Early hypermedia systems like Xanadu (Nelson 1974) and HAM (Campbell and Goodman 1988) were designed with a back end that supports the versioning of nodes and links. Modern hyperbases (Haake 1994; Wiil and Leggett 1992) also support versioning of various kinds. For example, HyperForm (Wiil and Leggett 1992) can version any class of objects in the hypermedia data model being used.

Hypermedia researchers generally consider versioning to be in the purview of the hypermedia database. In particular, the means of storing version trees should be transparent to the user.[2] In the case of Dexter-based hypermedia, versioning should be provided by the database independently of the storage layer's class structure; in other words, the database should be able to version any object.

An outstanding question is how to coordinate the versioning of structural objects in the HDB with third-party document formats stored in the file system or in an external document management system. To our knowledge, no open hypermedia system can align structure versions with content versions in a general way. Solving this problem will almost certainly require extensions to the runtime layer and open hypermedia protocols, but more research is needed to design such facilities.

16.4 Concurrency control and event notification at the runtime layer

While access and availability can be specified as attributes of storage layer objects, locking and notification support is more complicated and requires

---

2. Version trees are usually stored using either copies of whole files or deltas, records of changes from one version to the next. The latter technique is typical of classical file system versioning mechanisms like RCS (Tichy 1983) and its successors.

```
SessionMgr: Class
(
    subscribe:...
    unSubscribe:...
    reload:...
    changeLock:...
    Reaction: Class(...)
    ...
)
```

Figure 65
Runtime operations that support notification and lock management.

extensions to the runtime layer. If the locking and notification mechanisms are generically available for objects in the HDB, then the storage classes, such as hyperspace, component, and refSpec, do not need to be extended. Nonetheless, the session manager needs operations to handle locking and to propagate event notifications received from the HDB server. These operations, attached to the sessionManager class, are shown in figure 65 and discussed in the following sections.

16.4.1 Concurrency control at the runtime layer

Management of locks and long-term transactions takes place at both runtime and storage layers. The HDB must assign and release locks for the objects as they are retrieved from and restored to the database. In addition, there are occasions when the HSP needs to explicitly request a lock on an object. For example, if a user has retrieved a component with a read lock and suddenly wishes to start modifying it, she should be able to call a ChangeLock operation requesting that the lock be upgraded. We propose to define ChangeLock for the sessionManager class so that the operation can be applied to hyperspaces, components, and refSpecs. ChangeLock operations can also apply to hyperspace entities at an arbitrary level of granularity, for instance, on a single attribute in an object or on an entire transitive closure of objects.

16.4.2 Event notification at the runtime layer

An application layer program generally requires a user interface for subscribing to event notifications, although some applications automatically subscribe for certain kinds of events. The subscription mechanism consists of Subscribe and UnSubscribe operations in the sessionMgr class of the runtime layer. These operations package relevant information about the subscription, including the set of objects covered, the event types to track, and a list of other users whose actions should be monitored. This information is sent to the HDB, which instantiates and registers a *reaction* object. Reaction objects are invoked when particular types of events occur for particular objects or sets of objects. Reaction objects may, depending on the implementation environment, accept code from the user to be executed upon receiving a notification.

When an event occurs, the HDB server generates a notification and propagates it to matching reaction objects in the HSPs. The reaction objects in turn propagate messages or procedure calls appropriate to the notification, to client editors or back to the database. The notifications are typically displayed by the applications and/or the hypermedia client in the application layer.

When a user receives a notification that a storage layer object has changed, she may wish to retrieve the new version of that object from the HDB. The Reload operation retrieves the latest version of a storage object, such as a hyperspace, component, or refSpec, from the HDB server. Reload may be invoked directly by the user or called automatically by runtime objects in reaction to event notifications.

16.5   An example of a collaborative hypermedia system

Devise Hypermedia (DHM) is a collaborative hypermedia system built from the Open Dexter framework. The Devise Hypermedia architecture is based on the collaborative hypermedia architecture in figure 63 (section 16.2). The collaborative version of DHM is implemented in a UNIX environment with UNIX processes implementing the HSP and the HDB. However, the architecture is not restricted to UNIX; we have implemented runtime client processes on Apple Macintosh and Wintel platforms that communicate with an HDB server on UNIX by means of TCP/IP. The HDB for Devise Hypermedia is implemented on a multiuser object-oriented database (Andersen et al. 1992). As described in the preceding section, we augmented this general-purpose database to support flexible locking and event notifications.

In this section, we discuss some of the design decisions made in the DHM implementation of collaborative hypermedia, and give examples from the user interface for the UNIX X-Windows prototype version of DHM. Together with engineers from the bridge construction project, we codeveloped a hyperspace which we used to experiment with new ways of organizing the engineering materials in hypermedia structures (Grønbæk et al. 1993).

16.5.1   Storage and retrieval

An object-oriented database stores objects according to a conceptual schema based on a programming language specification of the object classes. Objects are stored in and retrieved from the database in a way that is transparent to application programmers. The database itself is usually an object-oriented program, in which transactions are specified as classes. The facilities described in this and the next section belong to the interface of a transaction class and are listed in figure 66.

The Create operation is used to turn an object, identified by a reference, into a persistent root, in other words, a persistent object and a name used to retrieve it from the HDB server. The Create operation directs the database to store the object and its transitive closure the next time the client commits or checkpoints the enclosing transaction. Storing the transitive closure causes every object that can be reached from the root object through references to become persistent. Calling the Create operation grants the client a write lock on each created object. Subsequent calls to the Get operation retrieve the persistent object and its transitive closure from the database.

16.5.2   Long-term transactions

As called for by Halasz (1988), the OODB implementing the Devise Hypermedia database supports transactions of arbitrary length. Each call to Get to retrieve an object specifies a lock parameter. Currently there are only two lock values, write and read, but the OODB can be extended to include others, such as those described in section 16.3.2.[3] It's important to note that retrieving the transitive closure of an object is a logical operation. The physical retrieval is implemented by an incremental algorithm that ensures that only the objects actually being accessed are read into memory. A client can also explicitly reload an object along

---

3. DHM's read lock allows multiple users to have simultaneous read access to the same object. However, the OODB can also support "exclusive read" locks that allow only one reader at a time.

```
Transaction: Class
( ...
    Start:...
    Checkpoint:...
    Commit:...
    Abort:...
    Subscribe:...
    UnSubscribe:...
    Notify virtual:...
    Create:...
    Get:...
    Reload:...
    Update:...
    ChangeLock:...
    ...
)
```

Figure 66
Operations in the transaction class.

with its transitive closure. For example, the client, notified about a change to the object, may choose to retrieve the new version from the database.

Three operations are used to store changes to objects in the database: Update, Checkpoint, and Commit. Update, operating on a persistent object and its closure, directs the database to store changes made to these objects, the next time the client invokes Checkpoint or Commit on the transaction. Checkpoint is an operation that writes all the changes made during the transaction to the database. The Commit operation is a superset of Checkpoint; it saves changes, but also releases the lock and closes the transaction. The fine-grained specification of exactly which objects are to be stored is also used to distribute notifications for update events. An exception is raised if Update is invoked on an object that is open with only read access.

The lock for an object that has been retrieved from the database can be changed dynamically, usually during long-term transactions. Often users change the locks of objects in advance of modifying them or in order to release them for other users. The ChangeLock operation applies to all objects in the transitive closure of the given object. Changing the lock to one with higher permissions than those of the current lock forces a reloading of the objects to be locked.[4]

4. The user can optionally be asked for confirmation before the reloading is performed.

Changing the lock to one with lower permissions forces a checkpoint, since the objects may have been changed. When a write lock is released, another client can obtain a write lock, change the objects, and commit the changes to the OODB.

16.5.3 Examples of event notifications in Devise Hypermedia

Devise Hypermedia supports event notifications for several of the situations described in the preceding section. A DHM user subscribes to notifications by specifying an event type, a target object or class, and a user or group. Distribution of notifications occurs in the HDB server when a client performs Checkpoint, Commit, Start, Abort, or ChangeLock on a transaction. Upon receiving the notification, the client activates the applicable reaction objects, which in turn present the notifications in the user interface. Notifications enable users to monitor the activities of other users sharing the same hyperspace. Users can also directly inspect a notification log, as well as attributes of hyperspaces and components, to learn about other users' modifications.

Through a dialog box users subscribe to notifications about object retrieval, creation, updating, and access changes made by other users of the hyperspace. Subscriptions apply to specific objects or entire classes of objects. Figures 67–69 show how the DHM user interface manages component event notifications.

The user subscribes to notifications from a component browser or a specific editor. In figures 67–69, the user chooses to receive a notification and then later performs a Refetch on the appropriate object. If the Immediate Update option in figure 68 is checked, the reloading takes place automatically. In the next section we show how such facilities can support various collaboration situations.

16.6 Use of collaborative hypermedia support

The bridge construction project described in chapter 2 illustrates the importance of providing hypermedia support for asynchronous modes of cooperation. The shared materials include CAD drawings, pictures and videos of bridge elements, letters, procedure handbooks, scanned documents, spreadsheets, case records, and reports. One promising area for the application of hypermedia involves maintaining the rich set of relationships among case records, letters, reports, and work procedure handbooks. A hypermedia service can support the engineers' navigation through the material and their cooperative management of cases. For example, engineers need to monitor, and sometimes approve, changes to the

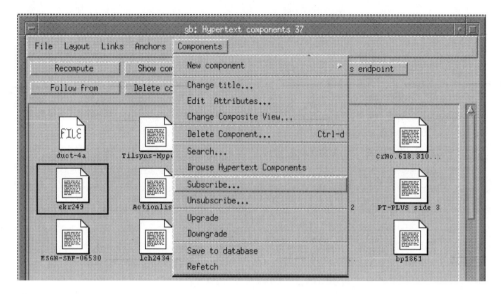

Figure 67
A Browser window that represents components in a hyperspace using icons. Selecting the Subscribe item in the Components menu brings up the dialog box shown in figure 68.

construction process for specific bridge elements, addenda to work procedure handbooks (SAB), and annotations made to drawings, reports, and the like.

The collaborative tasks of writing and gathering materials provide another opportunity for hypermedia support. At Great Belt, for example, engineers write and research reports together. Typically one engineer acts as editor, while others contribute and comment.

In this section, we present a series of abstracted use scenarios to illustrate the cooperation support a Dexter-based collaborative hypermedia system can provide. The scenarios offer detailed enactments of the asynchronous cooperation modes (1–4) from section 16.1 in the context of an open Dexter-based hypermedia system. The scenarios are abstract versions of work situations from the engineering project described by Grønbæk et al. (1993); they are formulated here using Dexter and HDB terminology.

16.6.1 Immediate updating for changed documents and structures
In the following scenario two users want the documents displayed on their screen updated as changes are made by other users.

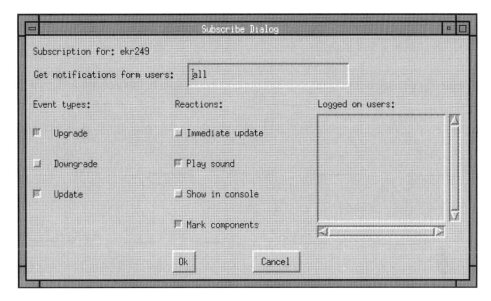

Figure 68
The dialog box for subscribing to notifications of component events. The subscribing user specifies the type of event, the desired reaction, and the set of users to monitor.[5]

Scenario: Jens and Susanne both start a session on hyperspace H1. Jens obtains a write lock on component C1. Susanne opens C1 with read access and subscribes to immediate updates when C1 is changed by other users. Susanne's instantiation for C1 now automatically updates itself whenever an update event notification appears, by reloading the most recent version of C1 stored in the HDB. Notifications of Jens's changes to C1 appear on Susanne's screen as soon as Jens commits them to the database.

16.6.2 Recording changes to shared documents and structures
In this scenario, users are again informed about changes colleagues make to particular documents. But rather than being immediately updated as in the previous scenario, change messages are written to a file or displayed in a console window.

5. Upgrade and Downgrade are events generated when a user changes a lock to one with a higher or lower value, respectively. The values in increasing order are read, exclusive read, write, and exclusive write.

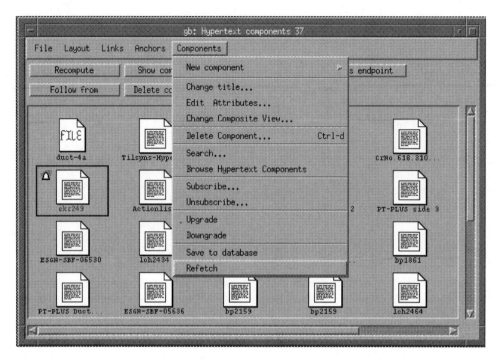

Figure 69
Invoking Refetch from the component browser window. The ekr249 component is marked with a bell indicating that an update notification was received. The user examines the changes by reloading the component using the Refetch command from the Components menu.

Scenario: Three users, Jens, Susanne, and Søren, start a session on hyperspace H1. Susanne opens C1 with read access and subscribes to the logging of changes to C1. Jens opens C1 with a write lock, and Susanne is notified with the following message in a console window: "Jens opened C1 with write lock Thursday 26.11.92 at 11:28:08." When Jens makes changes to C1 and commits them to the database, Susanne's console displays a second message: "Jens modified C1 Thursday 26.11.92 at 12:00:11." Then when Jens releases the write lock, Susanne sees: "Jens released the write lock for C1 Thursday 26.11.92 at 12:01:00." Later, Søren opens C1 with a write lock, whereupon this message appears in Susanne's console window: "Søren opened C1 with write lock Thursday 26.11.92 at 13:10:08."

16.6.3   Maintaining mutual awareness

The next two scenarios illustrate how users employ notifications to stay aware of their colleagues' work on shared structures.

Scenario 1:   Jens and Susanne both start a session on hyperspace H1, subscribing to notifications about who uses H1. Their console windows show a list of users who are currently invoking operations on H1. When Søren later starts a session on H1, his name appears on Jens's and Susanne's consoles.

Scenario 2:   Jens, Susanne, and Søren are working on the same case, for which Susanne is responsible. They start a session on the hyperspace H1. Susanne makes a composite CS1 containing components C1, C2, C3, and C4, corresponding to the currently active documents on the case. Susanne uses the Composite Subscribe command to subscribe to notifications of changes occurring to components contained in CS1. As a result, Susanne is notified whenever another user performs updates, lock changes, or other transactions on the four subcomponents.

   This illustrates the value of subscribing to events for entire classes of objects.

Scenario: Jens, Susanne, and Søren start sessions on hyperspace H1. Susanne subscribes to the logging of text component creation in H1, since she wishes to track any new annotations being made. Jens creates a new text component C1 in H1, edits the content and saves it, and Susanne is notified with a message to that effect on her console.

16.6.4   Exchanging locks

We next illustrate how users exchange a lock on part of the structure during a long-term transaction.

Scenario: Jens, Susanne, and Søren have all started a session on hyperspace H1. Jens obtains a write lock on component C1. Susanne and Søren both open C1 with read access. Søren subscribes to the logging of changes to C1. At some point Susanne requests a write lock on C1; she is immediately informed that Jens already has a write lock on it. Susanne calls Jens on the phone and asks him whether he is willing to save his changes and release the write lock. Jens agrees, saves his changes, and downgrades the write lock to a read lock, allowing Susanne to obtain a write lock. During this exchange, Søren receives notification messages to the effect that Jens saved changes, Jens released a write lock on C1, and Susanne obtained a write lock on C1. Finally, Jens subscribes to notifications of all changes to C1. Any subsequent changes to C1 that Susanne makes and commits now trigger notification messages to both Jens and Søren.

16.6.5 Simultaneous linking

In this scenario, multiple users manipulate link structures in a shared part of the hyperspace.

Scenario: Jens and Susanne each start a session on hyperspace H1, open text component C1 with read access, and subscribe to immediate updates on C1. Jens creates a public link from a text region in C1 to a text region in component C2. Jens commits the change by momentarily upgrading to a write lock on the anchor list of C1. Susanne's view of C1 is immediately updated with the new link marker. Susanne makes a second public link from C1 to component C3 and commits the change, causing Jens's view of C1 to be updated as well.

The foregoing scenarios illustrate the support for cooperation on shared hyperspaces that is possible with a Dexter-based collaborative hypermedia architecture, together with a multiuser HDB that supports access management, locking, and event notifications.

Problems arise, however, when we attempt to develop collaborative hypermedia that takes greater advantage of third-party applications for editing the contents of components. Unfortunately, most third-party applications are single-user and typically run on file systems that lack the access management, locking, and notification mechanisms built into an HDB. Even document management systems tend to lack the locking and notification support at the document level that could supplement the corresponding facilities of the HDB. For example, it is difficult to ensure that changing a Microsoft Word document triggers an event notification for the corresponding component. It is also difficult to use file system attributes to track changes to documents made independently of the hypermedia service. In short, the challenge is to develop an efficient *open* collaborative hypermedia service, one that can be integrated in the users' non-CSCW-enabled office environment.

16.7 Patterns for collaborative hypermedia

The five design patterns that follow outline our recommendations for integrating a hypermedia database to support collaboration with facilities for access management, concurrency control, event notifications, and versioning.

Title: Collaboration

Context: Open hypermedia systems that can integrate heterogeneous applications, be distributed, and support collaboration. Hypermedia structures are maintained as objects separate from the content.

Problem: To support users in authoring and navigating shared hypermedia structures.

Solution(s): At the storage layer of the architecture, integrate or implement a hypermedia database that can handle access management, locking, event notifications, and versioning of hypermedia structures and contents. At the runtime layer, implement a hypermedia service that manages multiple user sessions and provides access to a collaborative HDB.

Examples: Hyperform, HyperDisco, Devise Hypermedia, and SEPIA.

Related patterns: Depends on Access Management, Concurrency Control, Event Notification, and Versioning in this section.

Title: Access Management

Context: Open hypermedia systems that can integrate heterogeneous applications, be distributed, and support collaboration. Hypermedia structures are maintained as objects separate from the content.

Problem: To manage user access to shared hypermedia material.

Solution(s): Implement or customize a database so as to support at least the availability and access options for hypermedia structures shown in figure 64.

The access dimension distinguishes permissions to read the material, change the material, and add new links and hypermedia structures. The availability dimension distinguishes who is granted access to the hypermedia material. The read/write forms of access correspond to UNIX file permissions. The annotate access mode allows users to annotate documents that they do not have permission to modify.

Examples: Intermedia, HyperDisco, and Devise Hypermedia.

Related patterns: See also Concurrency Control, Event Notification, and Versioning in this section.

Title: Concurrency Control

Context: Open hypermedia systems that can integrate heterogeneous applications, be distributed, and support collaboration. Hypermedia structures are maintained as objects separate from the content.

Problem: To support collaborative manipulations of hypermedia material that maintain consistency across structures as well as content.

Solution(s): Provide a concurrency control mechanism for the hypermedia database using one of two approaches:

Optimistic concurrency control. Multiple users can modify the same structure or content at the same time, but only the user who saves first is allowed to change the original entities. Other users who attempt to save the modified object receive exception messages directing them to store their own copy of it.

Optimistic concurrency control works best when the components' content are small enough that conflicts are rare.

Locking and long term transactions. Before modifying a structure or content object, the user obtains a lock on the object and its dependent objects. The lock is released either explicitly by the user or automatically by the system when the user re-stores the object.

Locking may require traversing a portion of the hyperspace. For example, locking a composite substructure requires locking all the components referenced by the refSpecs of the composite.

Examples: Optimistic concurrency control is used in KMS and Devise Hypermedia, while locking is used in HyperDisco.

Related patterns: See also Event Notification, Access Management, and Versioning in this section.

Title: Event Notification

Context: Open hypermedia systems that can integrate heterogeneous applications, be distributed, and support collaboration. Hypermedia structures are maintained as objects separate from the content.

Problem: To make users aware of each others' interactions with shared hypermedia material.

Solution(s): Ensure that the hypermedia database:

· Maintains lists of clients subscribing to notifications of particular events
· Detects events that affect objects in the database, including creations, deletions, updates, and lock changes
· Sends notifications to connected subscribed clients
· Stores notification messages for subscribers not currently connected to the database

Examples: DHM's object-oriented hypermedia database and HyperDisco.

Related patterns: See also Concurrency Control, Access Management, and Versioning in this section.

Title: Versioning

Context: Open hypermedia systems that can integrate heterogeneous applications, be distributed, and support collaboration. Hypermedia structures are maintained as objects separate from the content.

Problem: To support users' collaborative and individual authoring and revision of hypermedia structures and content.

Solution(s): Add support for versioning of hypermedia structure objects to the hypermedia database. An integrated document management system, if available, can support versioning of the documents that comprise the content of the structures. Ideally, the versioning mechanism for the structure and that for the external content are integrated through extensions of the runtime layer and the open hypermedia protocol. However, to our knowledge, no system supports such open integrative versioning.

Examples: Four systems that only support versioning of database objects: Xanadu, HAM, HyperForm, and CoVer.

Related patterns: See also Access Management, Concurrency Control, and Event Notification in this section.

17

Distributed Hypermedia

[I]t seems possible that a 'network of networks' will, even in this century, become the nervous system of the world and that its applications will significantly change the way we live and work. . . . The value of information networks will depend critically upon their connectivity and their ability to connect any one of many sources to any one or more of many destinations. (Licklider and Vezza 1988, pp. 178–179)

This chapter discusses the problem of distributing hypermedia structures over local area networks and on the Internet. First, we briefly introduce distribution and the long-standing vision of distributed hypermedia. We then discuss how our Dexter-based framework and architecture are used to distribute hypermedia structures, particularly over enterprise networks using shared file systems. The last part of this chapter considers general design issues, including when to replicate and when to distribute hypermedia structures. Our closing design pattern outlines the strategies for structure distribution used by several of today's hypermedia systems. The next chapter focuses on global distribution using the WWW infrastructure.

17.1 Distribution

The term *distribution,* or *distributed computing,* refers to various means of dividing a complex system into smaller communicating processes. The processes may run on the same machine or on different machines; they may also run on the same local area network (LAN) or on different LANs. In some cases, the processes communicate using a client/server protocol by means of which clients request services from server processes. Alternatively, the processes can communi-

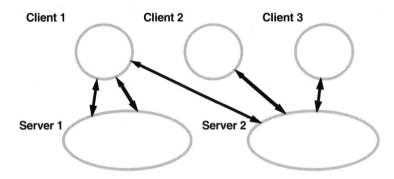

Figure 70
Peer-to-peer communication in which circular processes act primarily as clients; elliptical processes, as servers.

cate using a peer-to-peer protocol, a symmetric communication in which the initiative can originate with either party.

Distribution can be supported at different levels of abstraction. A common means of support is socket communication, in which data is decomposed into portable data formats and combined with operation encoding performed by the application programmer. Higher-level distribution support is provided by so-called distributed object systems, such as CORBA (Mowbray and Zahavi 1995), JAVA Beans/RMI,[1] Inter Language Unification (ILU),[2] and BETA (Brandt and Madsen 1993). These systems provide an analogous interface to objects in object-oriented programs. The distribution mechanism transparently invokes local procedures and passes object references as parameters to procedures on remote objects.

Unfortunately, because many systems that require integration still do not support a distributed object system, developers of open hypermedia system may need to support multiple distribution mechanisms.

17.2 Visions of distributed hypermedia

Over 30 years ago, the hypermedia pioneers Bush, Nelson, and Engelbart envisioned global distributed hypermedia databases that support searching, navi-

1. http://www.javasoft.com/beans/
2. ftp://ftp.parc.xerox.com/pub/ilu/ilu.html

gating, reusing, augmenting, and annotating what Nelson called the "docu-verse," a dynamic digital library containing the world's literature and scientific documentation.

Nonetheless, for several decades, hypermedia implementations were primarily local and nondistributed. NLS/Augment (Engelbart 1984b) was distributed over the early Arpanet, and a few systems like Intermedia and KMS (Akscyn et al. 1988) could be distributed in local area networks, but popular systems like HyperCard (Goodman 1987) and Guide (Brown 1987) were restricted to running on a single workstation. These early systems were all built around either a special kind of database, or a proprietary file format that made distribution especially challenging.

In the 1990s, however, parts of the pioneers' grand vision became a reality as the World Wide Web (Berners-Lee et al. 1992b) rapidly expanded. The web was constructed around simpler principles than the earlier systems: a tagged ASCII file format with embedded jump addresses, a uniform Internet addressing schema, and an enhanced file transfer protocol. The WWW has become a popular and efficient means of distributing information with simple hypermedia links over the Internet.

However, the vision proposed by Bush et al. and exemplified by the early systems includes people freely creating different types of links between documents in the docuverse. For example, Intermedia, the first system to use the term *web* for a hypermedia structure, was also the first to provide two-way links between blocks (the Intermedia precursors of Dexter anchors) outside the document content. Intermedia thus allowed users to create two-way links between documents they didn't own, activate different layers of links in the same body of documents, and inspect which documents were linked to a given document.

A few open hypermedia systems supporting distributed collaboration also appeared in the 1990s, including SP3/HB3 (Leggett and Schnase 1994) and HyperDisco (Wiil and Leggett 1997). Both support many of the early ideas about authoring, annotation, and collaboration that had been proposed for nondistributed hypermedia systems. However, the two newer systems are more limited than the WWW with respect to the volume and extent of distribution. As we discuss in the next section, this limitation is a function of the complexity in distributing open hypermedia and external hypermedia structures.

17.3   Challenges in distributing open hypermedia

Open hypermedia systems in general and the Dexter-based systems discussed in this book share the characteristic that hypermedia structures like links, composites, and paths, are maintained as objects apart from the data, that is, the documents being structured. Maintaining these separate structures imposes the challenges, discussed in chapter 14, of keeping the structures consistent with the content. The need to distribute structure in the form of hyperspaces and content raises new questions for open hypermedia system designers. Should structures reside on the same servers as the content they structure? Can we distribute the structures themselves? Should structures involving documents on several servers be replicated so as to be readily available when users access the documents? How do we guarantee the connection between a document editor and the relevant remote hypermedia service?

With regard to the WWW, these questions do not apply since on the web structure is typically embedded in content, and the content is easily distributed. Moreover, since links are only one-way, creation of a link only affects the source document; thus, only a local update is necessary.

For open hypermedia systems, there are several ways of addressing these design issues. In the SP3/HB3 system (Leggett and Schnase 1994), distributed and collaborative editing of shared documents and structures is supported by a process-oriented architecture. Links and anchors become processes and are responsible for behaviors such as monitoring document editing and traversing links established between remote documents. Persistent representations of links, called *associations,* are stored in distributed databases, in this case in instances of the HB3 hypermedia database. The choice of database depends on the association's owner rather than on where the associated documents reside. For example, private associations created by a user go into a local HB3 hyperbase on the user's workstation, while shared associations are stored in a group hyperbase running on a shared server.

The HyperDisco system (Wiil and Leggett 1997) supports distribution and collaboration for hypermedia structures and text documents. The structures and documents are stored in so-called workspaces, or local hypermedia databases that can be distributed over the Internet. Access to workspaces is facilitated by tool integrators, hypermedia runtime processes that connect to several workspaces at the same time. HyperDisco supports the creation of links across workspaces.

A cross-workspace link is replicated in all the workspaces that contain documents it references. Links are thus readily accessible from local documents in situations where remote servers are unavailable. However, this strategy creates a potential maintenance problem: a local change to a document must be communicated to all the workspaces that contain links to or from the document.

17.4   Open hypermedia services in distributed environments

As the preceding section argues, the design of distribution support depends on whether hypermedia structures are merged into the data or separated from it. Just as important is the question of how the file system gains access to documents. On the one hand, in a shared file system environment, such as a LAN or an intranet, content editors can be integrated directly with the open hypermedia service as described in chapter 14. The editors can then work on the content files in the locations where they are stored. On the other hand, in a wide area network (WAN) or on the Internet, though editors may still be integrated with the open hypermedia service, users usually retrieve a document using HTTP or FTP into a local environment before editing. Problems arise if multiple users fetch the same file for editing in different places without concurrency control for the HTTP and FTP ports on the remote server. This section primarily considers distribution issues that arise in a shared file system environment; the next chapter discusses the distribution of external structures on the Internet using the WWW infrastructure.

17.4.1   Open hypermedia distribution in a shared file system environment

Open hypermedia distribution and support for cooperation can be achieved in a shared file system environment by extending a single-user nondistributed architecture. When the documents structured by the hypermedia service reside at the same logical (or physical) address for editing as for viewing, we can apply the approach described in chapters 14 and 15 for the nondistributed situation. To enable distribution, the hypermedia service processes (HSPs) and databases (HDBs) must provide concurrency control and the other collaboration support mechanisms described in chapter 16. At the same time, distribution requires that the HSP communicate externally with, for example, a document management system, to coordinate access to the files and to guarantee that the concurrency control policy also applies to the structures managed in the HDB. In the distributed situation, the hypermedia service and database cannot solely control access to documents, since several HSPs may attempt to gain access to a single document whose structures reside on multiple HDBs.

The Dexter-based architecture depicted in figure 71 allows multiple clients and servers to be distributed on workstations and server hosts in a network. A local area network or a closed network in a distributed organization allows a tighter coupling between the interacting processes. For instance, all the workstations may act as trusted hosts while the shared file system (for example, UNIX NFS, Windows NT, or Apple Workgroup Servers) permits hypermedia-enhanced applications on any machine to access documents and the HSP. It is possible to use ordinary office applications to edit documents residing on servers on the network, provided that the users have write access to the files in shared directories.[3] A shared file system also makes it easy to track which files users open for editing.

In shared file system environments, we advocate a division of labor between clients and servers in which the HSP runs locally on the user's workstation and integrates applications using inter-application communication, as shown in figure 71. In this situation, the platform-specific communication facility (such as DDE or OLE automation on Windows) supports communication between the applications and the HSP. Communication between the HSP and the HDB can use TCP/IP or a distributed-object mechanism like CORBA or Java RMI, which provides a natural extension of the object-oriented approach used in the framework. We applied such a combination of mechanisms in the implementation of the distributed version of the Devise Hypermedia system. In DHM, communication between applications and the HSP is implemented by means of standard communication facilities such as DDE, AppleEvents, or TCP/IP sockets, whereas communication between the HSP and HDBs is implemented by means of a distributed-object mechanism (Brandt and Madsen 1993) supported by the implementation language Mjølner BETA (Knudsen et al. 1993; Madsen et al. 1993).

This shared file system approach to distribution meets some of the requirements posed by the Great Belt scenarios presented in chapter 2. In particular, users with proper access rights should be able to open files with their favorite applications anywhere in the distributed organization and apply the hypermedia structures residing on HDBs in the network to the documents they open. At Great Belt, different kinds of documents, for example, CAD drawings and

---

3. Unfortunately, however, addressing has to be based on physical paths to files unless a company-wide document-management system is used.

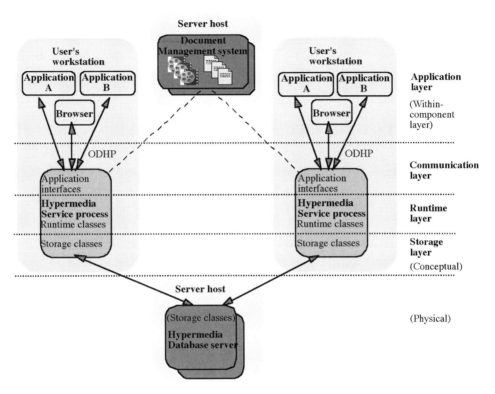

Figure 71
A possible distribution of clients and servers in a shared file system environment. The document management system, according to this architecture, belongs to the application layer since it manages content for hypermedia structures.

incoming and outgoing correspondence, are registered in separate special-purpose document management systems.

17.4.2 Open hypermedia distribution on the Internet

Shifting from a shared file system environment to the Internet complicates the work of distributing open hypermedia. On the WWW, remote documents are often edited first as a local copy and later uploaded to the server. In such situations, it is impossible to tell from looking at the file whether a copy is being edited somewhere else on the Internet. Such information has to be kept on the server hosting the document. This is not possible using current Internet protocols, but it may soon be achievable through an initative called WebDAV, Distributed Authoring and Versioning on the Web.[4] The WebDAV group is proposing an extension to HTTP that supports authoring and versioning. These facilities should support a distribution mechanism for open hypermedia that treats the web more like a shared file system. In the meantime, an approach like the one described in chapter 18 is needed.

17.5   Distributing and replicating hypermedia databases

Open hypermedia systems depend on data stored in a separate database apart from the documents. In a distributed environment, this dependency raises a number of organizational and infrastructural questions. How much overhead does hyperspace data add to a set of documents? Does a hyperspace have to reside on a single database server? Can a hyperspace be replicated on multiple servers? Hyperspace data is a critical resource for an open Dexter-based system; thus, in a distributed system, servers that manage critical application resources run the risk of becoming significant bottlenecks. This section discusses the problem of coordinating hyperspaces and their contents in a distributed environment.

17.5.1   The overhead involved in coordinating structures with contents

In an open hypermedia system, the information contents are usually stored apart from the hypermedia structures, although some system architectures and databases allow a mixture of content and structure storage in databases (Leggett and Schnase 1994; Wiil and Leggett 1997). In this section, we explore the computational overhead of keeping external structures in hyperspaces consistent with the contents maintained on file systems or in document management systems.

Choosing to store contents and structures on different servers requires access to several servers in addition to the one where the document resides. The additional overhead in access time is hard to estimate. For example, the time needed to establish server connections on the Internet is highly dependent on traffic load. In any case, open hypermedia services require efficient servers with high bandwidth access to reduce overhead to a minimum.

Fortunately, hypermedia structures are usually much smaller than their contents. For example, the graphic images in a document need much more space

4. http://www.ics.uci.edu/~ejw/authoring/

than the links that interconnect it with other documents. Thus, the fact that a hyperspace includes graphics-intensive documents as well as links does not make the hypermedia database storing the hyperspace a bottleneck. Assuming that the server access penalty is the same for content and structure, the bottleneck tends to occur when transfering and rendering the graphics. In less extreme cases, hyperspace data adds some minimal overhead to the transfer of information over the network.

Let's consider an example from Devise Hypermedia. A full-fledged DHM component sent over the network typically requires a few hundred bytes, depending on the number of its anchors, refSpecs, and user-defined attributes.[5] Establishing a link between anchors in two documents results in the creation of three components (two atomic components and a link component), which together require less than half a kilobyte of storage. Creating more links between the same documents only adds link components and anchors, not new atomic components. For example, creating five links between anchors in two documents adds as little as a single kilobyte in storage. For typical documents this overhead is negligible. Morever, the sizes of objects to be communicated can be compressed, further reducing the transfer overhead.

17.5.2 Distributing and replicating hyperspaces

When distributing Dexter-based hypermedia structures, we also need to consider how to distribute the structure objects themselves. The overarching hyperspace objects, in particular, may need to be distributed over several databases.

As discussed in chapter 8, hyperspaces represent an encapsulation of structure corresponding to a certain subject, task, or case, and belong to one or a group of users. The hyperspace contains a set of components that reference documents stored in arbitrary places on a shared file system. The structure and contents of a hyperspace as well as the hyperspace itself can be distributed. In this section, we discuss several approaches to the distribution of hyperspaces across multiple hypermedia database (HDB) servers.

A distributed hyperspace might have its attributes and overarching data structures stored on one HDB server, while the component data structures are distributed across other HDB servers. This approach is exemplified in the Hyper-Wave system (Maurer 1996) for the Internet, where a root collection on a central

---

5. This is a conservative estimate of the space overhead; specific databases may further compress the data.

server contains all other collections in a particular part of the world. Alternatively, to reduce bottlenecks and the dangers of server dropout, the shared hyperspace attributes and data structures could be replicated on each HDB server that contains a subset of the components. This approach corresponds to the KMS strategy of replicating the master file on all servers that store subsets of a frameset (Akscyn et al. 1988).

Hyperspace distribution requires HDB-to-HDB communication, which is reminiscent of Ted Nelson's (Nelson 1981) backend-to-backend (BEBE) protocol. Distributed-object systems and emerging OODB systems (Brandt and Madsen 1993; Mowbray and Zahavi 1995) support the distribution of aggregate objects over multiple physical servers. The HDB-to-HDB communication is necessary to keep the replicated objects updated and to access remote components in a way that is transparent to the client processes.

There are several options for tailoring the classes of our open Dexter framework to support the distribution of hyperspaces. One is simply to replicate all the hyperspace attributes and component set data structures. A reference in one of these data structures needs to resolve locally if the component reference is on the same server. Otherwise, the reference should transparently resolve to the appropriate remote server. This solution, however, requires replicating potentially large data structures.

Another option is to use nested hyperspaces, as described in chapter 8, to encapsulate one component subset for each HDB server. Each local hyperspace session is responsible for managing its local set of components; the session only accesses remote hyperspaces to resolve cross-hyperspace links. This solution reduces the number of references that have to be shared and replicated to those that belong to the root hyperspace; namely, references to each of the nested hyperspaces.

In a distributed-object environment, the object broker addresses distributed HDBs in a way that is transparent to the application programmer (Mowbray and Zahavi 1995). In a more conventional implementation, without object distribution, the addressing of remote components is handled explicitly, for example, by using a name service along with URL or URN addresses for remote HDBs. See Anderson (1997) for further discussion of these and other approaches to open hypermedia integration on the web.

As this section shows, the problem of distributing hyperspace structures turns on the question of which substructures should be distributed and which replicated to ensure local efficiency and independence of the root hyperspace server. The next section summarizes these design options in a pattern.

17.6   A pattern for distributed hypermedia

Our design pattern for this section outlines the strategies for structure distribution taken by several current hypermedia systems.

Title: Structure distribution

Context: Hypermedia structures maintained as objects separate from the content. Hypermedia support is provided for multiple users who are geographically separated, but working together on shared materials. Sharing includes browsing and editing, as well as creating new material.

Problem: To manage access to both local and remote hypermedia databases. Hypermedia services must maintain structures across multiple (remote) databases and coordinate user collaboration on remote and local material.

Solution(s):   Use distributed name services to allow hypermedia service processes to access both local and remote hypermedia databases. Support cross-database hypermedia structures, which can include links with endpoints in components from different databases, and composites whose members live in different databases. There are three main approaches to maintaining distributed hypermedia structures:

· centralized management
· structure replication
· centralized management combined with replication to support fault tolerance

In KMS and HyperWave, the basic containment structures (framesets and collections, respectively) are centralized: there is one top frameset or collection for the whole world. In KMS, the top frameset is replicated for fault tolerance.

  In HyperDisco there is no centralization; instead, links are replicated. Microcosm/DLS and DHM/WWW neither centralize nor replicate, but combine links from different distributed databases into the same web page. For a further description of DHM/WWW, see the design pattern Integrating Structures on the World-Wide Web in chapter 18.

Examples: HyperDisco, KMS, MicrosCosm/DLS, DHM/WWW, and HyperWave.

Related patterns: Depends on Structuring by Containment in chapter 8, Layering in chapter 12, and Collaboration in chapter 16.

18

Open Hypermedia and the World Wide Web

The Hyper-G project at Graz University of Technology builds upon the WWW and tackles some of its main shortcomings: in particular the lack of composite and hierarchical structures, the embodiment of links within documents and the inadequate provision for cross-server and focused searches. This is why we refer to Hyper-G as a "second generation" Web system. (Maurer 1996, p. 18)

This chapter discusses how to augment the web with Dexter-based hypermedia services that store anchors, links, and composites apart from the web pages. Although, as we discussed in chapter 4, the web has significant limitations with respect to dynamic link creation and sharing, its support for basic linking offers an effective tool for distribution. Rather than the naive goal of replacing the web with a Dexter-based system, we advocate augmenting the web with Dexter-based hypermedia services in order to support, for example, distributed work groups that share a body of web documents. In this chapter, we start by reviewing existing systems that provide external structures for web documents. Then we illustrate how the Dexter-based architecture and framework can be used to develop a general and platform-independent open hypermedia service for the web. Our closing design pattern compares two strategies for integrating structures maintained in hypermedia databases with the web.

18.1 External hypermedia structures for the web

Today's World Wide Web is still a far cry from the early visions of globally distributed hypermedia described in chapters 8 and 17. Fortunately, research involving web-based link services–storing link information apart from document contents–is well underway. Several systems already provide special-purpose hypermedia support for the web, including guided tour systems like Walden paths

(Furuta et al. 1997) and Footsteps (Nicol et al. 1995), and annotation systems such as ComMentor (Röscheisen et al. 1994). These systems preprocess the web pages, inserting navigation buttons and annotation markers to represent special-purpose structures, before the pages are presented to the user in an ordinary web browser.

HyperWave (Andrews et al. 1995; Maurer 1996) and Microcosm's Distributed Link Service (DLS) (Carr et al. 1995) go further in providing general support for link services. Both systems support the creation of nonembedded links to web pages. They store these links in hypermedia databases on Internet-based servers. These next-generation web systems are nonetheless in their infancy with respect to linking inside pages, particularly nontext pages; linking in the course of editing a document; distributing hypermedia databases; and supporting collaboration. For example, distribution on the web is based on the transfer of files via HTTP. Distributed object-based hypermedia systems could go beyond the web by supporting cooperative hypermedia linking of open third-party applications, as discussed in chapter 14.

Before discussing our proposal for Dexter-based web services, let's briefly review two of the existing systems that add external structures to the web.

18.1.1 HyperWave

HyperWave, originally called Hyper-G, was developed at Graz University of Technology in Austria, starting in 1993 (Andrews et al. 1995; Maurer 1996). It uses external hypermedia structures stored in an object-oriented database to support hierarchical navigation, linking, and attribute/content search for documents that reside on special servers. HyperWave provides a data model with classes such as the document, link, cluster, collection, and search. The document class corresponds to the Dexter atomic component; the link class to a Dexter bi-directional link with exactly two endpoints; and cluster, collection, and search to different forms of the composite. HyperWave employs its own SGML document format called HTF, which is HTML-compatible. Using special-purpose browsers–Harmony for UNIX and Amadeus for PC-Windows–users create external links to existing web pages, as shown in figure 72.

Using standard web browsers such as Netscape Communicator, users gain access to HyperWave pages, view attributes and metainformation, and perform HyperWave searches. However, only the HyperWave browsers support the creation of structure.

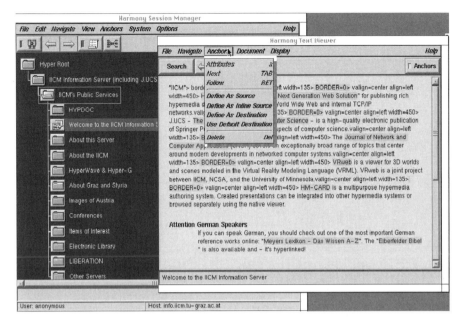

Figure 72
HyperWave's user interface. On the left side of the screen is an overview of a collection hierarchy; on the right side, a text viewer and the pull-down Anchors menu used to create links.

18.1.2 Microcosm's Distributed Link Service

Microcosm's Distributed Link Service (DLS) (Carr et al. 1995) was developed at the University of Southampton in the United Kingdom beginning in 1994 (Carr et al. 1995). DLS is built on Microcosm's open hypermedia system (Davis et al. 1992), and thus presents the Microcosm data model with its generic, local, and specific links stored in link bases, called *filters*. DLS is available through a pop-up menu, attached to the window title bar of the standard Netscape browser, as shown in figure 73. The menus let users connect to Microcosm link bases on the Internet, through which they follow and create links stored apart from the base web documents. Before the documents are presented in the browser, they are prepocessed by DLS to merge in the external links.

18.1.3 Weaknesses of the existing systems

HyperWave and Microcosm's DLS break new ground in providing value-adding hypermedia services to web documents. However, both systems have limitations

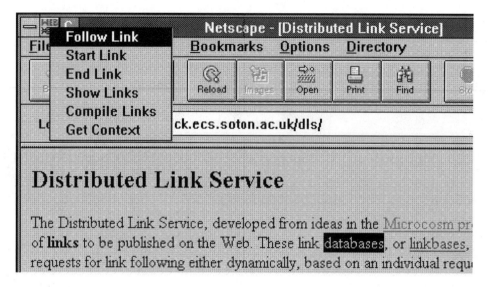

Figure 73
The Microcoms DLS interface on the Windows platform.

that we believe it is possible to overcome. HyperWave requires a special browser (and currently also a special text document format, HTF) to enable the user to take full advantage of the system, in particular, to create links and collections. Relying on a special browser and a special format forces developers to support plug-ins and maintain compatibility with new versions of HTML.

Microcosm has a slightly different limitation: supporting application independent hypermedia menus necessitates low-level patching of the browser in the window system of the given platform. This platform-dependence requires maintaining multiple window-system-specific pieces of code across new versions of browsers and window systems.

Finally, neither of the existing systems provides the collaboration support we describe in chapter 16.

18.2   Augmenting the web with Dexter-based hypermedia services

This section presents the design of a Dexter-based hypermedia service and the extensions required at all four layers of the architecture (Grønbæk et al. 1997a).

Providing Dexter-based hypermedia support for the web requires only modest extensions to the framework classes. The Dexter-based framework is sufficiently general to model the web and a web component with tailored anchors and locSpecs (for a discussion of locSpecs, see chapter 4). The difficulty lies in integrating the Dexter-based and WWW-based architectures rather than in integrating their respective hypermedia models.

18.2.1 Overall architecture integration

Architectural integration involves, in part, the work of tailoring described in chapter 13. In particular, the Dexter-based hypermedia service needs to be integrated with web browsers—in the application layer—to provide a user interface for the extended functionality, and with the communication layer to support communication between clients and the hypermedia service. There are several ways of providing application layer integration, as in the two previously discussed systems, HyperWave and Microscosm DLS. For the Dexter-based architecture, we propose the use of so-called applets, which it's preferable to write in a platform and browser independent programming language such as Java (Flanagan 1997). Applets are small programs that run in a restricted environment,[1] and are, at least in theory, platform neutral.[2] The communication between applet and HSP can be supported either by traditional CGI (common gateway interface) scripts or by a direct two-way communication facility such as TCP/IP, RMI (remote method invocation), or CORBA (common object request broker architecture). However, two-way symmetric communication is required in some cases, for example, to provide server notifications to clients in a collaborative setting, as described in chapter 16. Moreover, the runtime and storage layer classes must be specialized to model web documents. Figure 74 depicts the architectural integration of a Dexter-based hypermedia service with the web.

In figure 74, the applet in the application layer extends the user's favorite web browser so as to support communication with the DHM service. The browser extension connects to one or more hypermedia database servers that add link and composite structures to the web pages being visited. The browser can still

1. Because applets are compiled to run on a virtual machine, they need not be written in Java, though most still are.
2. However, in practice, they sometimes depend on the platform and, especially, the browser.

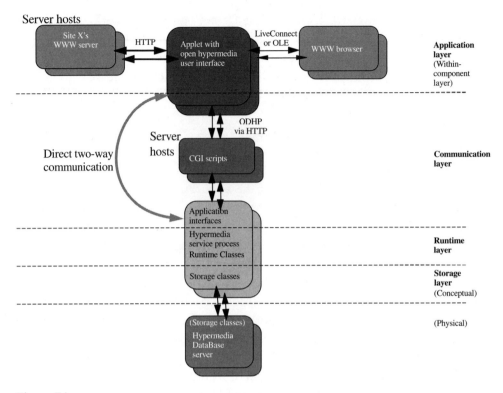

Figure 74
A Dexter-based architecture that augments the web with an open hypermedia service.
Web browsers and documents become part of the application layer of the architecture.
The modules from the communication level and below run on the server host; only the
modules in the application layer run on the client workstation.

communicate directly with web servers without going through the extension
module. However, the module is necessary to gain access to the external links
available in the document.

In the latest web browsers from Netscape and Microsoft,[3] designers can use
Java applets and scripting to integrate external structures with ordinary web
documents. In the next section, we discuss how to provide the functionality of a
Dexter-based service on the web through such standard browsers. Our description of the approach is organized according to the layers of the architecture.

3. As of this writing, the latest versions are Netscape Navigator 4.0 and Microsoft
Internet Explorer 4.0 (hereafter referred to as Navigator and Explorer). However, this
chapter mainly discusses experiences with version 3.x of both browsers.

18.2.2 Application layer integration

Most of the effort of integrating Dexter-based hypermedia with the web occurs at the application layer. In particular, integrators need to provide a platform-independent extension to the users' web browser. Toward that end, we recommend writing a general-purpose Java applet that manages browser integration and communication with the hypermedia service process (HSP). In the web architecture, HTTP and CGI scripts are typically used for communication between the browser and the HSP. Thus the HSP runs on a server host rather than on the users' workstations, as we propose in chapter 17 for environments with a common file system. This change increases the work load for the server hosts, although both the HSP and the hypermedia database (HDB) can be distributed across multiple hosts to improve performance.

The Java applet at the application layer should provide a user interface for the hypermedia service functionality and use the open hypermedia protocol to communicate with the HSP, as described in chapter 15. The applet should also manage the presentation of links in HTML documents.

Merging structure and content   As we discussed in chapter 4, integrating external hypermedia structures with content usually involves placing locators in the material and marking those placements (section 4.7). This section focuses on HTML, where marking placements requires inserting structural information directly into the material.

When augmenting the web with an external hypermedia service, we face two major client-side challenges:

1. To present the new links as naturally as possible

2. To maintain control over the document (and thus link) presentation

The most reasonable solution to the first problem is to make the links resemble ordinary links in the web document, and possibly to use a different color, which indicates the difference between an embedded link and an external structure. This markup requires access to the document before it reaches the browser, in order to insert external links. In addition, control over the displayed document must be maintained in order to continue to insert links from the HSP. Although we present our approach to these challenges for the Netscape Navigator browser, a similar method could be applied to MS Explorer.

In its present form, Navigator offers the powerful combination of (Java) applets, Javascript, and plug-ins. The Java language is supported by a variety of powerful and increasingly stable class libraries that ease the work of development. Javascript programs are interpreted when the HTML document is parsed, and as such can be used for HTML document creation. Javascript has suffered from continuous development, but is now fairly stable. Plug-ins are modules written for specific platforms and integrated in the browsers through a standard application programmer's interface. Plug-in modules are in widespread use for the rendition of data types not supported directly by the browser.

Our applet is composed of several threaded lightweight processes, linked together by a stream of data originating from the web server and the hypermedia service process and ending up in the Navigator frame, as diagramed in figure 75. Java threads are employed to maximize parallelism and performance. The data streaming is implemented so that new components can be added seamlessly as needed.[4]

The left side of figure 75 shows the flow of the HTML document through the applet, from the web server to the Netscape frame. The right side shows the transformation of a frame of HTML text, a single line that cites the Japanese author Kenzaburo Oe.

The URL of the original document is sent to the HSP, which returns an anchor encoded as a locSpec. The applet caches the locSpec information, and inserts a link containing a reference to the locSpec in the document, at the location indicated by the locSpec. This link is later encapsulated in Javascript, to ensure that the Navigator calls the applet when following links. Finally, the line is passed to a Javascript procedure printFrame which prints the line in a Netscape frame.

A user inputs the URL of the desired document either directly by typing in the applet window or indirectly by clicking on a link in the Navigator frame. The applet checks the URL for validity, and if no HTTP errors are reported, turns it over to the first part of the stream shown in figure 75. Standard Java library classes manage the task of actually retrieving the document.

The applet communicates with the HSP using CGI scripts, as described in section 18.2.3. The applet typically constructs messages for the HSP that contain an opcode and a locSpec. The server returns a stream consisting of locSpecs that

4. Currently, in Devise Hypermedia's WWW integration, links are inserted in the document stream according to their position and offset in the ogiginal HTML document. Because HTML documents are apt to change, we expect to extend the Java program to recognize the contents of link anchors. (See the Anchor Maintenance pattern in Chapter 14.)

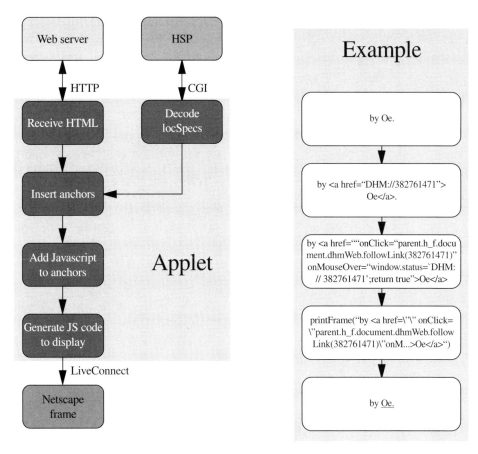

Figure 75
The architecture of an applet that merges external structures and the contents of web documents.

encode the locations of the anchors. The applet decodes this information and makes it available to the Java thread, which inserts links in the HTML stream. An exception is raised if the time stamp of an anchor is earlier than the time stamp of the document, alerting the user to the possibility that the anchor is corrupt as the result of recent modifications to the document.

The insertion of Javascript code takes place downstream from link insertion. In order to maintain control over the displayed documents, the applet must be used for each subsequent link traversal. To this end, we insert Javascript code in every link, including ordinary URLs, so that clicking a link calls our applet with the appropriate parameters, rather than directly causing the browser to retrieve a new document. However, in the recently released Netscape Communicator 4.x, Javascript control is no longer necessary, because the browser provides access to a richer set of events that occur in the browser frame. Applets in that context can catch every link-following event and do the necessary processing.

Finally, the Javascript PrintFrame function directs the LiveConnect interface to present the processed document to the user.[5] Once the document is generated and presented, the user can click any link, again causing the applet to execute the processing stream. A user can break out of this cycle by manually entering a URL or by selecting a bookmarked URL in the 3.x versions of Navigator, which cannot catch browser navigation events. The 4.x versions do permit catching such events, which makes it possible to have the applet permanently in control of the navigation.

An example of an applet user interface The document presented to the user consists of two frames. A hidden frame contains the applet and supporting Javascript functions; a second, visible frame contains the user's document. The following sequence of user interactions with DI IM/WWW applet (Grønbæk et al. 1997a) illustrates the idea.

Figure 76 shows how the applet can be used to display a web document in Netscape Navigator. The Hypermedia menu of the applet includes operations to create, follow, inspect, and delete Dexter-based links.

Figure 77 shows the link dialog box, which is required because, for security reasons, Netscape Navigator does not allow direct marking of links in the document frame. The user has selected the word *DEVISE* as source endpoint for a link; no destination endpoints have been selected.

Link traversal resembles ordinary web link following users click on hightlighted parts of the text. The main difference arises in situations where a link has more than one destination. In that case the applet presents to the user a list of the possible endpoints to visit, and the user decides which to open.

---

5. Netscape introduced LiveConnect to facilitate communication between JavaScript programs, Java applets and plug-ins (http://home.netscape.com/comprod/products/navigator/version_3.0/building_blocks/liveconnect/index.html). Java applets can manipulate JavaScript objects and methods, and vice versa, and both can control appropriate plug-ins.

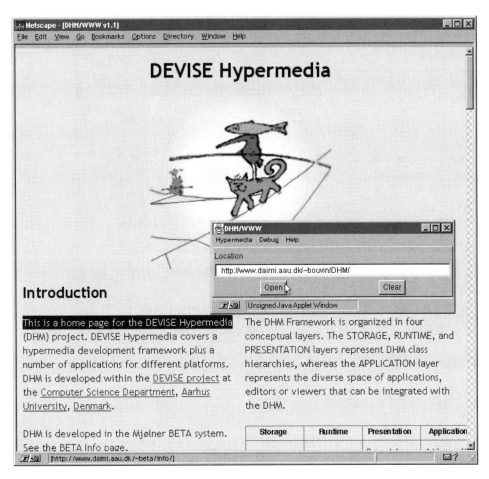

Figure 76
The DHM/WWW applet.

Finally, figure 78 shows the Inspect Anchor dialog box, which displays the anchor's locSpec information (described in chapter 4), including the context, actual selection, and position in the document.

The applet illustrated in figures 76–78 is a proof of concept; future improved versions of Java libraries and web browsers should enable smoother integration. In particular, we expect Java Beans (Microsystems,) and signed applets to make the Java environment versatile enough to obviate vendor-specific solutions. At the time of this writing, applets cannot detect text selection in a browser window, which makes it difficult to support elegant link creation, but recent extensions to Netscape Communicator are promising in this respect.

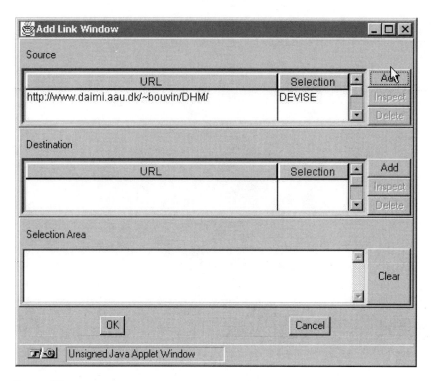

Figure 77
The DHM/WWW link dialog box.

Linking in non-HTML MIME types   So far, we have only explored the applet-based merging approach in relation to HTML documents. Non-HTML documents such as those created in Shockwave or Quicktime pose different challenges; the ability to create and follow links to and from placements in the documents is highly dependent on the openness of the proprietary plug-ins. Fortunately, Javascript can control many plug-ins. For instance, the Shockwave plug-in provides the operations GetCurrentFrame() and GotoFrame(), which can be used to request locSpec information and move within a ShockWave file given a locSpec. Marking link endpoints, however, requires a more elaborate mechanism, one that may include programmed extensions to the plug-in itself.

Bookmarking pages with external structures   Most web browsers let users create bookmarks for documents of lasting interest. For the purposes of integration, it is useful to bookmark documents together with their external structures. A

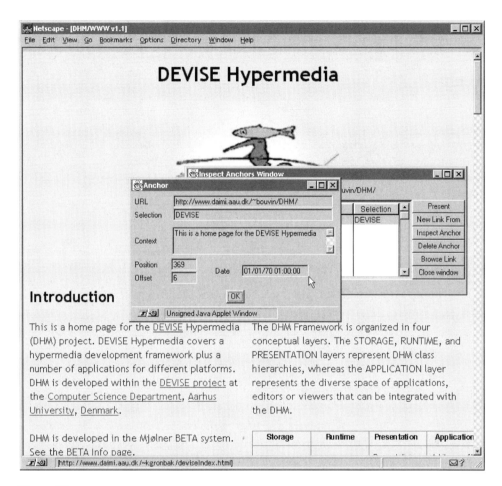

Figure 78
The DHM/WWW anchor inspection dialog box.

Dexter-based architecture can support such contextualized elements by virtue of the fact that hyperspaces residing in the hypermedia database (HDB) are addressable with ordinary URLs. An aggregate URL combines the address of a web document with links from multiple hyperspaces. Figure 79 shows an example of an aggregate URL from the DHM/WWW system.

This URL can be sent by email or used in other HTML documents just like any other URL. Following the link opens Randy Trigg's home page at the Xerox Palo Alto Research Center in California and merges it with two hyperspaces residing on an HDB at the Computer Science Department in Aarhus, Denmark.

```
http://www.daimi.aau.dk/cgidhm/dhmwww?((HyperSpace1,H
yperSpace2),http://www.parc.xerox.com/trigg))
```

Figure 79
An example of an aggregate URL that combines web documents with external structures.

```
http://www.daimi.aau.dk/cgidhm/sendhm?QUERY=webBrowse
r,0202,http://www.daimi.aau.dk/~bouvin/favoritebooks.
html,1,("http://www.daimi.aau.dk/~bouvin/favoritebook
s.html""Oe""Another good read is A Personal Matter by
Oe""374""2""853100323")
```

Figure 80
An invocation of the FollowLink operation using a CGI script.

This bookmark design merges multiple layers of links with web documents distributed over the Internet. For security reasons, however, the applet needs to be signed in order to permit it access to servers other than the one from which it was downloaded.

18.2.3 Communication layer integration

At the communication layer, a CGI script is used to implement the hypermedia service part of the open hypermedia protocol. The script simply decodes the query and starts a communication with the HSP. The HSP's response directs the CGI script to contact the applet before the script terminates. The CGI script and the HSP use simple socket communication.

Communication from the applet consists of a query containing an opcode and a locSpec (with URL, position, offset, time stamp, and so on). Figure 80 shows what the DHM/WWW applet sends when the user invokes FollowLink on an anchor in the document http://www.daimi.aau.dk/~bouvin/favoritebooks.html. The parameters include a locSpec, which in this case consists of the URL of the document, the selection and its context, the position and offset of the selection, and the last modification date of the document. The applet uses the modification date to determine whether the locSpec is not up to date with the document's most recent changes. In that case, the applet raises an exception and takes appropriate actions.

```
(1,2,("http://www.authors.jp/oe.html""Oe""Kenzaburo
Oe""70""2"
"850650404"),("http://www.daimi.aau.dk/japan.html""Ke
nzaburo Oe" "Yukio Mishima, Kenzaburo Oe and Musashi
Miyamoto are my""230" "12""852100133"))
```

Figure 81
A response generated by FollowLink.

The sendhm CGI script returns the locSpecs that match the given anchor, as shown in figure 81. The applet then retrieves the appropriate web document and presents the destinations to the user. If, as in this case, FollowLink results in more than one destination document, all links are presented to allow the user to select a destination. Again, the modification date registered by the hypermedia service is included to enable the applet to raise an exception if the anchors are not up to date. For more on ensuring consistency, see chapter 14.

The communication layer can also be implemented without using CGI; Java applets can communicate directly via TCP/IP or remote method invocation (RMI). The open hypermedia protocol can be used on top of these other carrier protocols as well. In fact, doing so is necessary in a collaborative setting, to allow HSPs to distribute event notifications to browser clients.

18.2.4   Runtime and storage layer extensions

The runtime and storage layers require only minimal extensions, including specializations of the Component, Instantiation, and Presentation classes, as described by Grønbæk and Malhotra (1994). In addition, the anchors are designed in accordance with the unifying concepts, refSpecs and locSpecs, proposed by Grønbæk and Trigg (1996). As discussed in chapter 14, the anchor locSpecs contain redundant information in the form of the position of the text string to be located, enabling detection and possibly repair of the locSpecs if the documents change after the link is established.

18.3   Support for collaborative work on web materials

One of the goals of introducing Dexter-based hypermedia in a web context is to support work groups in their collaborative use of shared web-based materials. Chapter 16 discusses collaborative hypermedia in some detail. In this section, we

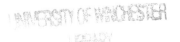

explore how the Dexter-based extensions to the web described in section 18.2 can be extended to support different aspects of collaboration on web materials. Users working with a browser augmented with Dexter-based hypermedia services should be able to:

· Create links to and from parts of web documents without having write access to them
· Follow both ordinary web links and DHM-based links imposed on the pages
· Structure web documents, using composites such as collections and guided tours
· Obtain CSCW support, for example, lock exchange and awareness notifications, for pages that a group of users share

In this section, we discuss the challenges that arise in designing collaboration support on the web. We assume that work group members are registered as users with a shared HSP and that they use an HTML editor that is integrated with an open hypermedia applet, which provides support similar to that of the DHM/WWW applet described in section 18.2.2.

18.3.1 Multiple hypermedia structures for the same body of materials
The approach illustrated in this chapter supports the imposition of multiple link and composite structures on the same body of web documents. In addition, it allows anyone to make links both into and from documents. This important step toward support for cooperative work recalls Intermedia's multiple webs over a single corpus of documents (Haan et al. 1992). Like the Intermedia group, we support annotation access, the ability for those who do not own documents to create links. But as Halasz explained in his "Seven issues paper" (Halasz 1988), full support for cooperative authoring requires both flexible transaction mechanisms and awareness notifications.

18.3.2 Locking and long-term transactions
An external hypermedia service can support asynchronous cooperation on web documents through turn taking and lock exchange. For example, let's assume that a group of people wants to establish a working environment in which they can cooperatively use and edit a set of web pages residing on one or more servers. They might use a Dexter-based hypermedia service to coordinate their work on

individual pages. A Java-based HTML editor could be tailored to request from the hypermedia service a write lock on the page to be edited before allowing changes. If the write lock were already taken by another user, the request would fail, and the requesting user would be told who possessed the lock.

18.3.3 Awareness notifications

A Dexter-based hypermedia service can support awareness notifications for web documents. However, the client DHM/WWW applet described in section 18.2.2 needs to be extended with mechanisms to subscribe to notifications on specific events. It also needs a thread that monitors notifications sent from the connected HSP. A user who is unsuccessful in obtaining a write lock on a given page managed by the HSP can then subscribe to a lock release for that particular page. Whenever the write lock is released, the applet receives a notification that it displays to the user.

Such cooperation support for web documents is weaker than the support we might provide for fully Dexter-based hypermedia structures. For instance, awareness notifications based on embedded HTML links are indistinguishable from changes to contents, since the links are not represented as objects in the hypermedia database. But the hypermedia service can provide full notification support for the link and composite structures created on top of the web pages and stored in the hypermedia database.

Finally, offering full-fledged Dexter-based hypermedia support for linking and collaboration on the web requires mature web browsers, plug-ins, and content editors that are more open to Java and Javascript access. There are at least two barriers to these goals: network restrictions and inadequate communication between applets and browsers (both Netscape and Explorer). For example, an applet that is not allowed to connect to servers other than the originating one can provide only limited support for distributed collaboration. Collaboration is also hindered by the inability of applets to catch browser events like text selection.

Because the technology is still in its infancy, augmenting the web with services that provide hypermedia structures outside the content of documents is a major challenge. If browsers become more open, as this chapter advocates, the web may yet support the dynamic link creation and world-wide collaboration envisioned by the hypermedia pioneers.

18.4   A pattern for open hypermedia on the World Wide Web

The design pattern in this section outlines techniques for integrating external structures into the web.

Title: Integrating External Structures with the Web

Context: Adding open hypermedia support to the web. Hypermedia structures are distributed in hypermedia databases that are separate from documents on the web.

Problem: To apply structures from one or more distributed hypermedia databases to arbitrarily chosen web pages.

Solution(s):   Maintain the separate hypermedia structures in hyperspaces, using distributed hypermedia services and databases.

Merge hypermedia structures into web documents as ordinary link tags immediately before presentation to the users. This can be done in two ways:

1. with a Java applet or an ActiveX control
2. through a proxy server

Using an applet or ActiveX control places both the user interface for manipulating the hypermedia structures and the HTML preprocessing on the client side, freeing the server from preprocessing responsibility. This approach requires that the applet catch ordinary web browser navigation events such as "back," "forward," "go," and bookmark manipulations, to trigger the preprocessing of the requested documents.

The second option places HTML preprocessing on the server side. The client side requires only a user interface module to access the functionality of the hypermedia service. However, the approach requires a proxy server through which every document is routed to trigger the preprocessing. The ordinary web browser functions need no special treatment; they continue to manage document requests in the usual way.

Regardless of the option they choose, designers can merge external structures with web documents by combining hyperspace URLs with the document URLs.

Examples: DHM/WWW takes the applet approach, while Microscosm/DLS, Walden paths, and ComMentor are proxy servers.

Related patterns: Depends on Structure Distribution in chapter 17.

IV

The Open Hypermedia Design Process

Parts II and III of this book treat the conceptual and technical design of open, distributed and cooperative hypermedia systems. This part focuses on contexts for the use of open hypermedia and a Dexter-based framework. In particular, we discuss the process of developing hypermedia systems and organizing a body of multimedia information into hypermedia structures to meet the needs of future users in a workplace.

Developing computer systems for workplaces is often difficult, in part because of the inadequacy of traditional specification-oriented approaches (Kyng and Mathiassen 1997). Over the last decade, several experimental and cooperative approaches to system development have gained widespread attention. Prototyping is an approach to development that enlists partial implementations early in the process. In contrast to specification-oriented methods, it does not assume that system design can be based solely on observation and detached reflection (Ehn 1988; Floyd 1984; Grønbæk 1989). Object-orientation is an approach to analysis, design, and programming that can make the relations between a system and the work it supports more explicit and thus simpler to maintain as the context of work changes (Madsen et al. 1993). Finally, participatory design engages end users during the design process when major decisions can still be made and changed at a reasonable cost. Some participatory design approaches, such as the Scandinavian tradition of cooperative design, combine user involvement with prototyping or mock-up techniques (Bødker et al. 1995; Grønbæk 1991).

In developing the Devise Hypermedia framework and variant systems, we addressed the problems of a real workplace (Grønbæk et al. 1993; Grønbæk and Mogensen 1994). Our development experiences led us to propose a new approach called cooperative and experimental system development, or CESD (Grønbæk et al. 1997b). The next two chapters illustrate how this approach contributes to the work of open hypermedia system design.

In particular, we advocate applying cooperative and experimental design techniques in specific settings to inform the development of general frameworks and products. We discuss how a general application framework can be developed in frequent interplay with cooperative design activities in specific application domains. The design activities result in various artifacts, including prototypes based on the general framework. Two development processes take place simultaneously: an application-domain-specific process, the development of specific variants of Devise Hypermedia for engineering; and a general process, the development of the Devise Hypermedia framework.

Chapter 19 describes the application domain-specific process by which we developed Devise Hypermedia. It discusses how we involved users from a specific workplace, a large engineering company, in the processes of designing a hypermedia prototype and of structuring information in hyperspaces.

In chapter 20, we describe the impact of our experiences developing and using open hypermedia in a specific workplace on the evolution of the general Devise Hypermedia framework. We relate these experiences to the scenarios described in part I and the general design patterns introduced throughout parts II and III.

19
Designing Open Hypermedia for a Workplace

... in place of the vision of a single technology that subsumes all others (*the* workstation, *the* ultimate multifunction machine), we assume the continued existence of hybrid systems composed of heterogeneous devices. Powerful technical systems on this view comprise not hegemonies but artful integrations. Design success rests on the extent and efficacy of our analysis of specific ecologies of devices and working practices, finding a place for our own technology within them. Design awards, by this reasoning, should be given not for discrete, decontextualized artifacts, but for the collective achievement of new, more productive interactions among devices, and more powerful integrations across devices and between devices and the settings of their use. (Suchman 1994, p. 34)

The Devise Hypermedia framework and variant systems, which form the basis for the theoretical work in this book, were developed in a series of projects conducted with potential user organizations. This chapter describes how this development took place, while the next chapter describes how our experiences in one user organization influenced the general framework design.

The work this chapter describes was funded under the European Union's Esprit programme. The Esprit projects EuroCoOp and EuroCODE analyzed the computing requirements for cooperative distributed work in organizations. These requirements informed the designs of general (CSCW) systems. In our case, a qualitative analysis of CSCW needs was carried out at the Danish Great Belt Link Ltd. (GB) (Grønbæk et al. 1993), a company responsible for the management and supervision of the largest bridge/tunnel project in the world (for further discussion of the Great Belt project, see chapter 2). The result of that analysis prompted us to explore the use of hypermedia to support GB's collaborative case handling. The requirements for open, collaborative, and distributed hypermedia discussed in parts I, II, and III of this book stem from our work with GB.

19.1   The Devise Hypermedia development project

This section gives an overview of how we organized the hypermedia development within the Esprit projects and how that development involved prospective users.

Development projects are often described in terms of such functions or concerns as analysis, design, implementation, testing, management, and the like. However, this perspective is less appropriate in a cooperative design context where most activities address several concerns at once. For instance, workshops with users can contribute to analysis, i.e. increasing understanding of the problem domain, as well as design, i.e. formulating visions of new systems and work practices. Similarly, prototyping activities can contribute to the work of analysis, implementation, and testing (Grønbæk et al. 1997b). We thus prefer to describe development projects by means of the activities planned or undertaken. Figure 82 depicts our sequence of activities at a level of detail corresponding to the high-level plan for the project.

This overview indicates the number of activities characterized by joint participation of prospective users and system designers, that is, those in which we applied various cooperative analysis and design techniques. The aim of these techniques, and of cooperative and experimental design more generally, is to pursue system development that enables democratic influence, supports participation of end users on their own terms, and is open-ended in its creation of visions. Interested readers can find detailed discussions of cooperative analysis and design techniques by Bjerknes et al. (1987), Bødker et al. (1995), Greenbaum and Kyng (1991), Grønbæk (1991), and Mogensen (1994). In this chapter, we focus on the use of such techniques in a hypermedia context.

19.2   Open hypermedia development in an engineering context

This section describes how we developed Devise Hypermedia prototypes conjointly with prospective users from a specific workplace, the Great Belt (GB) engineering company in Denmark.

Our overall research and development project had the goal of developing CSCW systems (Greif 1988) that could function in large-scale project groups. To gain an understanding of the need for computer support in such settings, we formed a design group with users from GB who were experienced bridge construction supervisors. This group, together with the involved researchers, con-

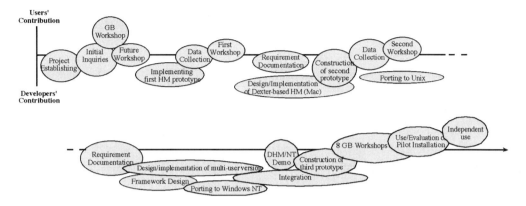

Figure 82
The flow of activities in the EuroCoOp/EuroCODE projects over four years from 1990 to 1995. GB stands for Great Belt ltd.

ducted the activities shown in figure 82. In the following six sections we describe these activities and discuss how the ideas of open, collaborative, and distributed hypermedia evolved through the project.

19.2.1 Initial inquiries and user workshops at Great Belt

The aim of the initial inquiries was to get an overall picture of the Great Belt organization, its objectives such as bridge construction, its practices, and so forth. We conducted interviews, studied GB's materials and work practices, and evaluated the current technology in use. This involved multiple visits to a construction site, a site office, and the headquarters in Copenhagen. To a large degree, GB determined the focus of the initial inquiries, by explaining and demonstrating what they considered relevant. Our understanding of Great Belt work practices and overall project goals led us to focus our inquiries on the work of sharing materials.

Some of these inquiries took the form of a modified *future workshop*, as Jungk calls it (Jungk 1986), in which we encouraged users to formulate critiques of current work practices as well as visions of new and improved practices. This workshop revealed that a central issue was the organization of huge amounts of heterogeneous material, including thousands of drawings, text documents, reports from multiple database systems, e-mail, pictures, and videos.

These materials could not all be accessed in the same way: some were filed in a central paper archive, some on the supervisors' shelves, others on a mainframe, a UNIX server, or local PCs. The special-purpose systems that managed the materials tended to introduce their own monolithic storage and access paradigms. Because of the heterogeneity of materials and systems, the supervisors first needed to consult one of the few experts in the relevant system in order to obtain important information.

The people at GB retrieved material by using keys such as filenames, keywords, and dates. With this kind of system, search is easy, provided that one knows at least part of the key; unfortunately, this is often not the case. Supervisors manage so-called actions that can include assessing a quality control form, coordinating work on a nonconformance report, and handling a change request. The necessary information is often hidden in similar cases from the past, previous correspondence on the issue, pictures or drawings of parts of the bridge, personal notes, videotapes about a particular procedure, and the like. Retrieving such relevant materials is difficult and cumbersome. For one thing, the proper key for searching the appropriate archive is seldom available. And even if the keys are known, the materials may well be distributed across multiple archives in different locations.

The future workshop resulted in several ideas for improved work procedures and computer support, including proposals to transcend GB's practice of retrieving materials by keyword. One idea was to follow threads through connected pieces of the material. However, it was almost impossible for the GB supervisors to imagine solutions based on hypermedia structures without seeing them firsthand. (The workshop took place long before the WWW became available to the public.) In the end, the future workshop provided the rationale for further explorations of hypermedia support for supervision.

Originally, we had planned to support asynchronous collaborative authoring of design diagrams, specifications, reports, and such. However, our analysis revealed that the primary problem for Great Belt supervisors was how to manage the huge amounts of heterogeneous materials described in chapter 2, in particular, how to organize the documents so they could be recovered when relevant materials or similar cases appeared at a later stage. The scenarios in chapter 2 illustrate some of these document management problems. An important result of the initial inquiries was thus that we turned our attention mainly toward the construction of hypermedia support for the management of heterogeneous materials.

19.2.2 Experiments with a HyperCard-based prototype

The future workshop identified the management of heterogeneous materials as the main problem for the supervisors and suggested hypermedia support as a possible solution. Subsequently, we explored this idea through cooperative prototyping, the goal of which was to let supervisors experience link creation and traversal as an alternative to keyword search.

Toward this end, we spent some two weeks developing a prototype with basic hypertext features on top of HyperCard. Figure 83 shows a change request in the form of a letter with an attached area for comments. The text in boldface represents anchors whose attached links are followed by clicking the mouse while pressing a command key. In addition, the user can provide keywords and use them as link anchors. The menu lists the basic hypertext functions.

Having built the hypertext prototype, we collected sample data to help GB supervisors relate the idea of hypermedia to their own work (Grønbæk 1991). We contacted supervisors to obtain a small collection of interconnected materials to enter into the prototype. Several supervisory documents were scanned with OCR and entered as components. Altogether, we entered approximately one megabyte of material, mostly text. Having prepared the prototype with example material, we conducted a series of sessions in which 10 to 15 supervisors and secretaries from Great Belt tried out hypermedia in the context of their own work. Their reactions called several aspects of the prototype into question, in fact, we modified both link structures and user interface during the sessions.

On the one hand, the session raised a number of issues that contributed to our understanding of the supervisors' work practices. First, many of the supervisors were concerned over the effort needed to enter all existing materials into hypermedia networks. In addition to interlinking recent materials for current cases, they also needed to establish links to old material. Although the entry of recent material and initial links is the province of journalization, supervisors, secretaries, and area managers alike would need to establish links as they discovered relationships between parts of materials.

The first prototyping session also raised several issues related to the design of hypermedia support at GB. First, the engineers needed to make links to parts of larger documents, such as handbooks and reports. Thus the hypermedia service would have to support anchoring link endpoints within a document. Second, the engineers often needed to represent one-to-many, or many-to-many relations

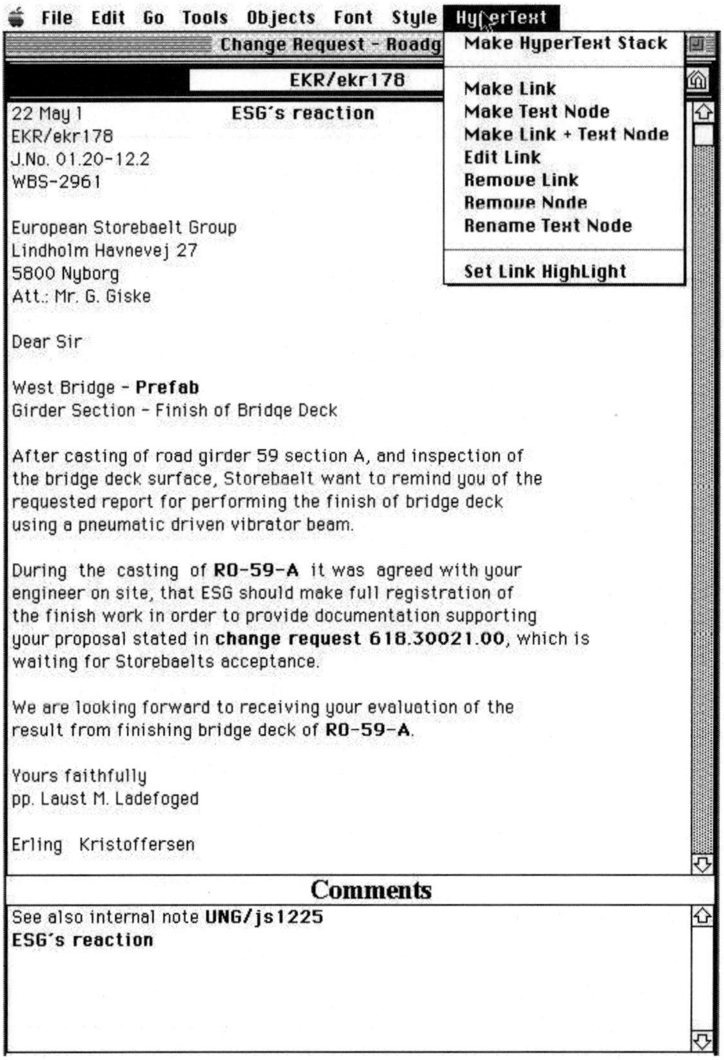

```
 File   Edit   Go   Tools   Objects   Font   Style   HyperText
```

```
                 Change Request - Roadg     Make HyperText Stack

                      EKR/ekr178            Make Link
22 May 1              ESG's reaction        Make Text Node
EKR/ekr178                                  Make Link + Text Node
J.No. 01.20-12.2                            Edit Link
WBS-2961                                    Remove Link
                                            Remove Node
European Storebaelt Group                   Rename Text Node
Lindholm Havnevej 27
5800 Nyborg                                 Set Link HighLight
Att.: Mr. G. Giske
```

Dear Sir

West Bridge - **Prefab**
Girder Section - Finish of Bridge Deck

After casting of road girder 59 section A, and inspection of
the bridge deck surface, Storebaelt want to remind you of the
requested report for performing the finish of bridge deck
using a pneumatic driven vibrator beam.

During the casting of **RO-59-A** it was agreed with your
engineer on site, that ESG should make full registration of
the finish work in order to provide documentation supporting
your proposal stated in **change request 618.30021.00**, which is
waiting for Storebaelts acceptance.

We are looking forward to receiving your evaluation of the
result from finishing bridge deck of **RO-59-A**.

Yours faithfully
pp. Laust M. Ladefoged

Erling   Kristoffersen

Comments

See also internal note **UNG/js1225**
ESG's reaction

Figure 83
Snapshot of a text node and the HyperText menu from the first prototype.

between materials. For instance, a letter often refers to several addenda. Third, the engineers wanted to annotate the image of a scanned letter without changing its content. Fourth, the supervisors asked for the ability to distinguish between types of link markers visually and to be able to see who established a link and when. Finally, the engineers said "Can't we use Microsoft Word for editing? We don't want to throw out our existing applications!" We interpreted these reactions as a request that the open hypermedia service integrate with existing applications in the organization, including word processors, spreadsheets, CAD systems, and the like.

We concluded from the prototyping activity that a company-wide system with hypermedia linking capabilities would address many of the problems encountered when managing large amounts of heterogeneous materials. It was also clear that we had to develop a hypermedia service that could integrate existing materials in their current form. The goal was to enable supervisors, secretaries, and area managers to establish links where and when they realized the need to interrelate parts of materials. Because the information already existed in multiple formats and applications, as discussed in chapter 2, the hypermedia system would need to support linking and structuring within the relevant applications and across the various formats.

19.2.3 Experiments with the first Dexter-based hypermedia prototype

To explore the required hypermedia functionality, we started developing a generic hypermedia package on the Macintosh based on the Dexter Hypertext Reference Model (Halasz and Schwartz 1990; Halasz and Schwartz 1994) and programmed in the Mjølner Beta System (Knudsen et al. 1993). This early version of the Devise Hypermedia system served as the platform for a second, Dexter-based, prototype that supported multiple component node types including Text, Draw, Movie, and File. For example, following a link to a File component launched the proper application with the attached file, thus offering simple integration of third-party applications. The prototype also supported a variety of composite types as well as bidirectional links with multiple endpoints (Grønbæk and Trigg 1994).

The Dexter-based prototype provided sufficient functionality for us to try reorganizing Great Belt materials into hypermedia structures, a task we planned to take up in a second round of workshops. In preparing for the workshops we considered two crucial questions: first, how to organize supervisory materials in hypermedia structures and, second, who should set up the initial links, and how, and when.

Preparation for the workshops   Both issues were addressed in a cooperative prototyping session prior to the second workshop. In advance of building the prototype, a designer from Aarhus University visited GB to collect material related to two supervision cases. We scanned the paper material (mostly letters from the contractor) and converted the digitized files into suitable formats. The prototype then interlinked the collected GB documents in a preliminary hypermedia structure.

Three weeks before the workshop, a few supervisors from GB evaluated the prototype. We responded to their comments with further work on the prototype and a set of scenarios (Kyng 1994) depicting the use of hypermedia at GB that included suggestions for links to be generated during the journalization of incoming documents. (The engineers were already considering the possibility of scanning incoming paper documents.) Examples of the scenarios appear in chapter 2.

A week later, we had two sessions with the supervisors from GB. In the first session, they went through the prototype, discussed alternate structures, and implemented a few of them. In the second, new material was entered, including the master file described in the scenarios in chapter 2. Proposals for three new features emerged from these sessions:

· Writable overlays for graphical components and third-party applications. The overlays would allow the engineers to create link markers without altering the material (which is important for legal reasons) and without knowing its internal representation.

· Visual representations of markers that reflect aspects of the associated link, including directionality and the type of destination.

· Graphical interfaces to the data, for example, a drawing of the bridge indicating links from the bridge elements to the appropriate master files.

In response to the second proposal, we added icons to the link markers, including <<, >>, ><, which denote backward, forward, and see also, respectively. We also designed a graphical interface that simulated an overlay, and completed our work on the two supervisory cases.

In addition to providing valuable input for the design of the prototype, the sessions highlighted two rather profound constraints on the use of hypermedia at GB. First, much of the supervisory work involved negotiations with the major contractor. For security reasons, it was not possible to interlink material from the two organizations. Second, the work of gathering materials from GB and converting it into suitable formats highlighted the inherent problems with GB's monolithic systems, especially their proprietary storage and access paradigms.

Just before the workshop, one of the supervisors joined us once again, primarily to get acquainted both with the hyperspaces we had built for the two cases and with the general concept of hypermedia. We had decided that he, rather than we, should demonstrate the prototype at the workshop, to ensure that the demonstration illuminated the potential role of hypermedia in the everyday work at GB. Though we had learned a great deal about work at GB, we were certainly not qualified supervisors.

The second set of workshops   The second round of workshops led us to adjust our technology and design visions and particularly highlighted the constraints on and potential for hypermedia at Great Belt. The workshops introduced general hypermedia ideas and our envisioned technologies and practices to approximately 20 people at Great Belt. We focused on how hypermedia could support their work tasks, and the requirements that using it would entail. One of the supervisors demonstrated DHM and several potential user groups used it in work-like settings. This meant that we had to move beyond supervision to confront the work tasks of other parts of Great Belt.

Participants gained hands-on experience with the current prototype and were thus better able to assess the various visions of hypermedia use at Great Belt. Together, we proposed improvements to the design of the Dexter-based prototype, including the addition of features like awareness notifications (such as notifications to supervisors when parts of the procedure handbook were updated), user-defined link types, and links from read-only documents. In addition, we developed elaborate ideas both about how Great Belt material should be structured, and about who would establish and use links, and where and when they would do so.

Although the supervisors considered the Dexter-based prototype to be promising, there were at least two obstacles to its introduction at Great Belt: the

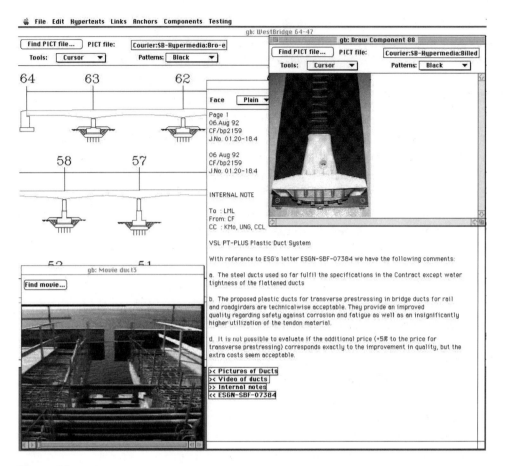

Figure 84
Picture, video, and text components in the prototype.

hardware platform (Great Belt used mainly PCs), and a lack of integration with the users' favorite applications, for example, they could not link from paragraphs in their text processor documents to objects in their CAD drawings.

19.2.4 Developing a Dexter-based framework and an object-oriented database

To address the limitations of the first Dexter-based prototype, we developed the Devise Hypermedia framework, a generic, open, platform-independent, multi-user hypermedia framework. Together with other groups at Aarhus University, we also designed and implemented a general-purpose object-oriented database (OODB) with support for cooperation.

19.2.5   Experiments in open hypermedia integration on Windows NT

The Macintosh prototypes helped us illustrate hypermedia ideas to our users and experiment with Dexter-based concepts. But to support the real work of GB users, we needed to integrate their favorite applications on GB's standard PC platform running Windows NT.

Our new platform-independent framework made it easy to port the DHM prototype to Windows NT. Subsequently, we improved this version of DHM with interapplication communication protocols that supported integration with third-party Windows applications. To respond to the needs of Great Belt in the face of resource constraints and limited technical possibilities, we chose to integrate with Microsoft Word, Microsoft Excel, and Bentley's Microstation. We extended these applications to facilitate creating, following, and inspecting links among, for example, parts of a Word document, a range of cells in an Excel document, and objects in a Microstation drawing. Chapter 20 discusses these integrations in further detail.

After completing the integration tasks, we conducted a pilot test that included installing the latest prototype in a network of five PCs supporting six Great Belt users (a secretary, the person responsible for quality information systems, three supervisors, and one manager). The new prototype was used to manage and interlink nonconformance reports and change requests at Great Belt over a three-month period.

The pilot test informed the further design of both the framework and the system. First, it led to suggestions for improving DHM. Second, it highlighted organizational issues related to the introduction and use of hypermedia. For example, one of the virtues of DHM as a general tool is its flexibility; however, in order to be useful at Great Belt, the system has to be customized for supervisors' particular practices. Last, but not least, the DHM vision and design were inspired by several challenges: how to support the interlinking of hundreds of thousands of maintenance documents, how to provide a generic way to integrate third-party applications that avoids the need to tailor each new one, and finally how to integrate third-party applications in a multiuser environment.

19.2.6   Exploring open hypermedia in other Great Belt work domains

After the three-month pilot test, Great Belt chose to continue using the DHM prototype for a new set of work tasks. At first, they used hardware borrowed from the project; later they acquired new hardware suitable for running Windows/NT, DHM, and the various third-party applications. Their goal at the time of this writing is to build an extensive hypermedia structure that organizes the material relevant to maintenance of the bridge, which is expected to last for at least 100 years.

The new hypermedia application has two main objectives. First, it should enable supervisors to track down all information relevant to a particular problem, for example, crumbling concrete on Pylon 17. This information must include quality documents, non-conformance reports and letters regarding the agreed solution, pictures of the problem, and so on. Second, the application should function as an inspection tool for planning and recording spot checks of the bridge. For example, a planned check would be entered into the system with links to "historical" material; after performing the check, the maintenance staff would update the hyperspace with new information.

Great Belt personnel are coordinating this project largely independently of the DHM design team. However, we have frequent discussions with the Quality manager about his experiences and possible design changes and enhancements. We are assessing the users' feedback with respect to its relevance for the general development of the DHM framework. Finally, we continue to fix bugs and make minor enhancements.

19.3   The interplay between general and specific hypermedia design processes

Grønbæk et al. (1997b) advocate a cooperative and experimental approach to system development (CESD) that is based on theory as well as experiences from the projects where Devise Hypermedia was developed. CESD includes a number of general directives on experimentation and cooperation in system development. We conclude this chapter by discussing three CESD directives that best illuminate the interplay between designing general hypermedia frameworks and specific hypermedia support for users.

19.3.1   The relations among theory, standards, and work practice

The work discussed in this book has been inspired by existing theories and standards, most notably the Dexter Hypertext Reference Model (Halasz and Schwartz 1994). At the same time, throughout our research project we have worked with potential user groups to understand their real-world needs in a way that informs our design work. The CESD approach includes two directives that deal with this interplay between theoretical work and user-centered design activities.

The first directive addresses the role of collaborative design experiments in relation to users' practice:

Experimentation is a means of analyzing actual practice that supersedes formal explanations or espoused theories.

In other words, system developers should not rely on preconceptions or theoretical assumptions about a given practice when analyzing it. Experimentation can draw attention to hidden aspects of the work practice and lead to new understandings. It can also constructively challenge existing work practices.

Prototyping experiments with prospective users that explore alternatives are central to cooperative design approaches (Bødker and Grønbæk 1991; Grønbæk 1991). Prototypes are concrete embodiments of abstract visions, usually employed to inform design. However, they can also improve our understanding of current practice, by revealing clashes between current practice and proposed alternatives. In addition, experimentation carried out in cooperation with prospective users can address issues that often exceed the scope of analysis carried out by outsiders. By drawing on the knowledge of participating users, developers investigate the reasons for specific actions, preferences for particular options, and so forth.

The second CESD directive concerns the role of theories and standards:

To compliment users' input, CESD design takes advantage of existing systems, research results, and standards.

Cooperative design approaches are sometimes criticized for reinventing the wheel by basing design only on users' ideas and current work practice. However, in most cooperative and experimental development projects, current technology, standards, and user interface guidelines play a significant role in shaping new designs. For example, a typical cooperative approach is to study the state of the art from a use perspective by inspecting analogous systems in use in other organizations (Kyng 1988). Developers in cooperative design projects also employ their computing expertise to identify technology platforms, standards, and user interface paradigms with which they envision technologies in use. The prototypes they build according to their current understanding of the problem domain can act as thought-provoking artifacts in cooperative workshops, extending the participants' understanding of alternatives as well as current practice (Mogensen 1994; Mogensen and Trigg 1992).

In our case, the Dexter Hypertext Reference Model (Halasz and Schwartz 1994) played a significant role in shaping the core functionality of the Devise

Hypermedia system, while the user workshops pushed the design toward an open architecture that enabled hypermedia functionality to augment the users' favorite applications (Grønbæk and Mogensen 1994). In this way, theory in the form of the Dexter model provided the basis for a practical hypermedia implementation. Its use in turn led us to improve the model.

19.3.2   The role of general frameworks

This book advocates the development of general object-oriented application frameworks that can be used to build variant systems with a common core and to support tailoring of the resulting systems. Our third CESD directive focuses on how to design a computer system that is open for tailoring and extension.

To maintain evolving opportunities for use, it is important to pay explicit attention to the creation of open points for tailoring flexible system architectures, and tools for tailoring during analysis, design, and implementation.

Fully tailorable systems with development environments that allow users to add arbitrary functionality or modify any system behavior do not exist today and probably never will. Instead, designers need to build systems that are prepared for tailoring in crucial places, so-called open points (Nørmark 1992), where variations in use can be anticipated. To provide this openness, tailorability must be considered during analysis, design, and realization (Trigg 1992). Places in the design where alternative competing solutions have been proposed are candidate locations for open points. Such open points offer generalized solutions that users can specialize to one of the alternatives.

Also noteworthy are the tools available for tailoring during development. Many of the current operating system architectures provide for scripting. For example, the light-weight interpreters of AppleScript, DDE with macros, and TCL/TK can open up applications for tailoring without granting access to the original development environment (Grønbæk and Malhotra 1994).

The Devise Hypermedia design provides such open points in its application framework using class hierarchies that embody alternative generalizations of central hypermedia functionality. We also took advantage of open points in the applications we integrated with our hypermedia system. Microsoft Word and Excel are examples of standard applications whose generalized functionality enabled us to add hypermedia features that were not anticipated by the Microsoft developers.

It is worth noting that most of the cooperative design techniques mentioned in this chapter can also be applied in small-scale development projects. In particular, the idea of separating development into general and specific foci can benefit smaller projects. For instance, a company standard for internal web pages might develop in conjunction with the design of particular pages for a specific department.

The challenge in a concrete project is to choose a level of generalizability that allows sufficient openness for the changing needs of the users. There are no general guidelines for such choices; however, the approach and examples given in this chapter and in writings on cooperative design (Greenbaum and Kyng 1991; Kyng and Mathiassen 1997) offer hypermedia designers a source of inspiration as well as specific techniques.

20

From Specific Workplaces to General-Purpose Designs

Too often design processes are institutionally separated from insights into the use of the designed artifact, and even designers themselves may use models and concepts that focus on the artifact without paying attention to the context in which the artifact is used. . . . [T]his is an important reason for many of the failures and breakdowns in contemporary systems development. (Grønbæk et al. 1997b, p. xi)

Every computer system in active use dwells in a complex technological and organizational context. Applications of hypermedia, in particular, are often associated with the changing character of information-handling practices in organizations. For example, the goal of moving paper documents online has led some organizations to explore hypermedia technologies. Furthermore, the increased visibility and awareness of hypermedia due to the WWW prompts the organizations to consider moving certain cross-departmental document work to intranets. In all such cases, we believe it is important for designers to engage the actual workplaces whenever possible. Involving users outside the laboratory requires investing extra time and resources, but as this chapter illustrates, the pay off for designers is improved hypermedia principles, frameworks, and products.

We start by briefly introducing our cooperative design approach and explaining how it can inform the design of general hypermedia products. We then discuss concrete examples of how the experiences at Great Belt influenced our open hypermedia principles and designs.

20.1 Cooperative design and general product development

Cooperative design is an approach to system development that actively engages users in the design process (Greenbaum and Kyng 1991). Based in current practice, it supports the envisioning of future possibilities. Cooperative analysis (Mogensen 1994) is a companion approach used to understand and change the constraints and possibilities of current practice. Done well, cooperative analysis and design reinforce and challenge one another in a dialectical interaction. Although such approaches have been considered difficult to pursue in product development settings (Grudin 1991), and thus applicable primarily to custom system development, our experience suggests otherwise. Cooperative analysis and design techniques in particular use settings can inform and improve the development of general products cost-effectively (Grønbæk et al. 1993; Grønbæk and Mogensen 1994).

Figure 85 illustrates how a general product application framework can be developed in continuous interplay with specific cooperative analysis and design activities that are based on prototypes built using the evolving general frameworks and principles.

The figure's two interlocking cycles show how the development of a specific hypermedia system can both gain from and contribute to the parallel development of general applications, design principles, and frameworks. The relationship between the domain-specific cycle and the general design is analogous to that between use sessions and the specific design. That is, concrete experiences of use and design trigger new understandings of obstacles and possibilities for general design. The double arrows in figure 85 indicate reciprocal relationships between pairs of activities, each affecting and informing the other.

In our case, the domain-specific cycle was conducted in collaboration with the engineering supervisors at Great Belt. Chapter 19 describes the cyclical activities of workshops, interviews, and cooperative prototyping. The general cycle resulted in the development of hypermedia design tools, a distributed object-oriented database interface, and general open hypermedia frameworks, all discussed in parts II and III of this book.

As we hoped, the specific and general cycles proceeded in parallel and in frequent interaction with one another. Before giving examples of how the domain-specific cycle informed general open hypermedia development, in the next section we discuss three issues that we believe were critical to the success of this project: (1) ongoing participation by developers, analysts, designers, and users, (2) long-term, resourced commitment from all sides, and (3) the use of mediating artifacts other than documents.

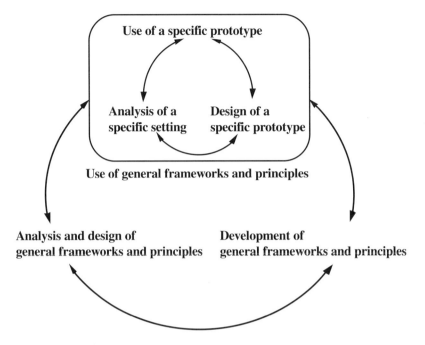

Figure 85
The interplay between general development and cooperative design activities in a specific use setting.

20.2   The roles of developers and artifacts

To enable a productive interaction between general design activities and particular work practices, we recommend reconsidering the division of labor that characterizes traditional system development. Typically, analysts perform user studies and then communicate the findings to implementers in the form of requirements documents. We advocate a tighter coupling of user-centered and general technical development. This requires on the one hand, that some technical developers be involved early in the project when much of the work is occuring at the use site. On the other hand, user-centered analysts and designers need to stay engaged as the balance shifts toward more focused product development. Having members of both groups involved throughout the project increases the chances that relevant knowledge of the use context is conveyed from the specific cycle to the general, and that technological innovations from the general cycle are applied to the specific cycle. We view this continuous involvement of analysts, designers, developers, and users as the most promising way to maintain the continuous customer focus deemed so valuable for product development (Young 1996).

There must also be a good faith commitment from all sides to invest time and resources in supporting the work of both cycles. The Work-Oriented Design project (WOD) provides an illustrative example (Blomberg et al. 1996). This participatory design project was conducted out of a research center of a large corporation; the use site was a nearby law firm. The WOD project, like the Great Belt, included work practice studies as well as cooperative prototyping in collaboration with participants from the law firm. The protoypes were built using technology from the corporation and were intended to influence products then under development. Though participants from the use site and their research colleagues considered the project a success, it had seemingly little influence on product programs (Blomberg et al. 1997). Given the pressures of product deadlines, the developers couldn't spend the time or resources necessary to engage the WOD project's specific cycle. In particular, project participants could not get access to prerelease versions of the product to support experiments at the use site. While researchers like Jonathan Grudin argue that it is hard for developers to get access to and commitment from users (Grudin 1991), the WOD project shows that gaining access to and commitments from developers can be just as problematic.

Finally, we recommend using a variety of artifacts to mediate the interactions between the work in the two cycles. In our approach, the specific cycle is not meant to generate authoritative guidelines or comprehensive requirements for the general cycle. Rather, it serves as a test-bed for development. In fact, at Great Belt, requirements documents and general product design specifications did not play a significant role in supporting the interaction between the domain-specific work and the design of general frameworks and principles. Instead, scenarios, prototypes, findings, and materials from the work practice were used to support communication between the members of the groups responsible for each of the cycles.

We used scenarios to focus the cooperative prototyping sessions and identify what Bødker and Grønbæk call *frame tasks* (Bødker and Grønbæk 1991; Grønbæk 1991). For the first cooperative prototyping session, we produced scenarios representing current and future work situations that hypermedia might support (Kyng 1994; Kyng 1995). In part, these examples were based on scenarios concerning collaborative writing and design that we had in mind from the beginning of the general development cycle. Later as a result of the specific cycle, we developed new scenarios involving integrated access to supervision materials. We also generalized some of the scenarios on cooperation to act as domain-independent general scenarios for cooperative hypermedia (Grønbæk et al. 1994).

Like the scenarios, our prototypes served as important mediators of the interaction between the general and the specific cycles. First, we collected the users' reactions to the first prototype as lists of findings, which we used, together with the prototype itself, as input for the general hypermedia design. Next, in the other direction, a prototype based on the DHM framework provided the basis for an experimental hypermedia application for engineering supervisors. The Great Belt workers' reactions to this prototype, together with our experiences building the prototype and configuring it with workplace data, were passed back to the general development group as printed lists of findings and in face-to-face meetings. Finally, the experiences from the pilot installation that we had transformed into scenarios, along with several successful integrations with third-party applications, informed our work on a more general solution.

On the basis of our experience at Great Belt, we believe that the interaction between cooperative analysis and design, on the one hand, and general technical development, on the other, can be mediated using scenarios, prototypes, and concise lists of findings. More traditional specifications of system architecture and object-oriented design were only used internally and quite late in the process. We therefore agree with Schrage (1996) that a prototype-driven approach to specification is appropriate in development processes that have a high degree of user involvement.

20.3   Influencing general hypermedia development

Throughout the process of general hypermedia development, the ongoing cooperative activities at Great Belt described in chapter 19 informed our understanding of requirements and the implications of our designs. We analyzed the constraints and potentials for hypermedia technology, gathered findings from cooperative prototyping sessions, and learned from the design and construction of hyperspaces for Great Belt. In addition, the need to coordinate the two cycles constrained our work in practical ways. For example, we needed to convert sample data smoothly from one version of the general prototype to another.

The fruits of our labors in the general cycle include a set of design principles for open hypermedia, a framework for object-oriented hypermedia development, and several running systems. The rest of the chapter offers concrete examples of how specific activities at Great Belt motivated the principles, frameworks, and design ideas presented throughout this book.

20.4   Extending the Dexter model's link construct

As explained in chapters 2 and 19, our choice to employ hypermedia in the first place was motivated by our meetings with engineers at Great Belt. In early workshops, they voiced the need to interconnect online documents created by different people, at different times, and for different purposes in the inspection process. Our experiences with the initial prototype demonstrated the need for links more powerful than HyperCard's embedded jumps. Thus the Dexter hypertext reference model and its multiheaded links stored apart from the content of components were particularly appealing.

Specifically, the Great Belt users asked for two features not easily supported by HyperCard links: the ability to see who built a given link and the ability to make different categories of links. Because the Dexter model represents the link as a kind of component, our links are able to take advantage of general attributes assigned to the Component class. The default component attributes in our Devise Hypermedia (DHM) framework include, among others, the ownership and update information that appears in figure 86. As explained in the Typing pattern in chapter 5, we support link types using attributes atttached to link components.

Link directionality was also important to the engineering supervisors at Great Belt. They asked that the interface make the direction of a link apparent and support bidirectional traversal. As shown in figures 87 and 88, the user interfaces of our hypermedia systems respond to these requests.

Supporting bidirectional link traversal was relatively easy. More problematic was the Dexter group's prohibition against dangling links, that is, the requirement that links have no fewer than two endpoints. Observing the work of engineering supervisors and others, we learned the value of flexible hypermedia structures. As explained in chapter 6, users might well build a link before

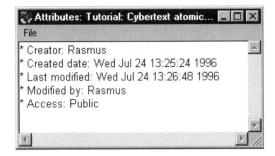

Figure 86
Ownership and update information for a component displayed in the Attributes window.

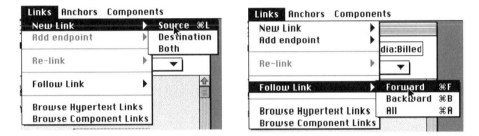

Figure 87
Support for directionality when creating and following links.

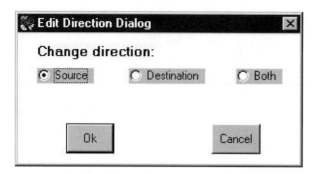

Figure 88
A dialog window used to change the direction of a given link endpoint.

identifying all its endpoints, or even before constructing the components containing those endpoints. Our frameworks and the Structuring by Linking pattern in chapter 6 reflect this looser approach to link endpoints in treating links with fewer than two endpoints as perfectly legitimate and even advantageous in some cases.

Moreover, following the original Dexter model, our framework supports multiheaded links. The users at Great Belt envisioned applications of such links; however, they were confused by the interfaces of the early prototypes, in which traversing a multiheaded link resulted in the immediate presentation of all endpoints. To address this problem, we added a mechanism to the framework to collect the endpoints resulting from a traversal. If there is more than one, the user selects the destinations to present, in a dialog box, as shown in figure 89. The user is also notified if there are no endpoints to present.

20.5   Heterogeneous materials and new component types

We chose the Dexter model primarily to address the heterogeneity of the engineer's materials. As the first scenario in chapter 2 describes, engineering supervisors often need to use a variety of online documents for the same task. Hypermedia systems like HyperCard that are essentially closed cannot address this degree of diversity. Fortunately, the Dexter model's notion of the component

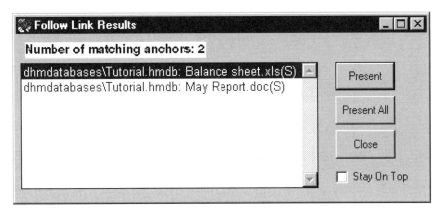

Figure 89
Feedback to the user when following a link results in multiple destinations.

as a wrapper for material that is outside the province of the hypermedia system is ideally suited to environments like Great Belt, where diverse applications manage documents in a variety of formats.

The diversity of Great Belt materials and applications had serious design implications. Specifically, we devised locSpecs as general means of identifying content in diverse materials, and refSpecs as building blocks for hypermedia structures. Our design principles based on locSpecs and refSpecs are reflected in the patterns of chapter 4, including Locating in Material, Placing a Locator, Embedded Interconnecting, and Externalized Locating.

An example of the heterogeneous materials at Great Belt is the short video sequences that engineers use to record problems at the construction site, such as those occurring during a glide casting process. We modeled such video sequences using the MovieComponent, a specialization of the basic Component class, used to display common movie file formats such as AVI for Windows and Apple's Quicktime. In the MovieComponent window shown in figure 90, users can create anchors for the movie as a whole or for segments of the movie. Below the viewing area and its controls, there are buttons for creating a new anchor for a selected segment. The extent of the current segment is shown, along with the controls just beneath the viewing area.

The list on the left identifies the movie segment anchors. Selecting an anchor causes the segment it marks to be made current. Users follow links from movie

Figure 90
The user interface for movie components.

anchors by selecting them and choosing the appropriate operation from the
Links menu. Following a link to a movie segment anchor causes the movie
segment to be played.

20.6   Extending the Dexter model's composite construct

The Great Belt engineering supervisors asked us for tools to view and structure
the hypermedia networks as well as query mechanisms to filter them. As explained in chapter 7, we chose the Dexter model's composite as our starting
point. In response to the supervisors' calls for different forms of structuring, we

extended the Dexter composites to support, for example, tree structures of container composites that resemble file system directories (Grønbæk 1994). At a deeper level, our design of refSpecs goes beyond the Dexter model to consolidate shared aspects of links and composites, such as endpoints. With flexibility as an essential design goal, our frameworks even permit components that can change back and forth from links to composites or function as a hybrid blend of both, as described in chapter 11.

20.6.1 Guided tours and tabletops

The guided tour is an example of a composite structuring mechanism we developed to address the supervisors' need to maintain paths through cases. A guided tour, as shown in figure 91, is a composite component that is capable of presenting a sequence of (nonlink) components to the user. It can be used for presentations or as an "in" tray holding components that the user needs to look at. Guided tours can be created manually by adding one component at a time to the tour.

Alternatively, existing composites can be converted into guided tours. For example, the history composite shown in figure 92 is maintained by the system to reflect the users' hypermedia activity. Converting a history composite into a guided tour lets the user quickly transform her recent traversal of a sequence of components into a presentation for later use.

The elements of a guided tour are often instances of another composite type called a tabletop, which we first described in 1988 (Trigg 1988). Tabletops store screen configurations of components meant to be simultaneously presented. Figure 93 shows the viewer for a tabletop that supports inspection and modification of its contents.

20.6.2 Transient and computable composites

Carefully considering the treatment of query mechanisms in hypermedia systems led us to revisit and extend Halasz's call for virtual composites to support cross-cutting notions of transient and computable components, as discussed in the Transience and Computability patterns in chapter 7. Our prototypes included basic capabilities for querying a hyperspace and collecting the returned components in transient composites (Grønbæk 1994). At the same time, we ensured that the framework was open to the inclusion of more advanced queries.

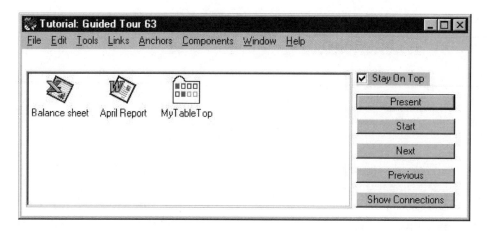

Figure 91
A guided tour composite whose tour consists of two documents and a tabletop composite. Pressing Start presents the first component and makes it current, Next replaces the current component with the next one, and Previous replaces the current component with the preceding one.

Our framework offers four main kinds of transient and computed browsers for viewing hypermedia components and anchors shown in figure 94.

The top three browsers are composite components, since they contain other components. In contrast, the bottom browser is a component that presents the anchors referenced by a given link's endpoints. The three browser composites work as follows:

· *Connected components browsers* graphically display all the links to or from a component, as well as the components at the endpoints of one or more of these links. To avoid confusion, links to links are not shown. An arrow pointing from a component to a link indicates that the endpoint corresponding to the component anchor is of type Source. An arrow pointing from a link to a component indicates that the endpoint is of type Destination. Endpoints of type Both act as both sources and destinations. All components (including links) can be double-clicked for editing. The user can reposition link and component icons to gain a clearer view of the connections.

· *Nonlink components browsers* display either all nonlink components of a hyperspace or only its atomic nonlink components. A specialized version of this

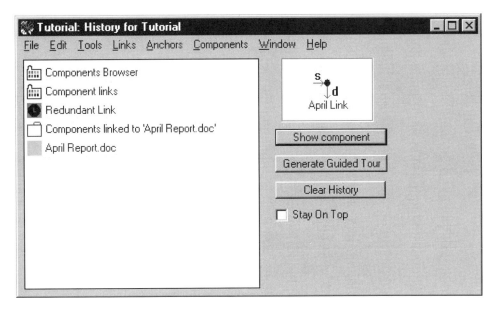

Figure 92
A viewer that shows an automatically updated history composite.

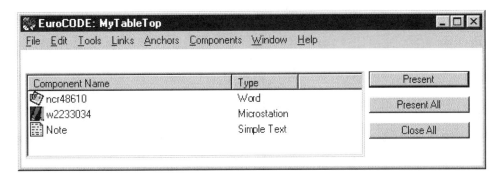

Figure 93
A tabletop viewer.

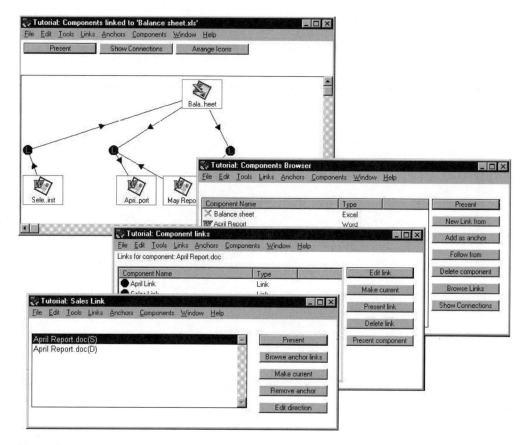

Figure 94
Four kinds of browsers; from top to bottom: a connected components browser, a nonlink component browser, a link browser, and an anchor browser.

browser, the Search composite, is used for displaying nonlink search results. This dynamic browser collects components whose titles, or attributes, match the search criteria specified by selecting the appropriate checkboxes. The default method of search is to match all components whose title includes the search string (ignoring case). The result of the search specified in figure 95 appears in figure 96.

· *Link browsers* display all the links belonging to a hyperspace, a component, or an anchor.

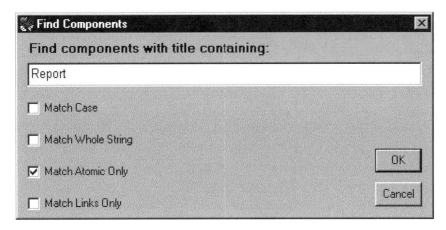

Figure 95
Specifying a search for atomic components with *Report* in the title (ignoring the case).

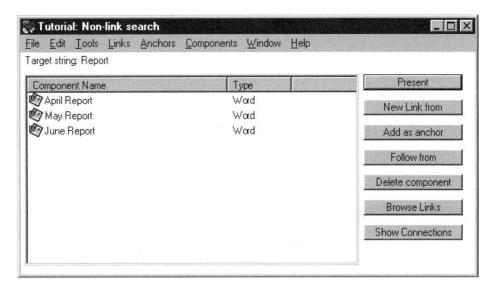

Figure 96
The search composite resulting from the search shown in figure 95.

20.7   Integrating third-party applications

One of the most important lessons from Great Belt was that a hypermedia system needs to integrate applications that exist in the workplace, rather than rely on new special hypermedia editors. This requirement is in keeping with calls for integration and open system design have been made by other researchers (Davis et al. 1992; Meyrowitz 1989). Our achitecture, with its support for third-party application integration, responds to these calls. However, the details of our design stem from the specific analysis at Great Belt.

We support three levels of integration, depending on the degree of openness provided by third-party applications, usually through communication protocols, APIs and the like:

· Whole component links for closed applications
· Links into semi-open applications
· A full-fledged linking interface from and within open applications

We use the File component to integrate closed applications. The application can be launched by following a link to the component or by opening a composite that has the component at one endpoint. However, links and composites cannot be anchored directly in the material managed by the closed application.

20.7.1   Microsoft Excel

We use a general protocol to integrate applications that are not closed. For example, we support simple local anchoring in Microsoft Excel for the Macintosh, using plug-in Excel modules that communicate with our protocol via AppleEvents, as described in chapter 15. We can thus support linking to and from Excel, as shown in figure 97, without having access to the source code of Excel. We have integrated other applications that similarly provide an externally accessible API.

20.7.2   Microsoft Word

Microsoft Word is an example of a program that allows full-fledged integration with an open hypermedia service. In our integration, shown in figure 98, the hypermedia functionality is available from the pull-down Hypermedia menu and through buttons added to the toolbar.

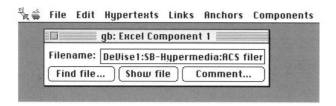

Figure 97
Integration with Microsoft Excel. The top image shows an Excel component in our open hypermedia prototype. The bottom image shows Excel with three buttons we've added to the standard toolbar. These buttons invoke New Link (N•), Add Endpoint (A•), and Follow Link (F•) on given selections. Cells acting as anchors for link endpoints are marked with a blue background.

Users construct anchors based on portions of material represented in Word using bookmarks. These anchors include selections of text, pictures, and drawing objects. In Word, an anchor is said to be *selected* if the cursor is inside it or if the current selection overlaps part of the anchor.

Certain operations are performed on all selected anchors. For example, Follow Forward traverses all links that have a source anchor appearing in the current selection. If the operation yields more than one anchor, a dialog box appears, from which the user can choose one or more links to follow. Delete Anchors removes all anchors in the current selection from the hyperspace.

Other operations apply to the current selection. For example, New Link creates a new link with the selection as a source anchor. Likewise, Add Anchor adds the selection to the current link as a destination anchor.

Finally, some operations pertain to the document as a whole. For example, Show Connections presents the components linked to the current document using the connected component browser shown in figure 94.

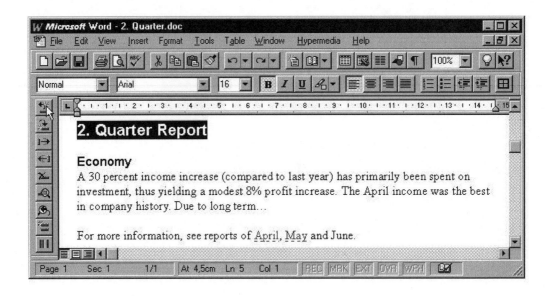

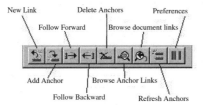

Figure 98

An extended Microsoft Word application and the added toolbar. The window shows
Microsoft Word augmented with a Hypermedia menu and toolbar. The toolbar enlarged
in the lower image appears vertically at the left side of the Word window and includes a
subset of the operations accessible from the menu.

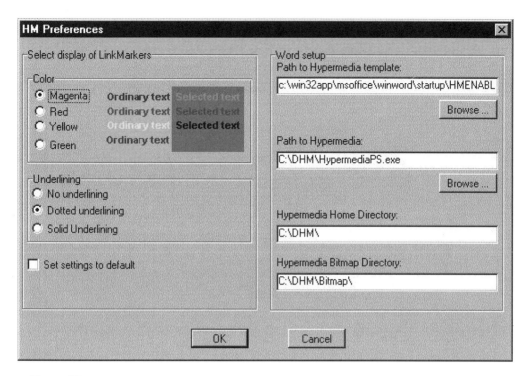

Figure 99
The hypermedia service preference dialog box for Microsoft Word.

The preferences window, displayed in figure 99, is used for editing Word settings related to the open hypermedia service. The user specifies the appearance of anchors and sets, or changes the location of hypermedia service files.

In summary, integrating third-party applications gave us experience with customization tools ranging from macro languages to window systems extensions. The Application Integration pattern of chapter 15 and the Application Tailoring and Anchor Maintenance patterns of chapter 14 identify some of the lessons we learned from these design experiences and offer design recommendations.

20.8   Annotating scanned letters and pictures

The engineers at Great Belt expressed the desire to link from and to documents for which they otherwise didn't have write access. Furthermore, the links needed

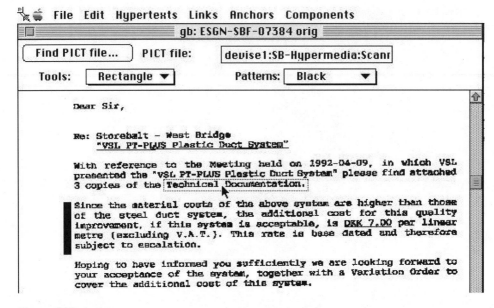

Figure 100
Annotating scanned images in a special-purpose editor. The black change bar to the left and the transparent rectangle around *Technical Documentation* indicate anchors for link endpoints.

to be anchored in the material of the document. To meet this need, we suggested link-based annotations using an overlay on the scanned document image, a proposal also made by Laura DeYoung (1989) in her studies of the auditing domain. The following three solutions illustrate the range of integration strategies possible, depending on a particular application's openness and the format of the material to be annotated.

· Build a specialized draw component as described in chapter 13 that includes support for background images. Annotations are in the form of links to graphical objects overlaid on the image as shown in figure 100.

· Integrate with Microsoft Word, a text editor in which graphical objects can be overlaid on inserted pictures, such as scanned document images, and used as anchors for links.

· Use Bentley's Microstation to create a new drawing with a reference to the original, so that the original can be viewed but not changed. The user can then select any Microstation object to be an anchor on top of the original drawing, as shown in figure 101.

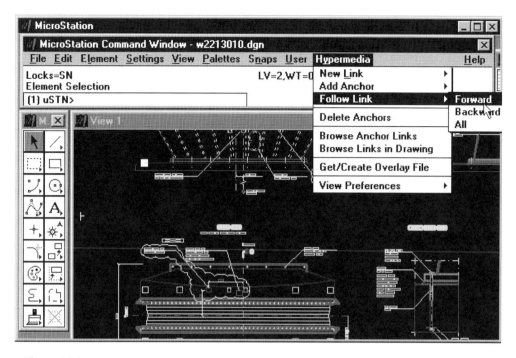

Figure 101
The Microstation integration, including support for overlays.

In Microstation, any element of a drawing can be designated as an anchor. Multiple selections are supported, but considered as separate anchors. (For example, when the user creates a new link, each selected element becomes an endpoint anchor.) Users cannot place anchors directly in write-protected Micro-Station drawings. Instead, the system positions the new anchors automatically in a transparent overlay on the drawing. Even users who have write permission for the original drawing may want to use an overlay to separate anchors from the drawing. The Create Overlay command in the Hypermedia menu serves this purpose.

20.9 Supporting cooperation

The engineering supervisors at Great Belt work together frequently, especially when producing and revising documents. The requirement that a hypermedia system support the sharing of materials used in such supervision activities greatly informed our design of cooperation-aware navigation and annotation facilities.

The first two prototypes we built for Great Belt explored the potential for hypermedia within a large-scale engineering setting and did not attempt to support cooperation. Nonetheless, some of the user's reactions implicitly or explicitly raised multiuser and cooperation issues. For instance, it was important for Great Belt users to manage access rights and identify those responsible for particular documents and annotations. The supervisors also needed to monitor updates to case-related materials. By means of cooperation support at the database level, we extended the DHM framework to become an environment for the development of cooperative hypermedia. The patterns in chapter 16 offer design recommendation on topics like concurrency control, event notification, and access management.

20.10   Integrating with the World Wide Web

Many organizations have or are planning to install an intranet (Rein et al. 1997), in part to improve the potential for collaboration in distributed organizations.[1] However, supporting distributed collaboration requires a hypermedia technology that is more than a tool for publishing and browsing. Such organizations need a hypermedia platform that enables collaboration on dynamically changing data and documents. Furthermore, the platform's designers ought to draw on earlier experiences developing collaborative hypermedia systems (for example, Augment, KMS, and Intermedia).

For example, in the engineering domain, rather than circulate documents on floppy disks or by email, organizations need to create dynamic working documents that are accessible on the company intranet for remote annotation and modification. At the same time, they also need to make available static documents such as company standards, laws, regulations, and product documentation, on both Internet and intranet.

Case handling in organizations typically involves coauthoring of reports and notes, as well as commenting on, annotating, and updating existing documents. Most organizations strive to achieve a homogeneous and standardized way of handling their documents, and the web is in many respects a step toward de-facto standards for data formats and protocols. However, the web constitutes a step

---

1. For more on intranets, see http://www.internet.ibm.com/whitepapers/intranet1f.html.

Figure 102
A web component viewer.

backward in publishing quality and performance compared with existing desktop publishing tools and special-purpose technical applications. Hence, the modern intranet-based organization will have to cope with heterogeneous systems and data formats.

Jointly managing traditional working documents and web documents requires integrating third-party applications with web browsers. The first version of Devise Hypermedia included support for a simple WWW component. These web components, like file components, represent documents using unique identifiers, in this case, URLs that can be automatically retrieved from a web browser, as figure 102 shows.

The later version of DHM/WWW described in chapter 18 supports web integration through an applet whose interface appears in figure 76. Though the interface is reminiscent of the extensions made to the various office applications, architecturally the hypermedia service process has moved from the user's workstation to a server on the network.

To integrate third-party applications with the web, the open hypermedia client and the WWW applet need to communicate using the same protocol or interface to the open hypermedia service running on the network. The applet described in chapter 18 already communicates through an open hypermedia interface. Thus we only need to separate the hypermedia client interface from the hypermedia service described in chapter 14 and turn it into a kind of "shim" (Davis et al. 1996) translating between the protocol supported by the office applications and the TCP/IP protocol used on the Internet. Such integration is currently being developed both for the Devise Hypermedia framework (shown in figure 103) and for the open hypermedia systems working group (OHSWG) protocols.[2]

2. http://www/csdl.tamu.edu/ohs/

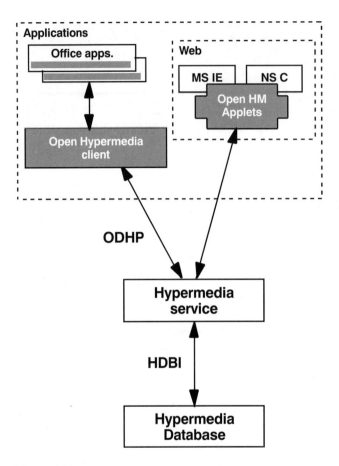

Figure 103
Integration with the web of open hypermedia support for traditional office applications.

20.11 Applying Dexter-based open hypermedia in new domains

Though the examples in this chapter are from prototypes developed for Great Belt, we believe that our general frameworks support the development of hyper-media systems for other domains and organizations. We have begun applying these principles and frameworks to the domains of collaboration support in organizational intranets and community support on the Internet. For instance, a DHM/WWW successor system is being explored as a tool for consultants super-vising customers in the use of domain specific law materials. The law texts will be published on government web servers, and the consultants will use the open hypermedia functionality to annotate and explain the paragraphs. At the same time, consultants and customers will use the open hypermedia service to link from reports they write with Microsoft Word to specific phrases in the law text not previously marked as HTML targets.

We expect to encounter many similar application domains that need seamless linking between traditional office applications and the web. In particular, intranet applications often require the integration of databases with hypermedia technology. In the context of the web, this integration has begun with the design of forms for updating and accessing databases and programs that format database query results into HTML pages. However, to provide seamless open hypermedia integration on intranets, open hypermedia frameworks need to support the structuring of such dynamic or intentionally specified content.

Epilogue

As one telephone company official complained in 1909, "The telephone is going beyond its original design, and it is a positive fact that a large percentage of telephones in use today on a flat rental basis are used more in entertainment, diversion, social intercourse and accommodation to others than in actual cases of business or household necessity." (Feenberg 1995, p. 165)

The last few years have been marked by explosive and unprecedented growth in public awareness of the power and potential of hypermedia. For the first time, the terms *hypermedia* and *hypertext* regularly appear in the popular press. The World Wide Web has brought link traversal to anyone who can afford a computer, a modem, and the monthly charge of a service provider. But we are far from a networked world order. The web today is probably at the stage of the telephone in the early 1900s. As the epigraph suggests, the web is well on its way toward "going beyond its original design."

Predicting the future under these circumstances is difficult if not foolhardy. Instead, our goal in this epilogue is to discuss tendencies, trajectories along which technological development seems to be moving. In each case, there are implications for hypermedia design, some of which may force us to rethink old assumptions.

We start by considering the boundary between online materials and the physical world, and the role hypermedia is playing in blurring and sometimes crossing this boundary. In the second section, we return to the topic of multimedia from chapter 10, exploring the potential for web-based linking into and out of dynamic media like audio and video. The third section outlines the current trends and emerging standards for two critical areas that we discussed in chapters 13 and 14, integration and tailorability. In the fourth section we revisit another topic from chapter 10, hybrid forms of navigation that are relevant to questions of formality and scale. Finally, in the last section, we discuss the role of open hypermedia in infrastructures that support emerging communities.

Linking to the physical world

Significant strides in network connectivity and embedded computing (Weiser 1993) suggest new possibilities for hypermedia systems that cross the boundary between physical and electronic worlds (Arai et al. 1997). With the latest Internet protocols (IP) (Hinden 1996), we can expect orders of magnitude to increase in the number of available Internet addresses. Moreover, we may soon see the addition of networking capabilities to the computer chips that are found in everyday devices such as microwave ovens, automobiles, and thermostats. This advance will enable hypermedia designers to link to network-aware physical devices that were formerly isolated.

The WWW already offers examples of intersections between electronic and physical worlds, including links to networked printers, robots, a video camera atop a San Francisco skyscraper, and a soft drink machine in a university computer science department. Already, such links are beginning to support computations that affect the physical world. For example, a link to a video camera in the Netherlands offers web viewers the ability to pan and zoom (see http://www.vin.nl/webcam/).

For Dexter-based hypermedia system design, these developments add a real-time variability to the content of a component. Thus, future locSpecs will represent new kinds of real-time selections, such as the set of all instrumented ventilation shafts in a particular building that are closed, or all the places in the country whose temperature is above 35 degrees centigrade.

Online representations that dynamically reflect the state of real-world activity are fairly common. One example is an electronic board in a police dispatcher's office that shows the last reported position of each vehicle. Another is a bedside display in an intensive care unit that indicates the state of a patient's vital signs. What it might mean to link to locations in such dynamic representations and how such links might function in practice remains to be seen. In any case, following a link will mean something different as online links begin to correspond more closely to real-world connections. For example, link traversal in the intensive care ward might involve moving a patient, delivering drugs, or responding to an alarm.

The merging of multimedia and telecommunications

Television and telephone are moving onto digital networks, and vice versa. This merger of telecommunications and multimedia has an impact in the area of "dynamic" or multimedia content for hypermedia structures. In this book, we've discussed the use of links and other hypermedia structures to organize and synchronize the elements of multimedia presentations. Having access to multimedia over the network leads to new possibilities for linking, in particular, into and out of time-based streams of video and audio.

Today, search engines on the WWW act as computed link services for co-occurrences of text across web pages. We're already beginning to see search engines that can explore spaces of image files in repositories or on the web (Ogle and Stonebraker 1995). It is only a matter of time before the web supports real-time link resolution into running multimedia sources, including audio and video streams from around the globe. This kind of search will be based on the signal processing characteristics of the materials (Chang et al. 1997).

Less intuitive, but just as useful, is the notion of links *out of* multimedia streams (Roschelle et al. 1990; Sawhney et al. 1996). In Open Dexter terms, such linking might involve the direct embedding of a locSpec in an audio or video component. Alternatively, traversal might start from a transient locSpec based on a selection of video frames. If the link were computed, its resolution might require matching time-based characteristics against stored refSpecs. As the Internet's bandwidth increases to meet the demands of networked multimedia, we can expect widespread examples of this sort of bidirectional integration of hypermedia and multimedia.

From competing formats to converging standards

Recently, there has been progress, as well as widespread attention in the trade press, regarding two of the most critical open hypermedia concerns, integration and tailorability. We are guardedly optimistic that the competing formats of today will lead to the convergent standards of tomorrow, and that hypermedia, in the richest sense, will not be left behind.

Though we hope for a convergence of standards, we believe heterogeneity in other arenas is here to stay. It is unlikely that a single vendor will be able to control and support any single fully integrated environment. Open systems and open hypermedia will continue to play an important role in the future.

Integration

Several of today's foremost high-technology corporations are making significant progress on the integration front. Netscape, through its browser plug-ins, has created a kind of encapsulated application environment that can support new formats, browsers, and editors. Such browser-based environments offer powerful integration across networks and workstations. Meanwhile, on the workstation side, Microsoft continues to integrate at least its own products with protocols like OLE and DLL, and more recently, Active-X. OpenDoc is another promising attempt to integrate applications on the workstation that has the backing of a consortium of technology corporations. Finally, Sun is marketing Java Beans, their foray into network-accessible component software.

We hope these efforts will lead to the development of personal workstations whose application infrastructure incorporates network access at the level of the operating system. For example, a cell in a generic spreadsheet application might be continually updated with the wind speed from a remote weather station accessed over the Internet.

Most important from our perspective, is that hypermedia linking and structuring be embedded deep in any convergent infrastructure. It will not be enough to support only the locSpec-style linking of today's web. We believe the proposals outlined in this book can form the basis of such a structure-enabling infrastructure.

Tailorability

Tailorability, the degree to which a wide spectrum of users can modify and extend their computing environments, has received welcome attention from system designers in recent years. On the workstation side, many of the more sophisticated programs support some kind of macro or scripting language (such as Visual Basic, Lingo, and AppleScript). Meanwhile, Java is becoming a de facto standard for programming applications across the Internet. Nonetheless, there are problems: there is little consistency among application scripting languages, and Java is not particularly well-suited to casual tailoring, especially by nonprogrammers. What is needed is another convergence, spanning applications and platforms on the one hand, and levels of expertise on the other (MacLean et al. 1990).

The increasing need for tailorable software will affect our design methods as well. In doing cooperative design, or performing any other user-centered design practice, we will need to take present and future tailors into account (Trigg and Bødker 1994). These are the people who, though not trained as designers, are responsible for helping their colleagues survive the installation of new technology in their workplace. Their active involvement will surely improve the utility of tailorable hypermedia.

Navigating through hybrid structures

Although today the WWW manifests little in the way of structure beyond the minimum provided by HTML, we expect the situation to change soon. Both SGML-based structuring along the lines of XML and Hyper-G-like structure-based services are joining the familiar generic HTML pages. Cross-page structures, often carefully and idiosyncratically hand-maintained by local webmasters, are helping web users find their way.

Figure 104 shows several mechanisms currently available on the WWW for navigating through more or less structured materials, some of which are discussed in chapter 10. In the future, we as hypermedia designers need to support smooth transitions across the mechanisms in the rows and columns of the table. The boundaries between the rows suggest hybrid navigation forms that combine links, both absolute and computed, with graphical overviews. For example, Jon Kleinberg has developed a web-based search engine that incorporates the information present in embedded links (Kleinberg 1998). Even more challenging would be graphical overviews that somehow represent computed as well as absolute links.

The boundary between weak, broad mechanisms and powerful, focused mechanisms also deserves a closer look. In the Open Dexter terminology, the mechanisms that support link traversal in the top row correspond to locSpecs that represent less structured links like embedded URLs, and refSpecs that underlie structures like composites and multiheaded links. The fact that locSpecs are embedded in refSpecs means that the addressing/pointing mechanism is the same across both mechanisms.

Mechanism applicability	Weak, but broadly applicable	Powerful, but dependent on maintained structure
Behavior		
Link traversal	Embedded "go-tos"	Hyper-G link objects
Search	Web crawlers	"Finding aids" (Pitti 1994)
Graphical representations	Hyperbolic browsers (Lamping et al. 1995)	Crafted graphical views, Hyper-G browsers

Figure 104
Navigation on the web mechanisms.

Currently our search engines make minimal use of structure, although the need for structure-based search was one of Halasz's seven issues (Halasz 1988). The web does include specialized structure-based search, such as Hyper-G and DynaWeb. But the field has yet to see a major search engine combine standard web crawler data with such structural information.

Finally, we expect the graphical representations of the near future to degrade gracefully from human-crafted overviews of an organization's web sites to automatically generated local overviews for the spaces between well-maintained sites. For example, graphical overviews based on web crawler data (Munzner and Burchard 1995), can smoothly give way to structured crafted representations wherever they exist (for example, InXight's hyperbolic tree browser at www.inxight.com).

From collaboration to community building

To support cooperative work, designers usually consider the technological requirements for synchronous and asynchronous collaboration between two people or among the members of a small working group. Visions of networked computer support tend to focus on coauthoring, joint engineering design, and the like. But developments on the WWW suggest that we need to broaden our sights to community formation. Particularly interesting are the ways that evolving web-based communities move between the mostly transient space of email lists and the more static world of web pages. Trigg (1996) discusses such a community and possible implications for hypermedia design. The way we do cooperative design may also change as we find ourselves considering whole communities as users (Korpela et al. 1998).

This book and the collaboration between its authors started with the premise that hypermedia design should be accountable to the technology needs and work practices of particular user communities, in our case, the Great Belt engineers and administrators. The most ingenious ideas, fortuitous convergences, and well-designed architectures, frameworks, and running systems must in the end be useful for people whose work has nothing to do with hypermedia, and everything to do with engineering, supervising, bookkeeping, writing, and so on. In short, the future of open hypermedia depends on the degree to which the products of our work continue to be informed by the concerns and active participation of users and communities.

A

A Brief Survey of Hypermedia Systems

In this brief survey, we present overviews of a few of the most important hypermedia systems, past and present. The systems, designs, and models we've chosen vary along several dimensions: from research prototypes for tens of users to popular products aimed at a broad market, from low-level infrastructure support to application-level integrators, and from workstation-centric programs to client-server architectures.

Because our coverage is restricted to the systems mentioned elsewhere in the book, it is far from complete. Though notable hypermedia systems are absent, we hope that this appendix conveys the breadth of development and design work that is either explicitly or implicitly related to the open hypermedia topics covered in this book.

Each of our brief characterizations is limited in scope to the topics covered in this book. However, the significance of many of these systems extends beyond the field of open hypermedia. Therefore, we encourage readers interested in learning more to consult the references given with each description.

Amsterdam Hypermedia Model

The Amsterdam Hypermedia Model (AHM) extends the Dexter model to support time-based multimedia structures (Hardman et al. 1994). In particular, AHM generalizes the Dexter composite to support coarse-grained synchronization between time-based materials. AHM composites organize atomic components in parallel, alternative, and sequential presentations. A new component attribute, synchronization arcs, supports more fine-grained synchronization. Finally, the model has been used to implement a tool, CMIFed (Rossum et al. 1993) for the design of interactive multimedia presentations.

Aquanet

In the design of Aquanet (Marshall et al. 1991), Cathy Marshall and Frank Halasz addressed a problem Frank first identified in his "Seven Issues" paper (Halasz 1988), namely, the inadequate support for structure in most hypermedia systems. In the Aquanet system, links are virtually nonexistent. Instead, components are interconnected through structured relations that are typed and customizable. A crucial aspect of each relation is its graphical representation in the interface. Aquanet uses color and two-dimensional layout to convey the roles components play in larger structures. As it turned out, the formal nature of Aquanet structures created problems for some users. Marshall later addressed these problems in her VIKI system (discussed below), which supported informal, emergent structure (Marshall and Shipman 1995).

Augment (NLS)

Researchers working in hypermedia and computer supported cooperative work (CSCW) have learned that whatever insight one is most proud of was probably demonstrated and published at least 20 years ago by Doug Engelbart. Starting in the early 1960s, Engelbart's NLS and Augment systems were platforms for a series of innovative tools for information structuring and navigation (Engelbart 1984a). Engelbart's contributions include the mouse and chordset input devices, video conferencing, tiled window user interfaces, and outline-based structure editing.

Although Augment's built-in applications made it an essentially monolithic system, several of its innovations have been influential for work in open hypermedia. Through the ARPAnet, Augment offered the first medium for networked collaborative authoring (Engelbart 1984b). And as we discuss in section 6.1.1, Augment's link specifications and traversal behavior inspired the Dexter model's presentation specifications (Engelbart 1984a).[1]

Chimera

Chimera (Anderson et al. 1994), developed at the University of California at Irvine, is an open hypermedia system that integrates third-party applications

1. An overview of Engelbart's research contributions appears on the World-Wide Web at http://www.bootstrap.org/library.htm.

with an approach similar to that of the Sun Link Service, providing libraries and APIs for use at the source code level. Chimera has been integrated with a number of applications, including Framemaker and WWW browsers. A distinguishing feature of Chimera's data model is that an anchor belongs to a view of a document rather than to the document itself. Users can thus decorate documents with different anchors for different views.

Devise Hypermedia

Devise Hypermedia (DHM) (Grønbæk and Malhotra 1994; Grønbæk and Trigg 1994) is an open hypermedia system running under the UNIX, Macintosh, and Microsoft Windows operating systems. Used as a reference example throughout this book, the system's object-oriented application framework extends the Dexter hypertext reference model. Devise Hypermedia uses an object-oriented database server to store the hypermedia structures. It integrates several office and technical applications with each other and with the WWW. A product version called Hypervise is available for Microsoft Windows from Mjølner Informatics in Denmark.[2]

Dexter Hypertext Reference Model

The Dexter model (Halasz and Schwartz 1994) is not associated with a particular system implementation; rather, it models a range of existing systems both architecturally and in terms of their runtime behavior. It is best known for its division of responsibilities in a hypermedia system among the storage, runtime, and within-component layers, and for the concepts of the anchor and the presentation specification. Chapter 3 provides a detailed introduction to the model.

HAM

The Hypertext Abstract Machine (HAM) (Campbell and Goodman 1988) was the first abstract data model for hypertext. Before the publication of the Dexter model, the HAM was used to characterize, compare, and contrast the data models of KMS, NoteCards, and Intermedia. Along with Intermedia and

2. http://www.mjolner.dk/Hypervise

Xanadu, it inspired the Dexter model's separation of runtime and storage layers. The HAM was also used to build a system for software engineering, Neptune, that for the first time addressed problems of hypermedia versioning (Delisle and Schwartz 1986).

HOSS (HB1–HB4)

HOSS (Hypermedia Operating System Services) (Nürnberg et al. 1996) represents the latest development in the HBn/SPn series (Leggett and Schnase 1994) of hypermedia systems from Texas A&M University. HOSS separates the functionality of hypermedia systems into basic primitives to be provided at the operating-system level. The primitives are divided into data, structures, and behaviors. Data is the information contents of hypermedia applications; structures reflect the rich variety of inter-data relationships; and behaviors are computations coupled to structure. HOSS provides a layered architecture on top of an exisiting operating system, which is SUN Solaris in the current implementation.

HyperCard

HyperCard was the first widely used hypermedia system for personal computers (Goodman 1987). Until the WWW, HyperCard probably had the largest user community of any hypermedia system. In fact, because of their similar models of linking and browsing, the first WWW browsers resembled HyperCard with the addition of tagged text. HyperCard does little to support application integration or collaboration, and thus has not figured prominently in discussions of open hypermedia. Nonetheless, its scripting language, HyperTalk, confirmed, at least for the Macintosh user community, the power and flexibility of deeply tailorable hypermedia.

HyperForm and HyperDisco

HyperForm (Wiil and Leggett 1992) and HyperDisco (Wiil and Leggett 1997) are open hypermedia platforms that generalize previous hyperbases, such as HAM, which were designed to support a fixed hypermedia data model and a specific set of database services. In contrast, HyperForm and HyperDisco can manage the storage of a variety of hypermedia data models. Furthermore, the platforms allow hypermedia designers to create new combinations of database and collaboration tools in support of access control, versioning, and event notification. Both platforms provide open hypermedia services through so-called tool integrators. Finally, HyperDisco provides support for distribution of hyper-media structures.

HyTime

HyTime is a standard for structured document representation and interchange (DeRose and Durand 1994). Built on SGML, it adds support for linking and synchronization of multimedia documents. Though not oriented toward system development, it has been influential in the open hypermedia community. For example, its structured, customizable format for locating within and across documents comprises one of the literature's most comprehensive definitions of the locSpec.

Intermedia

Along with KMS and NoteCards, Intermedia was one of the most influential hypermedia systems of the 1980s, with dedicated users and a diverse set of researchers (Yankelovich et al. 1988). Intermedia was the first system to support anchor-based, bidirectional links, stored in separable webs apart from the content of the documents. The Intermedia group conducted wide-ranging and ground-breaking research in such areas as multimedia (Catlin and Smith 1988), collaboration (Catlin et al. 1989), graphical browsing (Utting and Yankelovich 1989), and educational applications of hypermedia (Ess 1991). Perhaps most relevant for this book are Intermedia's object-oriented architecture (Meyrowitz 1986) and its use of generic databases as hypermedia back ends (Haan et al. 1992).

KMS (ZOG)

KMS has the longest and most illustrious history of any hypermedia system still in use. It started as ZOG at Carnegie Mellon University in the 1960s (McCracken and Akscyn 1984). After moving out of the university into the commercial world in the 1980s, it became KMS and is still in active use today

(Akscyn et al. 1988). Running on UNIX platforms, KMS has attracted a dedicated user population that appreciates its radical user interface, snappy link traversal, and canvas-like component editor. KMS supports collaboration and versioning, the latter still a rare feature in hypermedia systems. Like the web, KMS has a single component type, the frame, but unlike the web, KMS can easily represent hierarchical as well as linked interconnections. The structured component we propose in chapter 11 is inspired in part by the KMS frame.

Memex

Most hypermedia researchers agree that Vannevar Bush's memex (Bush 1945) is the progenitor of the modern notion of hypertext as navigable interlinked information. For example, both Doug Engelbart and Ted Nelson credit the memex as a major early influence (Kahn et al. 1991). Interestingly, for Bush, the *trail* rather than the link was the fundamental structuring entity (Trigg 1991). Beyond the mechanisms of trail creation and navigation, Bush articulated a vision of collaborating scholars, in particular, the idea that one scholar could pass along a research finding in the form of a trail to another. The trail carries along copies of the content it structures, and is thus a perfect example of the subhyperspace copying and moving we discuss in section 8.2.

Microcosm

The team of researchers and developers at Southampton University and Multicosm, Ltd. have articulated and implemented the vision of open hypermedia as well as anyone (Hall et al. 1996). Their primary contribution from an open hypermedia perspective is a set of tools for interconnecting third-party applications, including those that are minimally tailorable. Microcosm supports the integration of closed applications through a so-called Universal Viewer, which patches the user interface of an arbitrary application with funtionality to catch selections and invoke link services. A related contribution involves links "outside the data" that are implemented using link filters, a kind of link service for applications running on a single workstation. The Distributed Link Service (Carr et al. 1995) is an extension of Microcosm that translates many of their ideas into the context of the web. Like Intermedia, the Microcosm researchers have also addressed problems of multimedia integration (Lewis et al. 1996).

MultiCard

MultiCard (Rizk and Sauter 1992), developed at INRIA in France, is an open hypermedia system whose hypermedia toolkit allows programmers to create and manipulate distributed hypermedia structures. Applications to be integrated must support M2000, a rich library-based protocol for development-time integration. MultiCard also includes an advanced language for writing scripts, which can be assigned to nodes, groups (composites), and anchors. Finally, MultiCard provides a set of special-purpose authoring tools for hypermedia.

OLE/DDE

The libraries and APIs of OLE and its predecessor DDE support interapplication integration on the Microsoft Windows platform (Brockschmidt 1995). Cross-program data exchange and command invocation enable users to build "hot" or "warm" links that serve as active or passive channels, respectively, for data transfer between programs, for example, from a selection of spreadsheet cells to a table in a word processing document. OLE also supports HyperLinks, which are hypermedia links from one OLE container to another. As in HTML, these links are embedded in the data of their source container.

NoteCards

NoteCards was one of the best known research hypermedia systems of the 1980s (Halasz et al. 1987). Based on a metaphor of note cards and file boxes, it was intended to meet the needs of information workers ranging from intelligence analysts to doctoral dissertation authors. The size of the NoteCards user community was limited by its technology platform, the Xerox InterLisp environment. Nonetheless, for those with access to that platform, it provided a means of integrating standard text and graphics editors in customizable, extensible ways (Trigg et al. 1987). Several of the hypermedia tools developed by NoteCards users and developers were influential in the hypermedia community, including the graphical network browser, used to visualize and manage networks of hundreds of cards and links (Trigg and Irish 1987); the guided tour and Table-Top cards (Trigg 1988); and the history card, used to monitor asynchronous collaborative work among multiple authors (Irish and Trigg 1989).

From the perspective of open hypermedia designers, NoteCards' most important contribution may be its extensible card type mechanism, a precursor to the extensible component types we discuss in chapter 13. Also relevant to our concerns, but less heralded, are its cross-notefile links and operations for demarcating, copying, and moving the subnetworks of a notefile.

In the end, NoteCards may be best known as the straw man for Frank Halasz's brilliant "Seven Issues" paper (1988). Perhaps the most heavily cited journal article ever published on hypermedia, Halasz's paper lays out the major research directions for the 1990s on the basis of a careful analysis of the strengths and weaknesses of NoteCards. In a field that changes as fast as this one, it is a testament to Halasz's foresight that the field's most popular required reading is now 10 years old.

SEPIA

SEPIA (Streitz et al. 1992) is a cooperative hypermedia authoring environment. It provides persistent and shared data storage, a hypermedia data model with composites, comprehensive authoring functionality, and support for cooperative work. SEPIA subscribes to a model for authoring based on activity spaces, which provide activity-dependent views of the hyperdocument being authored. SEPIA supports asynchronous and synchronous cooperation among multiple authors by means of shared access to hyperdocuments and integrated audio and video conferencing. SEPIA's authoring tools are the built-in editors and graphical browsers; as far as we know, SEPIA does not support the integration of third-party applications.

Sun Link Service

Although Amy Pearl's Sun Link Service (Pearl 1989) never developed a large user community, it is generally credited with being the first network-based link service for third-party applications. Its anchor specifications and protocols for communication between link service applications inspired the separation of responsibilities modeled by the Dexter group's within-component layer. The Sun Link Service required that application developers integrate a small standard hypermedia library with their application at development time. This library provided, among other things, communication with the link service and standardized link marking.

VIKI

Cathy Marshall's VIKI system (Marshall and Shipman 1995; Marshall et al. 1994) introduced the notion of spatial hypermedia, an implicit means of determining structure based on the layout features of representations of components. Given an arrangement of component and composite icons in a window, VIKI can automatically cluster the components according to proximity, color, shape, and other features. These spatially determined structures are a perfect example of the computed, transient composites we discuss in chapter 7.

The World Wide Web and HTML

Invented only six years ago by Tim Berners-Lee, the World Wide Web (WWW) (Berners-Lee et al. 1992a; Berners-Lee et al. 1992b) brought the term *hypermedia* wide recognition. More important, it fundamentally altered the possibilities for broad-based distributed access to information (Berners-Lee et al. 1994). We believe that the web will be a crucial component of the world's computing and telecommunications infrastructure for the foreseeable future.

The web's success is due in large part to its adoption of certain open hypermedia principles, including linking across Internet hosts, extensible protocols, and scripting. However, we hope that this book clarifies the degree to which the web and HTML still fall short of offering the open hypermedia support users need. Uni-directional links embedded in HTML tags and the lack of support for annotations and collaborative authoring are among the topics that need to be addressed.

Fortunately, the web community, particularly, the World Wide Web consortium (W3C), is taking strides in these and other areas. Perhaps most exciting from our open hypermedia perspective is the work toward a standard for web-based distribution and versioning called WebDAV.[3] Once standardized, the resulting protocol will support distributed annotation across the Internet.

Xanadu

Along with Vannevar Bush's memex, the Xanadu system is the most influential hypermedia system that was never built. Created by Ted Nelson (Nelson 1981),

3. http://www.ics.uci.edu/~ejw/authoring/

along with the terms "hypertext" and "hypermedia," the Xanadu vision inspired many of those in the field today. The design includes sophisticated versioning of links and content, universally unique identifiers of spans of content, and a clean separation of frontend and backend functionality. The Xanadu transclusion suggested a new notion of the link as a dynamic maintainer of identity between copies of content (Nelson 1995). Xanadu was always conceived of as world-wide, with access based on a pay-per-use (and pay-per-link-traversal) economic model. There has never been a complete implementation of Xanadu although partial prototypes have been demonstrated.

B

Open Dexter Hypermedia Protocol

This appendix provides a closer look at the messages that comprise the Open Dexter Hypermedia Protocol (ODHP). We start by describing the format of messages in each direction between an HSP (hypermedia service process) and a hypermedia-extended application. The subsequent sections present message types for the four subprotocols: connecting, basic linking, extended browsing and management, and multiuser.

Messages from HSP to hypermedia-extended applications

The exact form of the messages sent from the HSP to an external application varies with each application. The examples in this appendix are messages sent to Emacs on a UNIX platform. Emacs receives the text string and interprets the commands and parameters it contains. Communicating with Word and Excel on the Windows platform is slightly different. The messages are implemented as calls to Word and Excel Visual Basic macros that are invoked directly from the hypermedia service. For those applications, the op codes are irrelevant.

Messages from hypermedia-extended applications to HSP

The general form of a message sent from hypermedia-extended applications to the hypermedia service is as follows: "UserName,ApplicationID,opCode, ...". In contrast to the messages sent in the other direction, the messages to the HSP obey the same format for every application.

Parameter types

The following types of parameters are encoded in the messages:

Parameter	Explanation
userName	the login name of the user
applicationID	an identifier that uniquely identifies the running instance of an application, e.g. a DDE name in Windows or a four letter signature on a Macintosh
hyperSpaceID	a unique identifier for a hyperspace object, here encoded as a pair of integers. Hyperspaces are usually also assigned a human readable name, HyperSpace Name.
compID	a unique identifier for a component object, here encoded as a pair of integers.
opCode	an integer encoding of the command in question
accessCode	a code that determines the access and availability rights for a given object
N	an integer used to tell the HSP/application that a list of parameters of a certain length is at the end of the message
nodeSpec	a unique identification of the content for a component. Typically this is a document identifier, e.g. a full file name and path or a document management system ID.
docType	a MIME-type for a document
locSpec	an application-specific specification of a location inside a document
pSpec	an application-specific encoding of information relevant to the presentation of a given document or an anchor inside a document
direction	an integer identifying the direction of the endpoint to be SOURCE, DESTINATION, BOTH or NONE.
linkType	a number encoding the type of link in question
lockValue	a number encoding the lock type on a component, e.g. read, write
responseCode	a number encoding the result of an operation, where 1 = success, 0 = failure, and numbers preceeded by '-' refer to specific messages describing the status of the operation

B.1.
Parameters appearing in the protocol.

Connecting protocol

The connecting protocol is made up of two messages for logging on and off of the hypermedia service.

```
Logon:                          1002
Usage:
Format: UserName,ApplicationID,opCode,password,clientid,
clientPortNo
Response: (ResponseCode)
Example: kgronbak@daimi.aau.dk,Webbrowser,1002,*****,
CORAL.daimi.aau.dk,7666
```

```
Logoff:                         1003
Usage:
Format: UserName,ApplicationID,opCode
Response: (ResponseCode)
Example: kgronbak@daimi.aau.dk,Webbrowser,1003
```

Basic linking protocol

The basic linking protocol supports creation, traversal and deletion of links to anchored parts of material managed by hypermedia-extended applications.

Messages from HSP to hypermedia-extended applications

```
IsOpen:                         12
Usage: Used to ask if a given document is open.
Format: ApplicationID,opCode,nodeSpec
Response: TRUE (= 1) or FALSE (= 0).
Example: emacs,12,/users/kgronbak/DHM/docs/interface.tex
```

```
PresentSelection:               13
Usage: Used to present an anchor within a given document.
Format: Application,opCode,nodeSpec,locSpec,pSpec
Response: (ResponseCode)
Example: emacs,13,/users/kgronbak/DHM/docs/interface.
tex,1,,
```

PresentDoc: 15
Usage: Used to present a document.
Format: ApplicationID,opCode,nodeSpec,pSpec
Response: (ResponseCode)
Example: emacs,15,/users/kgronbak/DHM/docs/interface.tex

DeleteDoc: 804
Usage: Used to inform the external application that a
component corresponding to a given document is being
removed from the hyperspace.
Format: ApplicationID,opCode,nodeSpec
Response: (ResponseCode)
Example: emacs,804,/users/kgronbak/DHM/docs/interface.tex

DeleteAnchors: 805
Usage: Used to inform the external application that some
anchors in a given component/document are being deleted.
Format: ApplicationID,opCode,nodeSpec,noOfArguments,
locSpec1, locSpec2,...., locSpecN
Response: (ResponseCode)
Example: emacs,805,/users/kgronbak/DHM/docs/interface.
tex,1,1

SaveDoc: 806
Usage: Used to inform the external application that the
component corresponding to a given document is being
saved (to disk).
Format: ApplicationID,opCode,nodeSpec
Response: (ResponseCode)
Example: emacs,806,/users/kgronbak/DHM/docs/interface.tex

SendAnchorList: 807
Usage: Used to send the anchorList for a given
component/document to the external application.
Format: ApplicationID,opCode, nodeSpec, N,{locSpec}*
Response: (ResponseCode)
Example: emacs,807,/users/kgronbak/DHM/docs/interface.
tex,1,0#836#852

CloseActiveChannel: 808
Usage: Used to inform external applications that an
active communication channel, e.g., a socket, is being
closed by the hypermedia service. This may happen in
UNIX implementations when the instantiation and
communication objects for a given component are closed.
Response: (ResponseCode)
Example: winword,808

Messages from hypermedia-extended applications to HSP

NewLink: 0
Usage: Creates a new link of a given type with a number
of endpoints determined by the given sets of
(nodeSpec,locSpec,direction).
Format: UserName,ApplicationID,opCode,NoOfEndpoints,
{nodeSpec, locSpec,direction}*,linkType,NoOfHyperSpaces,
{HyperSpaceId}*
Response: (LinkId,{EndPointId}*)
Example: kgronbak@daimi.aau.dk,WebBrowser,0,1, ("http://
www.daimi.aau.dk/~devise/front.html"),("Devise Homepage
http://www.daimi.aau.dk/~devise/ MainFrame ""DEVISE
""0""0""0""0""0"),3,2,1,1,888855764

AddEndpoint: 100
Usage: Adds a number of endpoints to the link determined
by LinkId.
Format: UserName,ApplicationID,opCode,NoOfEndpoints,
{nodeSpec,locSpec,direction}*,NoOfHyperSpaces,
{HyperSpaceId}*,LinkId
Response: ({EndPointId}*)
Example: kgronbak@daimi.aau.dk,WebBrowser,100,1,
("http://www.cit.dk/Coconut/introduction.html"),("Project
introduction http://www.cit.dk/Coconut/ display
""Coconut: Collaboration and Components,
(inter)Net-based Ubiquitous
Teleworking""0""0""0""0""0"),3,1,1,888855764,13

```
FollowLink:                          200
Usage: Follow links in the given direction from the
specified locSpecs.
Format:
UserName,ApplicationID,opCode,nodeSpec,noOflocSpecs,
{locSpec}*,direction
Response: (ResponseCode,N,{nodeSpec,locSpec,
endpointName}*)
Example: kgronbak@daimi.aau.dk,WinWord,200,("C:\My
Documents\Doc1.doc"),1,("HMB_4#75:82""""""0""0""0""0""0"),1

DeleteAnchors:                       300
Usage: Deletes the anchors corresponding to the given
locSpecs.
Format:
UserName,ApplicationID,opCode,nodeSpec,NoOflocSpecs,
{locSpec}*
Response: (ResponseCode)
Example: kgronbak@daimi.aau.dk,emacs,300, /users/
kgronbak/DHM/docs/interface.tex,1,4

SaveCompForDoc:                      501
Usage: save the component corresponding to a given
document.
Format: UserName,ApplicationID,opCode,nodeSpec
Response: (ResponseCode)
Example: kgronbak@daimi.aau.dk,WinWord,501,("C:\My
Documents\Doc1.doc")

DeleteCompForDoc:                    502
Usage: Delete the component corresponding to a given
document.
Format: UserName,ApplicationID,opCode,nodeSpec
Response: (ResponseCode)
Example: kgronbak@daimi.aau.dk,WinWord,502,("C:\My
Documents\Doc1.doc")

DocClosed:                           550
Usage: Received when the external application closes a
document.
```

```
Format: UserName,ApplicationID,opCode,nodeSpec
Response: (ResponseCode)
Example: kgronbak@daimi.aau.dk,emacs,550, /users/
kgronbak/DHM/docs/interface.tex
```

```
GetAnchorList:                    900
Usage: Get the anchor list for a component corresponding
to a given document.
Format: UserName,ApplicationID,opCode,nodeSpec
Response: (ResponseCode,{LocSpec}*)
Example: kgronbak@daimi.aau.dk,emacs,900, /users/beta/
DHM/v1.3/DRUN/dexterRuntime.bet
```

```
SetAnchorList:                    930
Usage: Update the anchors for the given document.
Format:
UserName,ApplicationID,opCode,nodeSpec,NoOflocSpecs,
{LocSpec}*
Response: (ResponseCode)
Example: kgronbak@daimi.aau.dk,emacs,930, /users/
kgronbak/DHM/docs/interface.tex,5,
0#614#627,2#1048#1065,6#1339#1353,7#1361#1375,8#1386#1405
```

Extended browsing and management protocol

The browsing and management protocol is optional and lets browsers and commands manipulate hypermedia structures directly from the user interfaces of hypermedia-extended applications. This involves no extra messages from the HSP to the application, since the new functionality consists of requests for information from the HSP.

Messages from hypermedia-extended applications to HSP

```
OpenHyperSpace:                   600
Usage: Used to open a hyperspace on the server with a
given ID (pair of integers).
Format: UserName,ApplicationID,opCode,N,
{HyperSpaceId,LockValue}*
Response: (N,{ResponseCode,HyperSpaceId,Lock}*)
```

Example: kgronbak@daimi.aau.dk,Webbrowser,
600,1,1,875045420,2

CreateHyperSpace: 601
Usage: Used to create a new hyperspace with a name and
access properties.
Format: UserName,ApplicationID,opCode,N,{HyperSpaceName,
accessCode}*
Response: (N,{ResponseCode,HyperSpaceId}*)
Example: kgronbak@daimi.aau.dk,Webbrowser,601,1,
HyperSpace6,2

SaveHyperSpaceAs: 602
Format: UserName,ApplicationID,opCode,HyperSpaceName
Usage: Save the current hyperspace under a new name.
Response: (ResponseCode)
Example:kgronbak@daimi.aau.dk,Webbrowser,602,HyperSpace6

SaveHyperSpace: 603
Format: UserName,ApplicationID,opCode
Usage: Save the current hyperspace.
Response: (ResponseCode)
Example: kgronbak@daimi.aau.dk,Webbrowser,603

GetHyperSpaceNames: 604
Usage: Retrieves the set of available hyperspaces for a
given user from the hypermedia server.
Format: UserName,ApplicationID,opCode
response= (ResponseCode,N,{"HyperSpaceName",
HyperSpaceId}*)
Example: kgronbak@daimi.aau.dk,Webbrowser,604

DeleteHyperSpace: 610
Usage: Deletes the hyperspace with the given ID from the
server.
Format: UserName,ApplicationID,opCode,N,{HyperSpaceId}*
Response: (N,{ResponseCode,HyperSpaceId}*)
Example: kgronbak@daimi.aau.dk,Webbrowser,610,1,5,
885224679

GetHyperSpaceAttrs: 611
Usage: Retrieves a given hyperspace's attribute list
Format: UserName,ApplicationID,opCode,HyperSpaceId
Response: (ResponseCode,AttributesList)
Example: kgronbak@daimi.aau.dk,Webbrowser,611,5,
885224679

InspectAnchors: 400
Usage: Show information about the anchors corresponding
to the given anchor values.
Format: UserName,ApplicationID,opCode,nodeSpec
Response: (ResponseCode)
Example: kgronbak@daimi.aau.dk,emacs,400, /users/
kgronbak/DHM/docs/interface.tex

InspectCompLinks: 450
Usage: Show information about the links with anchors in
the given document.
Format: UserName,ApplicationID,opCode,nodeSpec
Response: (ResponseCode)
Example: kgronbak@daimi.aau.dk,emacs,450, /users/
kgronbak/DHM/docs/interface.tex

SaveCompAs: 508
Usage: Save a component under a different name and let
it refer to a new document.
Format: UserName,ApplicationID,opCode,nodeSpec
Response: (ResponseCode)
Example: kgronbak@daimi.aau.dk,emacs,508, /users/
kgronbak/DHM/docs/interface.tex,1,/users/kgronbak/DHM/
docs/interface2.tex

GetCompAttributes: 910
Usage: Retrieve the value for some predefined attribute
for a given document type.
Format: UserName,ApplicationID,opCode,nodeSpec
Response: (ResponseCode)
Example: kgronbak@daimi.aau.dk,emacs,910, /users/
kgronbak/DHM/docs/interface.tex

SetCompAttributes: 920
Usage: Set the value for some predefined attribute for a
given document type.
Format: UserName,ApplicationID,opCode,nodeSpec
Response: (ResponseCode)
Example: kgronbak@daimi.aau.dk,emacs,920, /users/
kgronbak/DHM/docs/interface.tex

CreateComposite: 950
Usage: Creates a composite of a given type on the server
Format: UserName,ApplicationID,opCode,HyperSpaceId,
nodeSpec,Type
Response: (ResponseCode,compId) where compId is the uid
of the composite component created.
Example: kgronbak@daimi.aau.dk,Webbrowser,950,1,
881244672,("GT3"),501

AddCompsToComposite: 960
Usage: Adds components to the composite specified by
compID.
Format: UserName,ApplicationID,opCode,HyperSpaceId,
compID, noOfNodeSpecs,{nodeSpec}*
Response: (ResponseCode)
Example: kgronbak@daimi.aau.dk,Webbrowser,960,
(1,881244672), (10,881317409), 1,http://www.daimi.aau.dk/

DeleteCompsFromComposite: 970
Usage: Deletes components from the composited identified
with compID.
Format: UserName,ApplicationID,opCode,HyperSpaceId,
compId, noOfNodeSpecs,{nodeSpec}*
Response: (ResponseCode)
Example: kgronbak@daimi.aau.dk,Webbrowser,970,
(1,881244672), (10,881317409), 1,http://www.daimi.aau.dk/

Multiuser protocol

These messages are relevant when several users are simultaneously sharing a hyperspace. Primarily, they support locking and event notification.

Messages from HSP to hypermedia-extended applications

```
SetAccessMode:              801
Usage: Used to inform the external application about the
lock status of a given component.
Format: ApplicationID,opCode,nodeSpec
Response: (ResponseCode)
Example: emacs,801,/users/kgronbak/DHM/docs/interface.tex

ChangedOnServer:            803
Usage: Used to inform the external application that a
given component has been changed by another hypermedia
client.
Format: ApplicationID,opCode,nodeSpec
Response: (ResponseCode)
Example: emacs,803,/users/kgronbak/DHM/docs/interface.tex

NotifyNewComponent:         2000
Usage: If the users subscribes to information about
creation of certain component types, this message
informs the user whenever a new component of that type
is created
Format: opCode,hyperSpaceId,docType,nodeSpec,compId.
Response: (ResponseCode)
Example: 2000,1,875045420,106,"C:\My Documents\Doc4.doc",
4,875117860
```

Messages from hypermedia-extended applications to HSP

```
RefetchComps:               503
Usage: Refetch the components corresponding to the
listed documents from the database.
Format: UserName,ApplicationID,opCode,N,{nodeSpec}*
```

Response: (ResponseCode)
Example: kgronbak@daimi.aau.dk,emacs,503,2, /users/
kgronbak/DHM/docs/interface.tex, /users/kgronbak/DHM/
docs/protocol.tex

SubscribeComps: 504
Usage: Subscribe to specific notifications for
components corresponding to the given set of documents.
Format: UserName,ApplicationID,opCode,N,{nodeSpec}*
Response: (ResponseCode)
Example: kgronbak@daimi.aau.dk,emacs,504,1, /users/
kgronbak/DHM/docs/interface.tex

UnsubscribeComp: 505
Usage: Unsubscribe to specific notifications for the
given documents.
Format: UserName,ApplicationID,opCode,N,{nodeSpec}*
Response: (ResponseCode)
Example: kgronbak@daimi.aau.dk,emacs,505,1, /users/
kgronbak/DHM/docs/interface.tex

SubscribeNewNComps: 3000
Usage: Subscribe to notifications on events involving
creation of new components corresponding to the given
types of documents
Format: UserName,ApplicationID,opCode,HyperSpaceId,N,
{docType}*
Response: (ResponseCode)
Example: kgronbak@daimi.aau.dk,Webbrowser,3000,1,
875045420,1,100

ChangeLock: 506
Usage: Change the lock on the component corresponding to
a given document.
Format: UserName,ApplicationID,opCode,nodeSpec,LockValue
Response: (ResponseCode)
Example: kgronbak@daimi.aau.dk,emacs,506, /users/
kgronbak/DHM/docs/interface.tex,1

GetDocLockStatus: 800
Usage: Get the lock of a component corresponding to a
given document.
Format: UserName,ApplicationID,opCode,nodeSpec
Response: (ResponseCode)
Example: kgronbak@daimi.aau.dk,emacs,800, /users/
kgronbak/DHM/docs/interface.tex

GetActiveUsers: 970
Format: UserName,ApplicationID,opCode,HyperSpaceId
Response: (ResponseCode,NoOfUsers,{UserName}*)
Example: kgronbak@daimi.aau.dk,Webbrowser,970,6,
877534760

Bibliography

Ahmed, S., Wong, A., Sriram, D., and Logcher, R. (1991). *A Comparison of Object-Oriented Database Management Systems for Engineering Applications* (Research Report No. R91–12).

Akscyn, R. M., and McCracken, D. L. (1993). Design of Hypermedia Script Languages: The KMS Experience. In *Proceedings of ACM Hypertext '93* (pp. 268–269), Seattle, Wash. New York: ACM Press.

Akscyn, R. M., McCracken, D. L., and Yoder, E. A. (1988). KMS: A Distributed Hypermedia System for Managing Knowledge in Organizations. *Communications of the ACM 31*(7), 820–835.

Alexander, C. (1964). *Notes on the Synthesis of Form.* Cambridge, Mass.: Harvard University Press.

Alexander, C., Ishikawa, S., Silverstein, M., Jacobson, M., Fiksdahl-King, I., and Angel, S. (1977). *A Pattern Language.* New York: Oxford University Press.

Amann, B., Scholl, M., and Rizk, A. (1994). Querying Typed Hypertexts in Multicard/O2. In *Proceedings of the ECHT '94 European Conference on Hypermedia Technologies* (pp. 198–205), Edinburgh, Scotland. New York: ACM Press.

Andersen, P., Brandt, S., Hem, J. A., Madsen, O. L., Møller, K. J., and Sloth, L. (1992). *Workpackage WP5 Task T5.4, Deliverable D5.4: Distributed Object-Oriented Database Interface.* (EuroCoOp deliverable No. ECO-JT-92–3). Jutland Telephone and Aarhus University.

Anderson, K. M., Taylor, R. N., and E. James Whitehead, J. (1994). Chimera: Hypertext for Heterogeneous Software Environments. In *Proceedings of the ECHT '94 European Conference on Hypermedia Technologies* (pp. 94–107), Edinburgh, Scotland. New York: ACM Press.

Andrews, K., Kappe, F., and Maurer, H. (1995). Serving Information to the Web with Hyper-G. *Computer Networks and ISDN Systems, 27*(6).

Apple Computer (1991). *Macintosh™ Reference. System 7.* Cupertino, Calif.: Apple Computer, Inc.

Arai, T., Aust, D., and Hudson, S. E. (1997). PaperLink: A Technique for Hyperlinking from Real Paper to Electronic Content. In S. Pemberton (ed.), *CHI 97* (pp. 327–334), Atlanta, Ga. New York: ACM Press.

Baldazo, R., and Vaughan-Nichols, S. J. (1995). Web Publishing Made Easier. *Byte* (December): 170.

Beeman, W. O., Anderson, K. T., Bader, G., Larkin, J., McClard, A. P., McQuillan, P., and Shields, M. (1987). Hypertext and Pluralism: From Lineal to Non-Lineal Thinking. In *ACM Hypertext '87 Proceedings* (pp. 67–88), Chapel Hill, N.C. New York: ACM Press.

Bentley, R., Appelt, W., U., B., Hinrichs, E., Kerr, D., Sikkel, S., Trevor, J., and Woetzel, G. (1997a). Basic Support for Cooperative Work on the World Wide Web. *International Journal of Human-Computer Studies: Special Issue on Innovative Applications of the World Wide Web.*

Bentley, R., Horstmann, T., and Trevor, J. (1997b). The World Wide Web as Enabling Technology for CSCW: The Case of BSCW. *Computer Supported Cooperative Work: The Journal of Collaborative Computing* 6(2–3): 111–134.

Berners-Lee, T., Cailliau, R., Groff, J.-F., and Pollermann, B. (1992a). World-Wide Web: An Information Infrastructure for High-Energy Physics. In *Software Engineering, AI and Expert Systems for High Energy and Nuclear Physics,* (pp. 1–9), La Londe-les-Maures, France.

Berners-Lee, T., Cailliau, R., Luotonen, A., Nielsen, H. F., and Secret, A. (1994). The World-Wide Web. *Communications of the ACM* 37(8): 76–82.

Bernstein, M. (1993). Enactment in Information Farming. In *Hypertext 93* (pp. 242–249), Seattle, Wash. New York: ACM Press.

Bieber, M., Vitali, F., Ashman, H., Balasubramanian, V., and Oinas-Kukkonen, H. (1997). Fourth Generation Hypermedia: Some Missing Links for the World Wide Web. *International Journal of Human-Computer Studies* 47(1): 31–65.

Bjerknes, G., Ehn, P., and Kyng, M. (eds.). (1987). *Computers and Democracy: A Scandinavian Challenge.* England: Avebury.

Blomberg, J., Suchman, L., and Trigg, R. (1996). Reflections on a Work-Oriented Design Project. *Human-Computer Interaction* 11(3): 237–265.

Blomberg, J., Suchman, L., and Trigg, R. (1997). Back to Work: Renewing Old Agendas for Cooperative Design. In M. Kyng and L. Mathiassen (eds.), *Computers and Design in Context* (pp. 267–287). Cambridge, Mass.: MIT Press.

Bødker, S., and Grønbæk, K. (1991). Cooperative Prototyping: Users and Designers in Mutual Activity. *International Journal of Man-Machine Studies* 34(3): 453–478.

Bødker, S., Grønbæk, K., and Kyng, M. (1995). Cooperative Design: Techniques and Experiences from the Scandinavian Scene. In R. M. Baecker, J. Grudin, and W. A. S. Buxton (eds.), *Readings in Human-Computer Interaction: Toward the Year 2000* (pp. 215–224). San Francisco: Morgan Kaufmann.

Bolter, J. D. (1991). *Writing Space: The Computer, Hypertext, and the History of Writing.* Hillsdale, N.J.: Lawrence Erlbaum Associates.

Brandt, S., and Madsen, O. L. (1993). Object-Oriented Distributed Programming in BETA. In R. Guerraoui, O. Nierstrasz, and M. Riveill (eds.), *Object-Based Distributed Programming, ECOOP '93 Workshop,* 791 (pp. 185–212). Kaiserslautern, Germany: Springer-Verlag.

Brockschmidt, K. (1995). *Inside Ole* (2nd ed.). Redmond, Wash.: Microsoft Press.

Brown, P. J. (1987). Turning Ideas into Products: The Guide System. In *ACM Hypertext '87 Proceedings* (pp. 33–40), Chapel Hill. New York: ACM Press.

Buchanan, M. C., and Zellweger, P. T. (1992). Specifying Temporal Behavior in Hypermedia Documents. In *ACM European Conference on Hypertext '92,* (pp. 262–271), Milan, Italy. New York: ACM Press.

Bush, V. (1945). As We May Think. *The Atlantic Monthly* (August): 101–108.

Campbell, B., and Goodman, J. M. (1988). HAM: A General Purpose Hypertext Abstract Machine. *Communications of the ACM* 31(7): 856–861.

Carr, L., Roure, D. D., Hall, W., and Hill, G. (1995). The Distributed Link Service: A Tool for Publishers, Authors and Readers. In *Fourth International World Wide Web Conference: "The Web Revolution,"* (pp. 647–656). Boston: O'Reilly.

Catlin, T., Bush, P., and Yankelovich, N. (1989). InterNote: Extending a Hypermedia Framework to Support Annotative Collaboration. In *ACM Hypertext '89 Proceedings* (pp. 365–378). Pittsburgh. New York: ACM Press.

Catlin, T. J. O., & Smith, K. E. (1988). Anchors for Shifting Tides: Designing a "Seaworthy" Hypermedia System. In *Proceedings of The 12th International Online Information Meeting* (pp. 15–25), London. Oxford and New Jersey: Learned Information.

Chang, S.-F., Smith, J. R., Beigi, M., and Benitez, A. (1997). Visual Information Retrieval from Large Distributed Online Repositories. *Communications of the ACM* 40(12): 63–71.

Clark, W. (1992). Motif Applications + LinkWorks = Hyperenvironment. In *ACM European Conference on Hypertext '92* (p. 295), Milan, Italy. New York: ACM Press.

Cockburn, A. (1996). The Interaction of Social Issues and Software Architecture. *Communications of the ACM* 39(10): 40–46.

Collier, G. H. (1987). Thoth-II: Hypertext with Explicit Semantics. In *ACM Hypertext '87 Proceedings* (pp. 269–289), Chapel Hill. New York: ACM Press.

Conklin, J. (1987). Hypertext: An Introduction and Survey. *IEEE Computer* 20(9): 17–41.

Conklin, J., and Begeman, M. L. (1988). gIBIS: A Hypertext Tool for Exploratory Policy Discussion. In *Conference on Computer Supported Co-operative Work: CSCW '88* (Sept. 26–28), Portland, Oregon. New York: ACM Press.

Coplien, J. O., and Schmidt, D. C. (eds.). (1995). *Pattern Languages of Program Design.* Reading, Mass.: Addison-Wesley.

Davis, H. (1995). To Embed or Not to Embed . . . *Communications of the ACM* 38(8): 108–109.

Davis, H., Hall, W., Heath, I., Hill, G., and Wilkins, R. (1992). Towards an Integrated Information Environment with Open Hypermedia Systems. In D. Lucarella, J. Nanard, M. Nanard, and P. Paolini (eds.), *European Conference on Hypertext (ECHT '92)* (pp. pp. 181–190), Milan, Italy. New York: ACM Press.

Davis, H., Lewis, A., & Rizk, A. (1996). OHP: A Draft Proposal for a Standard Open Hypermedia Protocol. In U. K. Wiil & S. Demeyer (eds.), *Proceedings of the 2nd Workshop on Open Hypermedia Systems* (pp. 27–53), Washington, D.C. Irvine, California: Department of Information and Computer Science, University of California, Irvine, ICS-TR-96-10.

Davis, H. C., Knight, S., and Hall, W. (1994). Light Hypermedia Link Services: A Study of Third Party Application Integration. In *Proceedings of the ECHT '94 European Conference on Hypermedia Technologies* (pp. 41–50), Edinburgh, Scotland. New York: ACM Press.

Delisle, N., and Schwartz, M. (1986). Neptune: A Hypertext System for CAD Applications. In *ACM SIGMOD '86* (pp. 132–142), Washington, D.C. New York: ACM Press.

DeRose, S. J. (1989). Expanding the Notion of Links. In *ACM Hypertext '89 Proceedings* (pp. 249–257), Pittsburgh, Pa. New York: ACM Press.

DeRose, S. J., and Durand, D. G. (1994). *Making Hypermedia Work: A User's Guide to HyTime*. Boston/Dordrecht/London: Kluwer.

DeYoung, L. (1989). Hypertext Challenges in the Auditing Domain. In *ACM Hypertext '89 Proceedings* (pp. 169–180), Pittsburgh, Pa. New York: ACM Press.

Ehn, P. (1988). *Work-Oriented Design of Computer Artifacts*. Stockholm: Arbetslivscentrum.

Ellis, C. A., Gibbs, S. J., and Rein, G. L. (1991). Groupware: Some Issues and Experiences. *Communications of the ACM 34(1)*: 38–58.

Engelbart, D. (1984a). Authorship Provisions in Augment. In *Proceedings. IEEE Compcon Conference* (pp. 465–472). San Francisco: IEEE.

Engelbart, D., and English, D. (1968). A Research Center for Augmenting Human Intellect. In *Proceedings of Fall Joint Computing Conference 33* (pp. 395–410), San Francisco: AFIPS Press. Republished in 1988 in *Computer Supported Cooperative Work: A Book of Readings*, Irene Greif (ed.) (pp. 81–105). San Mateo, CA: Morgan Kaufmann.

Engelbart, D. C. (1984b). Collaboration Support Provisions in Augment. In *AFIPS Office Automation Conference, OAC '84 Digest* (pp. 51–58). Los Angeles. San Francisco: AFIPS.

Ess, C. (1991). The Pedagogy of Computing: Hypermedia in the Classroom. In *Proceedings of ACM Hypertext '91* (pp. 277–289), San Antonio. New York: ACM Press.

Feenberg, A. (1995). *Alternative Modernity: The Technical Turn in Philosophy and Social Theory*. University of California Press.

Flanagan, D. (1997). *Java in a Nutshell : A Desktop Quick Reference*. Boston: O'Reilly.

Floyd, C. (1984). A Systematic Look at Prototyping. In R. Budde (ed.), *Approaches to Prototyping* (pp. 1–18). Berlin-Heidelberg: Springer-Verlag.

Foss, C. (1988). Effective Browsing in Hypertext Systems. *Proceedings of the Conference on User-Oriented Content-Based Text and Image Handling (RIAO 88)* (pp. 82–98), Cambridge Mass. Centre de Hautes Études Internationales d'Informatique Documentaire.

Furuta, R., III, F. M. S., Marshall, C. C., Brenner, D., and Hsieh, H.-w. (1997). Hypertext Paths and the World-Wide Web: Experiences with Walden's Paths. In M. Bernstein, L. Carr, K. Østerbye (eds.), *Hypertext '97* (pp. 167–176). Southampton, England, New York: ACM Press.

Gamma, E., Helm, R., Johnson, R., and Vlissides, J. (1994). *Design Patterns: Elements of Reusable Object-Oriented Software.* Reading, Mass.: Addison Wesley.

Garrett, L. N., Smith, K. E., and Meyrowitz, N. (1986). Intermedia: Issues, Strategies, and Tactics in the Design of a Hypermedia Document System. In *Proceedings from the Conference on Computer Supported Cooperative Work* (pp. 163–174). Austin, Tex.: MCC Software Technology Program.

Goodman, D. (1987). *The Complete HyperCard Handbook.* New York: Bantam Books.

Goodman, D. (1996). *Danny Goodman's JavaScript Handbook.* Foster City, Calif.: IDG Books Worldwide.

Gosling, J., and McGilton, H. (1995). *The Java Language Environment—A White Paper* (WWW No. http://java.sun.com/doc/language_environment/). Sun Microsystems.

Greenbaum, J., and Kyng, M. (eds.). (1991). *Design at Work: Cooperative Design of Computer Systems.* Hillsdale, N.J.: Lawrence Erlbaum.

Greif, I. (ed.). (1988). *Computer-Supported Cooperative Work: A Book of Readings.* San Mateo, Calif.: Morgan Kaufmann.

Grønbæk, K. (1989). Rapid Prototyping with Fourth Generation Systems—An Empirical Study. *OFFICE: Technology and People* 5: 105–125.

Grønbæk, K. (1991) Prototyping and Active User Involvement in System Development: Towards a Cooperative Prototyping Approach. Ph.D. diss., Computer Science Department, Aarhus University.

Grønbæk, K. (1994). Composites in a Dexter-Based Hypermedia Framework. In *European Conference on Hypermedia Technology (ECHT '94)*, Edinburgh, Scotland. New York: ACM.

Grønbæk, K., Bouvin, N. O., and Sloth, L. (1997a). Designing Dexter-based Hypermedia Services for the World Wide Web. In M. Bernstein, L. Carr, K. Østerbye (eds.), *Hypertext '97—The Eighth ACM Conference on Hypertext* (pp. 146–156), Southampton, England. New York: ACM.

Grønbæk, K., Hem, J. A., Madsen, O. L., and Sloth, L. (1994). Cooperative Hypermedia Systems: A Dexter-Based Architecture. *Communications of the ACM* 37(2): 64–75.

Grønbæk, K., Kyng, M., and Mogensen, P. (1993). CSCW Challenges: Cooperative Design in Engineering Projects. *Communications of the ACM* 36(6): 67–77.

Grønbæk, K., Kyng, M., and Mogensen, P. (1997b). Toward a Cooperative Experimental System Development Approach. In M. Kyng and L. Mathiassen (eds.), *Computers and Design in Context* (pp. 201–238). Cambridge, Mass.: MIT Press.

Grønbæk, K., and Malhotra, J. (1994). Building Tailorable Hypermedia Systems: The Embedded-Interpreter Approach. In *ACM Conference on Object Oriented Programming Systems, Languages and Applications (OOPSLA '94)*, Portland, Ore. New York: ACM Press.

Grønbæk, K., & Mogensen, P. (1994). Specific cooperative analysis and design in general hypermedia development. In R. Trigg, S. I. Anderson, & E. Dykstra-Erickson (eds.), *PDC'94: Proceedings of the Participatory Design Conference* (pp. 159–171), Chapel Hill: Computer Professionals for Social Responsibility.

Grønbæk, K., and Mogensen, P. (1997). Informing General CSCW Product Development through Cooperative Design in Specific Work Domains. *Computer Supported Cooperative Work (CSCW): The Journal of Collaborative Computing* 6(4): 275–304.

Grønbæk, K., and Trigg, R. H. (1992). Design Issues for a Dexter-based Hypermedia System. In *European Conference on Hypertext 1992 (ECHT '92)*, (pp. 191–200). New York: ACM.

Grønbæk, K., and Trigg, R. H. (1994). Design Issues for a Dexter-based Hypermedia System. *Communications of the ACM* 37(2): 40–49.

Grønbæk, K., & Trigg, R. H. (1996). Toward a Dexter-based model for open hypermedia: Unifying embedded references and link objects. In *Proceedings of Hypertext '96* (pp. 149–160), Washington, D.C. New York: ACM Press.

Grønbæk, K., and Wiil, U. K. (1997). Towards a Common Reference Architecture for Open Hypermedia. *Journal of Digital Information (JODI)* 1(2), <http://jodi.ecs.soton.ac.uk/Articles/v01/i02/Gronbak/>.

Grudin, J. (1991). Obstacles to User Involvement in Software Product Development, with Implications for CSCW. *International Journal of Man-Machine Studies* 34(3): 435–452.

Haake, A. (1994). Under CoVer: The Implementation of a Contextual Version Server for Hypertext Applications. In *Proceedings of the ECHT '94 European Conference on Hypermedia Technologies* (pp. 81–93), Edinburgh, Scotland. New York: ACM Press.

Haan, B. J., Kahn, P., Riley, V. A., Coombs, J. H., and Meyrowitz, N. K. (1992). IRIS Hypermedia Services. *Communications of the ACM* 35(1): 36–51.

Halasz, F. (1991). "Seven Issues" Revisited. Keynote address at the Hypertext '91 conference, San Antonio, <http://www.parc.xerox.com/halasz-keynote>.

Halasz, F., and Schwartz, M. (1990). The Dexter Hypertext Reference Model. In J. Moline, D. Benigni, and J. Baronas (eds.), *NIST Hypertext Standardization Workshop* (pp. 95–133). Gaithersburg, Md.: National Institute of Standards.

Halasz, F., and Schwartz, M. (1994). The Dexter Hypertext Reference Model. *Communications of the ACM,* 37(2): 30–39.

Halasz, F. G. (1988). Reflections on NoteCards: Seven issues for the next generation of hypermedia systems. *Communications of the ACM,* 31(7): 836 –852.

Halasz, F. G., Moran, T. P., & Trigg, R. H. (1987). NoteCards in a Nutshell. In J. M. Carroll & P. P. Tanner (eds.), *Proceedings of Proceedings of ACM CHI+GI '87 Conference on Human Factors in Computing Systems and Graphics Interface* (pp. 45–52), Toronto. New York: ACM Press.

Hall, W., Davis, H., and Hutchings, G. (1996). *Rethinking Hypermedia: The Microcosm Approach.* Boston: Kluwer.

Hardman, L., Bulterman, D. C. A., and van Rossum, G. (1994). The Amsterdam Hypermedia Model: Adding Time and Context to the Dexter Model. *Communications of the ACM* 37(2): 50–63.

Hills, M. (1996). *Intranet Business Strategies.* New York: John Wiley.

Hinden, R. M. (1996). IP Next Generation Overview. *Communications of the ACM* 39(6): 61–71.

Holtman, K. (1996). The Futplex System. In *ERCIM Workshop on CSCW and the Web,* Sankt Augustin, Germany.

Instone, K. (1996). Hypermedia Research and the World Wide Web Workshop. *ACM SIGLINK Newsletter* 5(2): 4–5.

Irish, P. M., & Trigg, R. H. (1989). Supporting Collaboration in Hypermedia: Issues and Experiences. In E. Barrett (ed.), *The Society of Text: Hypertext, Hypermedia, and the Social Construction of Information* (pp. 90–106). Cambridge, Mass.: MIT Press.

Johnson, R. E. (1997). Frameworks = (Components + Patterns). *Communications of the ACM* 40(10): 39–42.

Jordan, D. S., Russell, D. M., Jensen, A.-M. S., and Rogers, R. A. (1989). Facilitating the Development of Representations in Hypertext with IDE. In *ACM Hypertext '89 Proceedings* (pp. 93–104), Pittsburgh, Pa. New York: ACM Press.

Jungk, R. (1986). *Future Workshops—How to Create Desirable Futures.* London: Institute for Social Inventions.

Kacmar, C. J., and Leggett, J. J. (1991). PROXHY: A Process-Oriented Extensible Hypertext Architecture. *ACM Transactions on Information Systems* 9(4): 399–419.

Kahn, P., Nyce, J. M., Oren, T., Crane, G., Smith, L. C., Trigg, R., and Meyrowitz, N. (1991). From Memex to Hypertext: Understanding the Influence of Vannevar Bush. In *Proceedings of ACM Hypertext '91* (p. 361), San Antonio. New York: ACM Press.

Kibby, M. R., and Mayes, T. (1989). Towards Intelligent Hypertext. In R. McAleese (ed.), *Hypertext: Theory into Practice* (pp. 164–172). Norwood, N.J.: Ablex.

Kiczales, G. (1992). Towards a New Model of Abstraction in the Engineering of Software. In *IMSA '92 (Workshop on Reflection and Meta-level Architectures),* Tokyo. Palo Alto: Xerox. <http://www.parc.xerox.com/spl/groups/eca/pubs/papers/Kiczales-IMSA92/for-web.pdf>.

Kiczales, G., Rivieres, J. D., and Bobrow, D. G. (1991). *The Art of the Metaobject Protocol.* Cambridge, Mass.: MIT Press.

Kleinberg, J. (1998). Authoritative Sources in a Hyperlinked Environment. In *Proceedings of. 9th ACM-SIAM Symposium on Discrete Algorithms.* Also appears as IBM Research Report RJ 10076, May 1997 and at <www.cs.cornell.edu/home/kleinber>.

Knudsen, J. L., Löfgren, M., Madsen, O. L., and Magnusson, B. (1993). *Object-Oriented Software Development Environments—The Mjølner Approach.* Englewood Cliffs, N.J.: Prentice Hall.

Korpela, M., Soriyan, H. A., Olufokunbi, K. C., Onayade, A. A., Davies-Adetugbo, A., and Adesanmi, D. (1998). Community Participation in Health Informatics in Africa: An Experiment in Tripartite Partnership in Ile-Ife, Nigeria. *Computer Supported Cooperative Work* 7(2–3).

Kyng, M. (1988). Designing for a Dollar a Day. In *CSCW '88. Proceedings of the Conference on Computer-Supported Cooperative Work* (pp. 178–188). New York: ACM Press.

Kyng, M. (1994). Making Representations Work. In L. Suchman (ed.), *Representations of Work, HICSS Monograph, Hawaii International Conference on System Sciences—27* (pp. 19–35), Honolulu.

Kyng, M. (1995). Creating Contexts for Design. In J. Carrol (ed.), *Scenario-based Design: Envisioning Technology in Use*. New York: John Wiley.

Kyng, M., and Mathiassen, L. (eds.). (1997). *Computers and Design in Context*. Cambridge, Mass.: MIT Press.

Lamping, J., Rao, R., and Pirolli, P. (1995). A Focus+Context Technique Based on Hyperbolic Geometry for Visualizing Large Hierarchies. In I. R. Katz, R. Mack, and L. Marks (eds.), *CHI '95* (pp. 401–408), Denver. New York: ACM Press.

Landow, G. P. (1987). Relationally Encoded Links and the Rhetoric of Hypertext. In *ACM Hypertext '87* (pp. 331–343). New York: ACM Press.

Leggett, J. J., and Schnase, J. L. (1994). Viewing Dexter with Open Eyes. *Communications of the ACM* 37(2): 77–86.

Levy, D. M., and Marshall, C. C. (1995). Going Digital: A Look at Assumptions Underlying Digital Libraries. *Communications of the ACM* 38(4): 77–84.

Lewis, P. H., Davis, H. C., Griffiths, S. R., Hall, W., and Wilkins, R. J. (1996). Media-Based Navigation with Generic Links. In *Hypertext '96* (pp. 215–223), Washington, D.C. New York: ACM Press.

Licklider, J. C. R., and Vezza, A. (1978). Applications of Information Networks. *Proceedings of the IEEE* 66(11): 1330–1346.

Licklider, J. C. R., and Vezza, A. (1988). Applications of information networks. In I. Greif (ed.), *Computer-Supported Cooperative Work: A Book of Readings*. San Mateo, Calif.: Morgan Kaufmann.

D. Lucarella, J. Nanard, M. Nanard, and P. Paolini (eds.), *Proceedings of the Fourth European ACM Conference on Hypertext (ECHT '92)*, Milan, Italy. New York: ACM Press.

MacLean, A., Carter, K., Lovstrand, L., & Moran, T. (1990). User-Tailorable Systems: Pressing the Issues with Buttons. In J. C. Chew & J. Whiteside (eds.), *Proceedings of ACM CHI '90 Conference on Human Factors in Computing Systems* (pp. 175–182), Seattle, Wash. New York: ACM Press.

Madsen, O. L., Møller-Pedersen, B., and Nygaard, K. (1993). *Object-Oriented Programming in the Beta Programming Language*. Reading, Mass.: Addison-Wesley.

Magnusson, B., Asklund, U., and Minör, S. (1993). Fine-Grained Version Control for Cooperative Software Development (Research Report No. LU-CS-TR:93–112). Lund University, Department of Computer Science.

Malcolm, K. C., Poltrock, S. E., and Schuler, D. (1991). Industrial Strength Hypermedia: Requirements for a Large Engineering Enterprise. In *Proceedings of ACM Hypertext '91* (pp. 13–24), San Antonio. New York: ACM Press.

Malhotra, J. (1993). Dynamic Extensibility in a Statically-compiled Object-oriented Language. In S. Nishio and A. Yonezawa (eds.), *International Symposium on Object Technologies for Advanced Software (ISOTAS '93)* (pp. 297–314), Kanazawa, Japan. Springer-Verlag.

Malhotra, J. (1994). On the Construction of Extensible Systems. In *TOOLS EUROPE '94*, Versailles, France.

Marshall, C. C. (1987). Exploring Representation Problems Using Hypertext. In *ACM Hypertext '87 Proceedings* (pp. 253–268), Chapel Hill. New York: ACM Press.

Marshall, C. C., Halasz, F. G., Rogers, R. A., and William C. Janssen, J. (1991). Aquanet: A Hypertext Tool to Hold Your Knowledge in Place. In *Proceedings of ACM Hypertext '91* (pp. 261–275). San Antonio. New York: ACM Press.

Marshall, C. C., and Irish, P. M. (1989). Guided Tours and On-Line Presentations: How Authors Make Existing Hypertext Intelligible for Readers. In *ACM Hypertext '89 Proceedings* (pp. 15–26), Pittsburgh, Pa. New York: ACM Press.

Marshall, C. C., and Shipman, F. M. (1995). Spatial Hypertext: Designing for Change. *Communications of the ACM* 38(8): 88–97.

Marshall, C. C., Shipman, F. M., and Coombs, J. H. (1994). VIKI: Spatial Hypertext Supporting Emergent Structure. In *Proceedings of the ECHT '94 European Conference on Hypermedia Technologies* (pp. 13–23), Edinburgh, Scotland. New York: ACM Press.

Maurer, H. (ed.). (1996). *HyperWave: The Next Generation Web Solution*. Harlow, England: Addison-Wesley.

McCracken, D. L., and Akscyn, R. M. (1984). Experience with the ZOG Human-Computer Interface System. *International Journal of Man-Machine Studies* 21(4): 293–310.

Meyrowitz, N. (1986). Intermedia: The Architecture and Construction of an Object-Oriented Hypermedia System and Applications Framework. In *ACM Conference on Object Oriented Programming Systems, Languages and Applications (OOPSLA '86)* (pp. 186–201), Portland, Ore. New York: ACM Press.

Meyrowitz, N. (1989). The Missing Link: Why We're All Doing Hypertext Wrong. In E. Barrett (ed.), *The Society of Text* (pp. 107–114). Cambridge, Mass.: MIT Press.

Meyrowitz, N. (1991). Hypertext and Pen Computing. In *Proceedings of ACM Hypertext '91* (p. 379). San Antonio. New York: ACM Press.

Mjølner Informatics. (1990). *Sif–Mjølner BETA Source Browser and Editor*, No. MIA 90–11). Mjølner Informatics.

Mogensen, P. (1994) Challenging Practice: An Approach to Cooperative Analysis. Ph.D. diss., Aarhus University, Daimi PB-465.

Mogensen, P., & Trigg, R. H. (1992). Artifacts as triggers for participatory analysis. In M. J. Muller, S. Kuhn, & J. A. Meskill (eds.), *Proceedings of Participatory Design Conference (PDC '92)* (pp. 55–62), Cambridge, Mass. Computer Professionals for Social Responsibility, P.O. Box 717, Palo Alto, CA 94302-0717.

Monnard, J., and Pasquier-Boltuck, J. (1992). An Object-Oriented Scripting Environment for the WEBSs Electronic Book System. In D. Lucarella, J. Nanard, M. Nanard, and P. Paolini (eds.), *Proceedings of the Fourth European ACM Conference on Hypertext (ECHT '92)* (pp. 81–90), Milan, Italy. New York: ACM Press.

Monty, M. L., and Moran, T. P. (1986). A Longitudinal Study of Authoring Using NoteCards. Poster presented at CHI '86 Human Factors in Computing Systems conference (Boston, April 13–17, 1986).

Mowbray, T. J., and Zahavi, R. (1995). *The Essential CORBA—Systems Integration Using Distributed Objects*. New York: John Wiley.

Munzner, T., and Burchard, P. (1995). Visualizing the Structure of the World Wide Web in 3D Hyperbolic Space. In *VRML '95* (pp. 33–38), San Diego. New York: ACM Press.

Mylonas, E., & Heath, S. (1990). Hypertext from the Data Point of View: Paths and Links in the Perseus Project. In *Proceedings of ECHT '90 European Conference on Hypertext* (pp. 324–336), Versailles, France. New York: ACM Press.

Nanard, J., and Nanard, M. (1991). Using Structured Types to Incorporate Knowledge in Hypertext. In *Proceedings of ACM Hypertext '91* (pp. 329–343), San Antonio. New York: ACM Press.

Nanard, J., and Nanard, M. (1993). Should Anchors be Typed Too? An Experiment with MacWeb. In *Proceedings of ACM Hypertext '93* (pp. 51–62), Seattle, Wash. New York: ACM Press.

Nardi, B. A. (1993). *A Small Matter of Programming: Perspectives on End User Computing*. Cambridge, Mass.: MIT Press.

Nelson, T. H. (1965a). A File Structure for the Complex, the Changing, and the Indeterminate. In *The 20th National ACM Conference* (pp. 84–100). New York: ACM Press.

Nelson, T. H. (1965b). The Hypertext. Paper presented at the International Documentation Federation Conference.

Nelson, T. H. (1974). *Computer Lib/Dream Machines*. Sausalito, Calif.: Mindful Press.

Nelson, T. H. (1981). *Literary Machines*. San Antonio: T. H. Nelson.

Nelson, T. H. (1995). The Heart of Connection: Hypermedia Unified by Transclusion. *Communications of the ACM* 38(8): 31–33.

Nicol, D., Smeaton, C., and Slater, A. F. (1995). Footsteps: Trailblazing the Web. Paper presented at the Third International World-Wide Web Conference, Darmstadt, Germany.

Nielsen, J. (1990). *Hypertext and Hypermedia*. San Diego: Academic Press.

Nørmark, K. (1992). From Hooks to Open Points and Back Again. No. Aalborg University (Technical Report).

Nürnberg, P. J., Leggett, J. J., Schneider, E. R., and Schnase, J. L. (1996). Hypermedia Operating Systems: A New Paradigm for Computing. In *Proceedings of the Seventh ACM Conference on Hypertext—Hypertext '96* (pp. 194–202), Washington, D.C. New York: ACM Press.

Ogle, V. E., and Stonebraker, M. (1995). Chabot: Retrieval from a Relational Database of Images. *IEEE Computer* 28(9).

Pearl, A. (1989). Sun's Link Service: A Protocol for Open Linking. In *ACM Hypertext '89 Proceedings* (pp. 137–146), Pittsburgh, Pa. New York: ACM Press.

Pitti, D. V. (1994). The Berkeley Finding Aid Project: Standards in Navigation. In A. Okerson (ed.), *Scholarly Publishing on the Electronic Networks: Filling the Pipeline and Paying the Piper* (pp. 161–166). Washington, D.C.: Association of Research Libraries.

Pree, W. (1997). Essential Framework Design Patterns: Why "Hot Spot" Identification Helps. *Object Magazine* (March): 34–37.

Raskin, J. (1987). The Hype in Hypertext: A Critique. In *ACM Hypertext '87 Proceedings* (pp. 325–330), Chapel Hill. New York: ACM Press.

Rayward, W. B. (1994). Visions of Xanadu: Paul Otlet (1868–1944) and Hypertext. *Journal of the American Society for Information Science* 45(4): 235–250.

Rein, G. L., McCue, D. L., and Slein, J. A. (1997). A Case for Document Management Functions on the Web. *Communications of the ACM* 40(9): 81–89.

Rizk, A., and Sauter, L. (1992). Multicard: An Open Hypermedia System. In D. Lucarella, J. Nanard, M. Nanard, and P. Paolini (eds.), *European Conference on Hypertext (ECHT '92),* (pp. pp. 4–10), Milan, Italy. New York: ACM Press.

Röscheisen, M., Mogensen, C., and Winograd, T. (1994). Shared Web Annotations as a Platform for Third-Party Value-Added Information Providers: Architecture, Protocols, and Usage Examples (Technical Report CSDTR/DLTR). Stanford University, Stanford Integrated Digital Library Project, Computer Science Dept.

Roschelle, J., Pea, R., and Trigg, R. (1990). VIDEONOTER: A Tool for Exploratory Video Analysis (IRL Report No. IRL90–0021). Institute for Research on Learning.

Rossum, G. V., Jansen, J., Mullender, K. S., and Bulterman, D. C. A. (1993). CMIFed: A Presentation Environment for Portable Hypermedia Documents. In *ACM Multimedia '93* (pp. 183–188), Anaheim. New York: ACM Press.

Rumbaugh, J., Blaha, M., Premerlani, W., Eddy, F., and Lorensen, W. (1991). *Object-Oriented Modeling and Design* (1st ed.). Englewood Cliffs, N.J.: Prentice Hall.

Sawhney, N. N., Balcom, D., and Smith, O. (1996). HyperCafe: Narrative and Aesthetic Properties of Hypervideo. In *Proceedings of Hypertext '96* (pp. 1–10), Washington, D.C. New York: ACM Press.

Schmucker, K. J. (ed.) (1986). Introduction to MacAPP. In *Object-Oriented Programming for the Macintosh* (pp. 83–129). Hasbrouck Heights, N.J.: Hayden Book Company.

Schrage, M. (1996). Cultures of Prototyping. In T. Winograd (ed.), *Bringing Design to Software* (pp. 191–205). New York: ACM Press.

Shackelford, D. E., Smith, J. B., and Smith, F. D. (1993). The Architecture and Implementation of a Distributed Hypermedia Storage System. In *Proceedings of ACM Hypertext '93* (pp. 1–13), Seattle, Wash. New York: ACM Press.

Shneiderman, B. (1987). User Interface Design for the HyperTies Electronic Encyclopedia. In *ACM Hypertext '87 Proceedings* (pp. 189–194), Chapel Hill. New York: ACM Press.

Smith, J. B., and Smith, F. D. (1991). ABC: A Hypermedia System for Artifact-Based Collaboration. In *Proceedings of ACM Hypertext '91* (pp. 179–192), San Antonio. New York: ACM Press.

Soergel, D. (1977). An Automated Encyclopedia—A Solution of the Information Problem? *International Classification* 4(1,2).

Sørgaard, P. (1987). A Cooperative Work Perspective on Use and Development of Computer Artifacts. Paper presented at the 10th Information Systems Research Seminar in Scandinavia (IRIS).

Spivey, J. M. (1989). *The Z Notation*. Hertfordshire, England: Prentice-Hall.

Stallman, R. (1984). EMACS: The Extensible, Customizable, Self-Documenting Display Editor. In D. R. Barstow, H. E. Shrobe, & E. Sandewall (eds.), *Interactive Programming Environments* (pp. 300–325). New York: McGraw-Hill.

Star, S. L., and Ruhleder, K. (1996). Steps Toward an Ecology of Infrastructure: Design and Access for Large Information Spaces. *Information Systems Research* 7(1): 111–134.

Stotts, P. D., and Furuta, R. (1991). Dynamic Adaptation of Hypertext Structure. In *Proceedings of ACM Hypertext '91* (pp. 219–231), San Antonio. New York: ACM Press.

Streitz, N., Haake, J., Hannemann, J., Lemke, A., Schuler, W., Schütt, H., and Thüring, M. (1992). SEPIA, A Cooperative Hypermedia Authoring Environment. In D. Lucarella, J. Nanard, M. Nanard, and P. Paolini (eds.), *Proceedings of the Fourth European ACM Conference on Hypertext (ECHT '92)* (pp. 11–22), Milan, Italy. New York: ACM Press.

Suchman, L. (1994). Working Relations of Technology Production and Use. *Computer Supported Cooperative Work* 2(1–2): 21–40.

Sun Microsystems. (1997). *Java Beans: A Component Architecture for Java* (<http://splash.javasoft.com/beans/WhitePaper.html>). Sun Microsystems.

Tanenbaum, A. S. (1992). *Modern Operating Systems*. Englewood Cliffs, N.J.: Prentice-Hall.

Teitelman, W., and Masinter, L. (1981). The Inter-lisp Programming Environment. *IEEE Computer* 14: 25–34.

Tichy, W. F. (1983). RCS: A Revision Control System. In P. Degano and E. Sandewall (eds.), *Integrated Interactive Computing Systems* (pp. 345–361). Amsterdam: North-Holland.

Tompa, F. W., Blake, G. E., and Raymond, D. R. (1993). Hypertext by Link-Resolving Components. In *Proceedings of ACM Hypertext '93* (pp. 118–130), Seattle, Wash. New York: ACM Press.

Trigg, R. H. (1983). A Network-Based Approach to Text Handling for the Online Scientific Community. Ph.D. diss., Dept. of Computer Science, University of Maryland (University Microfilms #8429934).

Trigg, R. H. (1988). Guided Tours and Tabletops: Tools for Communicating in a Hypertext Environment. *ACM Transactions on Office Information Systems* 6(4): 398–414.

Trigg, R. H. (1991). From Trailblazing to Guided Tours: The Legacy of Vannevar Bush's Vision of Hypertext Use. In P. D. Kahn and J. Nyce (eds.), *From Memex to Hypertext: Vannevar Bush and the Mind's Machine,* San Diego: Academic Press.

Trigg, R. H. (1992). Participatory Design meets the MOP: Acountability in the Design of Tailorable Computer Systems. In T. Bratteteig, G. Bjerknes, and K. Kautz (eds.), *15th IRIS* (pp. 643–660). Larkollen, Norway: Department of Informatics, University of Oslo.

Trigg, R. H. (1996). Hypermedia as Integration: Recollections, Reflections and Exhortations. In keynote address: Hypertext '96 Conference, Washington, D.C. (<http://www.parc.xerox.com/trigg/HT96-keynote>).

Trigg, R. H., and Bødker, S. (1994). From Implementation to Design: Tailoring and the Emergence of Systematization in CSCW. In R. Furuta and C. Neuwirth (eds.), *Proceedings of the Conference on Computer Supported Cooperative Work (CSCW '94)* (pp. 45–54). New York: ACM Press.

Trigg, R. H., and Irish, P. M. (1987). Hypertext Habitats: Experiences of Writers in NoteCards. In *ACM Hypertext '87 Proceedings* (pp. 89–108), Chapel Hill. New York: ACM Press.

Trigg, R. H., Moran, T. P., and Halasz, F. G. (1987). Adaptability and Tailorability in Notecards. In *Human Computer Interaction—INTERACT '87* (pp. 723–728). Amsterdam: North-Holland.

Trigg, R. H., Suchman, L., and Halasz, F. G. (1986). Supporting Collaboration in Notecards. In *Proceedings from the Conference on Computer Supported Cooperative Work* (pp. 153–162), Austin, Tex.: MCC Software Technology Program.

Trigg, R. H., and Suchman, L. A. (1989). Collaborative Writing in NoteCards. In R. McAleese (ed.), *Hypertext: Theory into Practice* (pp. 45–61). Norwood, N.J.: Ablex.

Trigg, R. H., and Weiser, M. (1986). TEXTNET: A Network-Based Approach to Text Handling. *ACM Transactions of Office Information Systems* 4(1): 1–23.

Utting, K., and Yankelovich, N. (1989). Context and Orientation in Hypermedia Networks. *ACM Transactions on Information Systems* 7(1): 58–84.

Vlissides, J. M., Coplien, J. O., and Kerth, N. L. (eds.). (1996). *Pattern Languages of Program Design 2*. Reading, Mass.: Addison-Wesley.

Weiser, M. (1993). Some Computer Science Issues in Ubiquitous Computing. *Communications of the ACM* 36(7): 74–84.

Weiser, M. (1993). Some Computer Science Issues in Ubiquitous Computing. *Communications of the ACM* 36(7): 74–84.

Wells, H. G. (1938). *World Brain*. London: Methuen.

Wiil, U. K. (1991). Using Events as Support for Data Sharing in Collaborative Work. In K. S. Gorlin, (ed.), *Proceedings of the International Workshop on CSCW*. Berlin: Institut für Informatik und Rechentechnik.

Wiil, U. K. (1993). Experiences with HyperBase: A Multiuser Hypertext Database. *SIGMOD RECORD* 22(4): 19–25.

Wiil, U. K., and Leggett, J. J. (1992). Hyperform: Using Extensibility to Develop Dynamic, Open and Distributed Hypertext Systems. In D. Lucarella, J. Nanard, M. Nanard, and P. Paolini (eds.), *Proceedings of the Fourth European ACM Conference on Hypertext (ECHT '92)* (pp. 251–261), Milan, Italy. New York: ACM Press.

Wiil, U. K., and Leggett, J. J. (1997). HyperDisco: Collaborative Authoring and Internet Distribution. In M. Bernstein, L. Carr, K. Østerbye (eds.), *Proceedings of Hypertext '97* (pp. 13–23). Southampton, England. New York: ACM Press.

Wiil, U. K. E. (1997). *Proceedings of the 3rd Workshop on Open Hypermedia Systems*. (Scientific Report No. 97–01). The Danish National Centre for IT Research.

Wilson, D. A., Rosenstein, L. S., and Shafer, D. G. (1990). *Programming with MacApp (MacIntosh Inside Out)*. Reading, Mass.: Addison-Wesley.

Yankelovich, N., Haan, B. J., Meyrowitz, N. K., and Drucker, S. M. (1988). Intermedia: The Concept and Construction of a Seamless Information Environment. *IEEE Computer* 21(1): 81–96.

Young, L. D. (1996). Organizational Support for Software Design. In T. Winograd (ed.), *Bringing Design to Software* (pp. 253–267). New York: ACM Press.

Zellweger, P. T. (1989). Scripted Documents: A Hypermedia Path Mechanism. In *ACM Hypertext '89 Proceedings* (pp. 1–14), Pittsburgh, Pa. New York: ACM Press.

Index

References to drawings appear in italics.